National Monetary Policies and International Monetary Cooperation

LITTLE, BROWN SERIES IN ECONOMICS

Richard E. Caves, CONSULTING EDITOR

National Monetary Policies and International Monetary Cooperation

DONALD R. HODGMAN
University of Illinois

Little, Brown and Company   Boston

Library of Congress Catalog Card No. 73–13356

FIRST PRINTING

Published simultaneously in Canada
by Little, Brown & Company (Canada) Limited

PRINTED IN THE UNITED STATES OF AMERICA

Portions of Chapter 8 of this book previously appeared in the October
1973 issue of the *Bankers' Magazine*. Copyright © 1973 by Little, Brown
and Company (Inc.).

The author is grateful for permission to reprint material from his articles
in the following journals:

Journal of Money, Credit, and Banking, for "British Techniques of
Monetary Policy: A Critical Review," Vol. III (November, 1971), pp.
760–79. Copyright © 1971 by the Ohio State University Press. All Rights
Reserved. And "Selective Credit Controls," Vol. IV (May, 1972), pp. 342–59.
Copyright © 1971 by the Ohio State University Press. All Rights Reserved.

The Banca Nazionale del Lavoro *Quarterly Review*, for "The French
System of Monetary and Credit Controls," No. 99 (December, 1971), pp.
324–53.

Kredit und Kapital, for "European Monetary Integration: Problems and
Prospects," Vol. 5, Issue 3/1972, pp. 249–65.

Preface

Research for this book began in the fall of 1965 and continued through the fall of 1972. I have attempted to keep abreast of developments in national monetary and credit techniques, measures to influence international capital movements, and other relevant national policies through early spring of 1972. Although subsequent developments may alter particular details of the national systems studied in this book, I do not believe that important features of national practice and policy will be changed radically before the passage of considerable time. Moreover, a number of the recent changes represent cross-national borrowings or adaptations of practices already followed elsewhere. Thus, their novelty is limited.

By contrast, European monetary integration and reform of the international monetary system are under current and continuing international negotiation intended to result in new forms of international monetary cooperation. For this reason, despite personal doubts about the pace of progress and degree of novelty that may result in both these areas, I have followed developments closely until sending the manuscript to the publisher in late December 1972.

This book could not have been written without the extraordinarily generous assistance of a very large number of individuals in official and private capacities in the countries studied and in several international organizations. My primary debt is to central bankers in Belgium, France, Italy, Germany, the Netherlands, and the United Kingdom. Discussions with these officials and study of the sometimes voluminous materials they placed at my disposal provided the foundations for this book. Moreover, a number of central bankers have had the kindness and the patience to read drafts of country chapters

v

and to point out errors of fact or interpretation. I stress that they bear no responsibility for remaining errors of fact that may have crept in during further revisions nor for my interpretations. Indeed, in several instances, officials have strongly disagreed with interpretations that I have seen fit to leave unchanged in the final manuscript.

Other individuals to whom I am deeply indebted for their explanations of practice in the countries studied include officials in finance ministries and planning departments, officials in bankers' associations, commercial bankers, and officers in other financial institutions. I am grateful also for assistance from officials and professional staffs of these international organizations: the International Monetary Fund, the Commission of the European Communities, the Organization for Economic Cooperation and Development, and the Bank for International Settlements.

To Pierre Berger, Andrew D. Crockett, and H. R. Wortmann, I express my special thanks. My university colleagues Carl Arlt, William M. Bryan, and Case M. Sprenkle have provided constant professional stimulation. Alicia Mullor, Farhad Nomani, and Alan Pankratz helped greatly in their capacities as research assistants at various stages of the study.

Appreciation for financial assistance for my research is expressed to the Social Science Research Council, Irving Trust Company, The Board of Governors of the Federal Reserve System, the United States Treasury, and most of all to the University of Illinois. Financial assistance from the University of Ilinois was made available on various occasions through the Department of Economics, the College of Commerce and Business Administration, the Bureau of Economic and Business Research, the Center for International Comparative Studies, and the Center for Advanced Study.

Donald R. Hodgman

Contents

National Monetary Policies and International Monetary Cooperation

1 Introduction

For the six original members of the European Economic Community and for the United Kingdom, this book examines the instruments and techniques of monetary and credit policy within the framework of national financial institutions and national goals of economic policy. The performance of these national systems is evaluated herein, with a comparative analysis of factors that determine their effectiveness. Two concluding chapters of the book are concerned with the implications of its national findings for efforts to achieve European monetary integration and to reform the international monetary system.

Chapters devoted to individual countries are designed to be sufficiently self-contained that they may be read with understanding on a selective individual basis. There is a degree of standardization in topics covered, but each country chapter retains its own distinctive flavor. For each country, there is discussion of the role assigned to the central bank and to other monetary and credit authorities, the instruments and techniques they use, and the goals they seek to achieve.

In the countries studied, it is not possible to understand the rationale for central bank actions involving such traditional instruments as discounting, reserve ratios, and open market operations without extending the scope of the analysis to include aspects of the broader institutional and regulatory environment within which the monetary authorities function. Especially important are other central banking techniques, the structure of financial institutions and markets, conditions of access to the national money and capital markets, certain aspects of national budgetary and debt management policy, and measures by the authorities to influence international capital flows. The aim in the individual country chapters is to describe and analyze the instruments and processes of monetary and credit policy with sufficient attention to these other features of a country's more general "financial system" to allow realistic appraisal of the working of monetary and credit policy.

National authorities may differ in how they conceive of the actual or potential workings of monetary and credit policy and in how they assess the relative importance for policy of different targets such as money supply, bank liquidity, general liquidity, and interest rates. If a dominant theory can be identified as influencing official action, it is summarized and its importance for policy evaluated.

A commonplace to those who make international comparisons of economic performance is that monetary policy appears to have been effective in some countries far more than in others and on some occasions more than on others. This book explores the reasons for the variations. This aim has influenced the organization of topics covered in the country chapters and the substance of discussion in their sections devoted to evaluation and commentary. In addition, Chapter 8 presents a systematic, comparative treatment of factors that condition the effectiveness of monetary policy.

One further purpose of the research undertaken for this book has been to provide information and analysis relevant to international monetary cooperation. Comparatively few of us have had occasion to study carefully how any monetary and credit system works other than that of our own country. Yet to communicate intelligently on aspects of international monetary cooperation, we must have some degree of mutual comprehension of each other's systems.

Chapter 9 is concerned with international monetary cooperation in the form of plans and initial actions to organize a regional monetary union among members of the European Economic Community. Seven of the nine countries scheduled to be members of the EEC as of January 1, 1973, are covered in the present study. These seven include all the chief economic powers among the members of the EEC. In Chapter 9 are evaluated the problems and prospects of European monetary integration, with the aid of information drawn from the studies for individual countries.

Chapter 10 carries examination of international monetary cooperation one step further. This chapter explores the relevance of national differences in monetary and credit techniques, policy goals, and size and degree of openness of a national economy for rational preferences by national officials concerning certain key issues involved in reforming the international monetary system. These issues are (1) the degree of flexibility of exchange rates; (2) controls over international capital flows; and (3) the form and degree of interconvertibility of official reserve assets. On the basis of this discussion and that of the preceding chapter concerning prospects for European monetary integration, Chapter 10 concludes with some speculations about probable features of the international monetary system that is likely to emerge from reform negotiations.

The level of sophistication required of the reader involves a knowledge of the standard models and concepts of monetary economics at the undergraduate level. Moreover, a reader's comprehension will be aided by some familiarity with the functions and behavior of the monetary authorities, banks, and credit markets in his own national economy.

2 Belgium–Luxembourg

In this discussion the techniques of monetary and credit policy in Belgium and Luxembourg are treated together in view of the economic and monetary union of the two countries since 1921. Economically, Belgium is by far the dominant partner in the union; Luxembourg has no central bank and no capability for national monetary policy in the customary sense. Moreover, the two countries have a common foreign exchange authority. Therefore, we place primary emphasis on Belgian policies and institutions, although we briefly consider certain distinctive features of the financial organization and policy of Luxembourg.

Belgian national economic goals, like those of the Netherlands, have been conditioned by the smallness of the country's geographic area and the openness of the economy to external trade and capital movements. In 1971, exports of goods and services equaled 47.6 per cent of the value of Belgian gross national product.[1] This openness has led to continuing concern for the condition of the balance of payments and derivatively for sufficient domestic price stability to avoid inflation-induced loss of competitive position in international markets. Belgium has one of the best records for price stability within the European Economic Community. Capital movements through the balance of payments have been moderated by operation of a two-tier market for foreign exchange, in which the exchange rate for capital transactions is permitted to vary with the pressures of supply and demand in the market. Belgian national economic policy also

[1] "Les Instruments de la Politique Monetaire en Belgique," in *Bulletin de la Banque Nationale de Belgique*, XLVII Année, vol. 1, no. 5 (May 1972): xii.

4

has accorded a high priority to economic growth. This emphasis has found expression in a succession of laws to foster economic expansion through government aid and also through strong government intervention in the money, credit, and capital markets to secure an allocation of short- and long-term credit to selected investment objectives. Finally, there is evidence of substantial governmental concern with regional economic development to aid depressed and backward economic regions. In the areas of monetary and credit policy, these goals have fostered a key role for government intervention and control to secure an allocation of credit consistent with the government's set of priorities.

In formulating and executing policy, the monetary authorities in Belgium have been influenced less by explicit monetary and economic theory than the authorities of any other country in this study. Changes in policy and in the techniques of policy have been pragmatic responses to changes in problems perceived by the authorities. The increasing importance of international financial flows for Belgian financial institutions and markets has been one important stimulus that called for adaptive responses by the authorities. Another has been the decline in specialization by financial institutions, with resulting decrease in operational differences between deposit banks and other credit-granting institutions.

Other distinctive aspects of the environment for monetary policy in Belgium are the relatively high proportion of cash to bank deposits in the money supply (44–45 per cent on the average during the year 1971),[2] the weak role of budgetary policy in economic stabilization, and the two-tier foreign exchange market used to moderate international capital flows. The underdeveloped role of budgetary policy in economic stabilization has placed an excessive burden on monetary policy. The two-tier foreign exchange market has strengthened the hand of the monetary authorities in dealing with destabilizing capital flows. On balance, the high proportion of cash to the deposit component of the money supply has probably strengthened the influence of the monetary authorities. When the money supply expands owing to an increase in bank credit and deposits, the accompanying rise in cash in circulation drains bank reserves and thus keeps banks more dependent on central bank credit than they would be under circumstances of a smaller cash drain.

The examination of Belgian policy and institutions begins with a description of the central monetary authorities and their assigned roles. Then a brief survey of financial institutions and markets is followed by discussion of the instruments and techniques of monetary and credit policy. Subsequently, we turn our attention to policy regarding the domestic capital market and to controls over international capital movements as these relate to the tasks of the monetary au-

---

[2] "Les Instruments," Table 13.4, p. 74.

thorities. A brief consideration of the deficient role of the government budget in aggregate demand management follows. We then sketch some distinctive aspects of the Luxembourg financial system as this relates to that of its Belgian partner. A final section provides an evaluation and commentary focused on the Belgian system and describes reforms in this system that the central monetary and regulatory authorities have proposed.

THE CENTRAL MONETARY AUTHORITIES

The Banque Nationale de Belgique, the central bank, occupies the key position among the Belgian institutions concerned with monetary and credit policy. In Belgium, however, operational and legal responsibility for monetary and credit policy is distributed among a number of institutions. The entire structure of central banking functions appears to have developed gradually and pragmatically simply by new functions and sometimes new institutions having been added to cope with problems as they arose. The legislative process of adding new functions and assigning them to operating agencies does not seem to have been guided by any clear and consistent view of the principal policy functions a modern central monetary authority should perform. One cannot escape the impression that this loose organization of functions reflects an inadequate appreciation in the past for the analytical interdependence of these various aspects of monetary policy.

In recent years, however, the variety of difficult challenges posed to the monetary authorities by events, both domestic and international, has placed this unwieldy structure of monetary institutions under stress. The system has been able to function adequately only through improvisations and informal accommodations. Relief from the need for such expedients is currently (1972) being sought through an integrated set of proposed changes in various laws (for example, exchange controls, regulation of deposit banks, savings banks, and other financial intermediaries). The changes should strengthen the statutory powers of the Banque Nationale de Belgique so it can perform the customary functions of a modern central bank in implementing monetary policy. In part, the proposed changes seek added powers to aid in controlling domestic credit allocation and international capital flows.

The Banque Nationale de Belgique was established as a central bank in 1850 and given the privilege of note issue. In 1948, the state acquired 50 per cent of the stock of the Banque. It is now governed under the terms of the Organic Law of the National Bank, which dates from 1939, with its various amendments. The law provides for the governing machinery of the Banque and sets forth various functions that the Banque may perform. Among these, primary attention is given to discounts, loans, and advances, under the Banque's role as lender of last resort. The Banque is authorized also to issue bank notes, deal in gold and silver, accept deposits, purchase and sell government or government-guaranteed securities, and serve as cashier for the government. The law does not mention broad responsibilities such as preservation of the purchasing power of the currency or regulation of its foreign exchange value.

The amount of securities that the central bank may hold in its portfolio is subject to an upper limit fixed by agreement between the Minister of Finance and the Banque. The limits set under this agreement have made no significant provision for the central bank to engage in open market operations. Rather, they cover a non-interest-bearing consolidated claim against the government of 34 billion francs resulting from the Second World War, investment of the Banque's staff pension fund, and a credit line to the Belgian government that may not exceed 16 billion francs at present and one to the Luxembourg government that may not exceed 533 million francs.[3] In addition, the central bank is free to invest in government or government-guaranteed securities an amount equal to its capital, reserves, and amortization funds.

Primary operational responsibility for open market purchases and sales of securities does not belong to the central bank but to the Securities Stabilization Fund (*Fonds des Rentes*), organized in 1945. Since the establishment of this fund, the central bank has voluntarily refrained from open market operations without, however, relinquishing its right in principle to undertake such operations. The Securities Stabilization Fund operates in both the money and the capital markets. Its principal task in these markets has been to stabilize prices and yields on government securities with the purpose of increasing their attractiveness to investors. Thus, its operations have not been guided primarily by the aim of controlling the liquidity of the banking system as a measure to aid in economic stabilization.

The Institute for Rediscount and Guarantee (*Institut de Réescompte et de Garantie*), a government agency, is the key intermediary in the bankers' acceptance portion of the short-term money market. The Institute helps to regulate the money market in cooperation with the central bank and the Securities Stabilization Fund. The Belgian-Luxembourg Foreign Exchange Institute (*Institut Belgo-Luxembourgeois du Change*), organized in 1944, is the authority concerned with foreign exchange control. The Exchange Institute prepares foreign exchange regulations and is responsible for their enforcement. Its administrative and operational activities are delegated to the central bank.

Coordination of these various central banking functions is achieved by means of a system of interlocking representation on policy-making boards of the various organizations. The Securities

[3] National Bank of Belgium, *Report,* 1971, pp. 98, 128.

Stabilization Fund and the Exchange Institute are subject to the joint supervision of the central bank and the Minister of Finance. The president of the Institute for Rediscount and Guarantee normally is a director of the central bank. The Minister of Finance is represented in the affairs of the Banque Nationale de Belgique by a commissioner who has veto power over decisions of the central bank should these conflict with the interests of the state.[4] Legally, therefore, the central bank is clearly subordinate to the Minister of Finance, who represents the government. In practice, the Banque has exercised a substantial degree of autonomy in policy matters subject to the government in power by whom its management is appointed.

Other state organizations exercise authority in the realm of credit and financial regulation. Principal among these is the Banking Commission (*Commission Bancaire*), which as bank regulatory authority can require deposit banks to maintain certain balance sheet ratios such as cash and liquidity reserve requirements. The Banking Commission also regulates new public issues of fixed interest securities by private issuers. The Ministry of Finance regulates new issues of securities by the public sector including those by local authorities and by various semipublic financial intermediaries such as the Municipal Credit Institution (*Crédit Communal*), National Industrial Credit Company (*Société Nationale de Crédit à l'Industrie*), and others. The Central Office for Small Savings (*Office Centrale de la Petite Epargne*) regulates activities of private savings banks. In practice, the regulatory measures by these organizations that influence monetary and credit policy are coordinated by the participation of representatives of the central bank and the Ministry of Finance in their governing boards.

FINANCIAL INSTITUTIONS AND MARKETS

The financial institutions of primary importance for monetary and credit policy in Belgium include the deposit banks, private savings banks, public savings banks, the Postal Check Office, and a variety of semipublic financial intermediaries and funds. The relative importance of these different types of credit institutions is shown in Table 2.1 in terms of their asset totals at the end of 1971. Not shown in Table 2.1 are the resources of the Postal Check Office, which had checking accounts averaging 79.8 billion francs on a daily basis during 1971.[5] As Table 2.1 indicates, the state-controlled savings banks and financial intermediaries held approximately 41 per cent of

---

[4] Hans Aufricht, ed., *Central Banking Legislation*, vol. 2, *Europe*, International Monetary Fund (Washington, D.C.: 1967) arts. 29–30, p. 65. The post of government commissioner to the central bank Council is filled by the Directeur General de la Trésorerie et de la Dette Publique, i.e., the permanent secretary of the treasury.

[5] *Bulletin*, XLVII Année, vol. 1, no. 6 (June 1972): 85.

TABLE 2.1   Belgium: Assets of Principal Types
of Credit Institutions (year-end, 1971)

	Billion francs	*Percentage*
Deposit banks	915.0 [a]	48.2
Private savings banks	203.3 [a]	10.7
The General Savings and Pension Fund	253.6 [b]	13.4
Public financial intermediaries and funds	527.8 [c]	27.8
	1,899.7	100.0

Source: Bulletin de la Banque Nationale de Belgique, XLVII Année, vol. 1, no. 5 (May 1972).

[a] p. vii.

[b] Year-end 1970, p. viii.

[c] p. viii. Note: This item does not include the resources of the Securities Stabilization Fund, of the National Investment Company (*Société Nationale d'Investissement*), or of the Postal Check Office.

the combined assets of these credit-granting institutions (excluding the Postal Check Office) at the end of 1971. Other types of financial institutions that are found in Belgium include life insurance companies, consumer finance firms, investment banks, and mortgage banks. These are of only peripheral importance in relation to monetary and credit policy.

In Belgian usage, the term *deposit banks* applies to institutions that accept deposits up to two years in maturity and use them for credits or investments.[6] The primary business of deposit banks is extension of short-term credit, much of it by discounting commercial bills. Since 1959, however, banks have been authorized to invest freely in medium- and long-term loans and to purchase corporate as well as government bonds. During the past decade they have increased their medium- and long-term loans and investments as savings and time deposits have increased in importance relative to sight deposits in their balance sheets. Thus, deposit banks are active participants in the capital market as well as in shorter-term money and credit markets.

Deposit banks also are the channels through which new issues of private-sector securities reach the capital market. They may not invest in corporate equities but are permitted to hold these for periods up to six months in connection with their activities in floating new issues.

Three large branch banking systems dominate the deposit banking business. These are the Société General de Banque, Banque de

[6] Aufricht, p. 91.

Bruxelles, and Kredietbank. Together they accounted for 61.3 per cent of the assets of deposit banks at the end of 1971.[7] The share of the "big three" has been declining steadily in recent years by about 3 per cent per year.

Savings bank facilities are provided by the state savings bank network known as the General Savings and Pension Fund (*Caisse Générale d'Epargne et de Retraite*) and by private savings banks. The latter are supervised by the Central Office for Small Savings. The private savings banks invest the bulk of their funds in mortgages and in government securities. The General Savings and Pension Fund is the principal nonbank financial intermediary in Belgium. It obtains the bulk of its funds through savings deposits and savings certificates. This fund makes a large variety of loans and investments, principal among which are domestic commercial bills, loans to industry, bankers' acceptances, mortgage loans, treasury certificates, certificates of the Securities Stabilization Fund, and government and government-guaranteed bonds. The bulk of its pension and insurance funds are invested in government securities.[8]

The state operates the Postal Check Office to provide current account and bill-paying services to the public. Its funds in excess of those required for current operations are placed at the disposition of the Treasury.

The state sponsors a variety of financial intermediaries to channel medium- and longer-term credit into uses accorded high priority by public policy. These include institutions to foster industrial, agricultural, export, communal, and housing credit.

The Belgian financial markets of primary importance for monetary and credit policies are the short-term money market and the market for medium- and long-term government and government-guaranteed securities. Through these markets the monetary authorities influence monetary and credit conditions. The Rediscount and Guarantee Institute is the key intermediary in the bankers' acceptance portion of the money market, whereas the Securities Stabilization Fund plays an active policy role throughout the maturity spectrum in these markets. Direct intervention in these markets by the Belgian central bank is minor and without policy significance. In its role as lender of last resort, the central bank indirectly supplies funds to these markets when it extends credit to the Rediscount and Guarantee Institute, the Securities Stabilization Fund and the Treasury.

INSTRUMENTS AND TECHNIQUES OF MONETARY POLICY

Discussion of the instruments of monetary and credit policy is complicated slightly by the decentralization of such instruments among

---

[7] "Les Instruments," p. vii.
[8] *Bulletin*, XLVII Année, vol. 1, no. 6, pp. 91–92, Table 45.

the various institutions mentioned above.[9] Among available instruments are rediscount policy, minimum obligatory reserve requirements, open market purchases and sales of securities, and ceilings on bank credit expansion. In addition, certain bank deposit rates are fixed by the central bank in consultation with the Belgian Bankers Association, and bank lending rates are tied by convention and by official suggestion to the central bank's discount rate. Interest rates in both the money and the capital markets are dominated by the policies and actions of the Securities Stabilization Fund with the cooperation in the money market of the Rediscount and Guarantee Institute.

Rediscount Policy
The Banque Nationale de Belgique is the lender of last resort in the Belgian monetary system. The Banque discounts a variety of foreign trade and commercial bills with maturities up to 120 days. In the past it has applied preferential rates of discount to types of bills or uses of credit that national policy sought to encourage, for example, export credit. It has also refused to rediscount certain types of bills, notably those intended to finance consumer installment credit. The Banque also makes advances against secured promissory notes of banks, public institutions, a variety of private institutions, and individuals. The required security must be in the form of government or government-guaranteed securities, securities of the Municipal Credit Institution, obligations of provincial and local authorities, or specified international organizations. The vast bulk of the Banque's credit to the economy is extended through discounts rather than advances.

Most of the bills discounted by the central bank are not presented to it directly but reach it via the intermediation of the Rediscount and Guarantee Institute or one of the state-run financial intermediaries established to channel credit to specific categories of users. Among these are the public credit institutions that specialize in providing industrial, agricultural, professional, and mortgage credit.[10]

Prior to May 1, 1969, the Banque Nationale de Belgique had for many years set quantitative limits to the amount of discount credit for which individual banks were eligible. These limits were established for individual banks as a ratio to their capital and surplus and were intended to protect bank solvency rather than serve as an in-

[9] This section has profited greatly from the article "Les Instruments de la Politique Monetaire en Belgique," in *Bulletin*, XLVII Année, vol. 1, no. 5, pp. iii–lii.

[10] The list includes la Société Nationale de Crédit à l'Industrie, le Crédit Communal de Belgique, la Caisse Nationale de Crédit Professionnel, l'Institut National de Crédit Agricole, l'Office Central de Crédit Hypothécaire, la Société Nationale du Logement, and la Société Nationale de la Petite Propriété Terrienne.

strument of monetary policy. Banks were not informed of their limits, and these were rarely reached.

Beginning May 1, 1969, bank discounting and borrowing on advances, whether direct or via intermediaries, have been subject to a system of rediscounting and certification ceilings that are specific to individual banks. Counted against the ceiling are bills and acceptances already presented for discount to the central bank or to the Rediscount and Guarantee Institute and also foreign trade acceptances approved in advance for rediscount and bearing a central bank "visa" to this effect whether presented for discount or not. Until the recent past, a central bank visa qualified foreign trade bills for a privileged rate of discount. This privilege has been suspended since 1970. The new rediscount ceiling is defined as a percentage of the average volume of a bank's deposits in Belgian francs, notes, cash certificates, and capital for the preceding twelve months. The percentage can be varied, and has been, for reasons of monetary policy. It was set at 16 per cent of the specified liabilities in May 1969 and has since been as low as 9 per cent. The purpose of the ceiling is to permit the central bank to regulate the quantity of rediscounting by refusing to discount or certify for rediscount bills that otherwise meet its general standards for rediscountability. Thus, the measure strengthens the control the central bank exercises over the volume of credit it extends to the banking system.

The Rediscount and Guarantee Institute, a state agency, was organized in 1935 to assist banks in meeting liquidity needs by rediscounting assets not eligible for rediscount by central bank standards. It functions as the key intermediary in the bankers' and commercial acceptance portions of the money market. It is no exaggeration to say that the Institute "makes the market" by buying and selling bankers and commercial acceptances and serving as broker. It buys only from banks and sells only to a selected list of financial institutions: banks, public credit organizations, private savings banks, mortgage societies, and international organizations, and to some lesser extent to insurance companies. Nonbank firms and individuals are not permitted to participate in this market.

Funds used by the Institute to enable it to be a *net* purchaser in this market come from its own borrowings in the call money (or day-to-day) market and from rediscounting by it at the central bank. For example, during 1971, the Institute's daily average volume of acceptances negotiated was 25.4 billion francs, of which 17.9 billion were resold or placed in the market, 6.1 billion were financed by the Institute's borrowing of call money, and 2.6 billion were rediscounted at the central bank.[11]

On acceptances with no more than 120 days to maturity, the Institute discounts at a rate below that charged by the central bank.

[11] *Bulletin,* XLVII Année, vol. 1, no. 5, p. xxxix, Table 11.

Public credit institutions that engage in rediscounting follow a parallel policy so as to channel funds to priority credit uses. For this reason, the volume of bank discounting directly with the central bank is minor in comparison with that with the Institute and the public credit institutions. For example, average end-of-quarter data for 1971 show deposit bank discounts of 19.5 billion francs at the Rediscount and Guarantee Institute, 7.9 billion at other public credit institutions, and 0.1 billion at the Banque Nationale de Belgique. The same data show an additional volume of discounting of 6.7 billion francs at "other national discounters" [not further identified], and 1.4 billion discounted with foreign sources, and they indicate that the Rediscount and Guarantee Institute refinanced 3.1 billion with the central bank.[12]

In interpreting statistics on rediscounting, one should be aware that only that portion of rediscounting that reaches the central bank directly or indirectly or takes place abroad adds to the domestic money supply. The remainder simply represents internal short-term credit flows that redistribute existing money balances.

The Belgian central bank regards its policy on rediscount rates and ceilings as an important mode of action to influence the economy but is aware of limitations on the effectiveness of these measures. Commercial bank lending rates are conventionally linked to the central bank's rediscount rate, but limited movement in these rates does not exert much influence on the demand for bank credit. Moreover, effects on domestic liquidity of changes in the central bank's rediscount rate tend to be offset by short-term capital movements between the Belgian and foreign money markets. Bank time deposit rates, once tied firmly to the rediscount rate, since 1961 have been set independently of that rate by consultation between the central bank and the Belgian Bankers Association. Although the central bank rediscount rate has been altered frequently in recent years, the authorities probably regard such changes as having more indicative than substantive importance in the current environment for monetary policy.

Open Market Operations

Open market operations are the responsibility of the Securities Stabilization Fund (*Fonds des Rentes*), which is jointly managed by the central bank and the Ministry of Finance. The Securities Stabilization Fund was established in 1945 to regulate the market for medium- and long-term public securities. In 1959, the scope of the Fund's activities was extended to include the market for short-term public securities and the very short-term money market. The Fund has an endowed capital of 2.8 billion francs. It obtains the bulk of its resources by borrowing in the call money market, by a weekly

[12] Ibid., p. xvii.

auction of its four-month certificates, and by a line of credit of 4 billion francs at the Banque Nationale de Belgique.

The Fund has as a primary task to stabilize the market for public securities of all maturities. *Public securities* is defined as including securities issued or guaranteed by the central government as well as securities issued by local government authorities, the Municipal Credit Institution, the Telegraphs and Telephones Board, and the Belgian National Railways Company. In the markets for these securities, the Fund exercises a dominant influence on both the level and the term structure of interest rates. To withdraw liquidity from the banking system, the Fund may sell its own certificates and deposit the proceeds in its account at the central bank. To supply liquidity, it can reverse the process and even draw on its line of credit with the central bank. The Fund is a net borrower in the call money and short-term security markets and a net investor in longer-term securities of the central government, of various other government entities, and of official credit institutions.

Despite these capabilities of the Securities Stabilization Fund together with the complementary activities of the Rediscount and Guarantee Institute in the acceptance portion of the money market, open market policy cannot be considered a principal instrument of monetary policy in Belgium. A superficial explanation for this is the absence of broad participation in the market for short-term public securities in Belgium. But a more fundamental reason has been the government's desire to provide priority access for public borrowing at low and stable rates of interest in both the money market and the capital market.

The Belgian money market has three main subdivisions: (1) the market for day-to-day, or call, money; (2) the bankers' and commercial acceptances market; and (3) the market for short-term certificates issued by the Treasury, the Securities Stabilization Fund, and the public highway authority. The call money market is regulated with a view to serving the changing liquidity needs of deposit-taking and credit-granting institutions, to financing foreign trade, and to stabilizing the interest rates on public securities. Besides the regulatory agencies, participation in the market is limited to public and private financial institutions with deposit obligations having maturities of three months or less. The privilege of borrowing net is reserved to the Rediscount and Guarantee Institute and to the Securities Stabilization Fund. Other participants may borrow only to meet liquidity needs and not for investment purposes, and they may not be net borrowers on the average during any calendar quarter.

In the section of the money market dealing in short-term certificates, the Treasury, the Securities Stabilization Fund, and the public highway authority are the sole borrowers. Banks are the principal buyers of the four-month certificates of the Securities Stabilization Fund, whereas the state savings network is the principal subscriber to Treasury certificates. There is also a substantial volume of special Treasury certificates that is placed privately with the public financial institutions.

The acceptance market is the domain of the Rediscount and Guarantee Institute. There, as we have seen, only banks may be net borrowers, and lenders come from a restricted list of financial institutions.

Nonbank firms and individuals are barred from participation in all three sectors of the money market either as borrowers or as investors. This is partially a reflection of the view that the market should not compete with banks for the deposits of firms and individuals. But more basically, their exclusion reflects the government's determination to channel the flow of credit through regulated institutions and markets so as to allocate credit to government and other priority uses at moderate rates of interest that neither impose too heavy an interest burden on the government budget nor discourage desired investment in housing and various forms of social infrastructure and productive capital.

Reserve Ratios

Statutory authority to prescribe cash reserve requirements and other required balance sheet ratios rests with the Banking Commission (*Commission Bancaire*), established in 1935 as a separate agency to regulate banks in order to preserve their liquidity and solvency. From 1946 to 1962, the Banking Commission required banks to fulfill a capital ratio (*coefficient de solvabilité*), a cash ratio (*coefficient de trésorerie*), and a cover ratio (*coefficient de couverture*). The cash ratio was set at 4 per cent of liabilities of maturity of one month or longer and could be met by holding cash, call loans, or deposits at the central bank. The cover ratio applied to liabilities up to two years and required the holding of cash and government securities in amounts calculated by a detailed formula. The cash ratio was supposed to protect the liquidity of banks. The cover ratio was intended to ease the task of budgetary policy by preventing banks from liquidating too rapidly their extensive holdings of government securities accumulated during the war and to guarantee that any expansion of bank resources would be accompanied by additions to bank portfolios of government securities. These ratios could be changed by the Banking Commission only with the agreement of the Ministry of Finance and the Ministry of Economics. Throughout the period 1946–62 they remained fixed. No attempt was made to use them as instruments of monetary policy.

In 1961, the authorities rescinded the cash and cover ratios and introduced a new system of minimum cash reserves intended to provide the monetary authorities with an instrument that could be altered to influence bank liquidity. Under this system, the required reserve is calculated as a percentage of sight, time, and savings

deposits. It can be met by holding sight deposits in Belgian francs
at the central bank, or if the Banking Commission so rules, by sight
claims against the Securities Stabilization Fund or in the form of
special Treasury bills deposited with the central bank. This instrument has been very little used. There appear to be two reasons for
this. One is the legal confusion concerning the role of the Banking
Commission in relation to that of the central bank in using the
instrument. The other difficulty is that the banks' response to an
increase in the reserve ratio has been to reduce their purchases of
Treasury certificates, thus putting pressure on the financing of the
government budget. When last used, from July 1964 to July 1965,
the minimum cash reserve ratio was set at 1 per cent.

From May 1969 to May 1970, the Banking Commission used a new
asset coefficient referred to as the reinvestment coefficient (*coefficient
de remploi*). This coefficient established a required minimum ratio
between certain liquid assets held by banks and their obligations
with maturities up to two years. Among the principal assets eligible
to satisfy the requirement were cash assets, rediscountable commercial
bills, and public bills and longer-term public securities. The purpose
of the reinvestment coefficient was to prevent banks from liquidating
rediscountable bills and government securities in response to the
authorities' initiatives to restrict bank rediscounting.

Certain conclusions emerge from this review of various ratios that
commercial banks in Belgium have been required to observe in
recent years. The authorities do not hesitate in principle to apply
such ratios. Their hesitancy stems rather from legal confusion concerning the respective roles of the Banking Commission and the
central bank in using these measures and in their apparent reluctance to accept the consequences of tighter credit conditions for
market interest rates and the cost of financing the government debt.
There is also the problem of international, short-term capital flows
in response to interest rate differentials between Belgian and foreign
financial markets.

Loan Ceilings

We have seen that the three classical instruments of monetary policy,
that is, rediscount policy, reserve asset ratios, and open market operations, have been of limited effectiveness in Belgian circumstances.
It is not surprising, therefore, that recent years (beginning with
1964) have witnessed an increasing reliance on credit ceilings. The
Banque Nationale de Belgique administers credit ceilings for deposit
banks, whereas appropriate supervisory agencies such as the Central
Office for Small Savings administer them for other credit institutions.
These ceilings have been applied in a flexible manner by the relevant
authorities. They were in constant use from April 1969 until they
were suspended in late September 1971, with the modes and intensity
of rationing varying according to circumstance. Typically the burden

of credit restriction has fallen on the private sector of the economy, with no restrictions imposed on credits to the public sector. Within the private sector, export credits have been exempt, and installment credit, personal loans, and other consumption loans have been singled out for special credit restriction. A bank that exceeded its ceiling was subject to penalty by having its rediscount line reduced by at least the amount of the excess.

Interest Rate Policy

Until 1962, bank deposit rates were tied to the central bank's rediscount rate by a rigid formula. From that date, bank deposit rates have been regulated by the central bank in consultation with the Belgian Bankers Association. Interest rates on deposit accounts with balances in excess of 5 million francs are not regulated. Bank lending rates on shorter maturity loans are tied by convention and by official suggestion to the central bank's rediscount rate. Rates on longer-term bank loans take as a benchmark the lending rates of the National Industrial Credit Company (*Societé Nationale de Crédit à l'Industrie*).

Interest rates in both the money and capital markets are strongly influenced then by the policies and actions of the Securities Stabilization Fund with the cooperation in the money market of the Rediscount and Guarantee Institute. Lending rates for the public credit institutions specialized to various types of credit, for example productive investment, exports, and housing, are established by their respective administrations. The central bank has influence in such decisions through its representation in their governing boards. For example, the governor of the central bank is chairman of both the Council of Public Credit Institutions and the board of the Central Office for Small Savings.[13]

Clearly, the Belgian authorities exert substantial influence on both the structure and the level of interest rates throughout the maturity spectrum. This influence derives not only from administrative participation in the setting of rates but also from the dominance granted public institutions acting as intermediaries in both the money and the capital markets. This influence on the cost and availability of credit is strengthened by regulations affecting access of borrowers to the capital market and by policies designed to influence capital movements between the Belgian money and capital markets and the counterpart markets in other countries.

CAPITAL MARKET POLICY

Our consideration of capital market policy takes us beyond the realm of monetary policy in the narrow sense of central bank policy. How-

---

[13] Ibid., p. xxvii.

ever, in the Belgian financial system, capital market controls complement monetary policy and foreign exchange controls; they contribute
to a broader framework of controls and regulations designed to
achieve goals of national economic policy. Essentially, the government, through the Ministry of Finance and the Banking Commission,
completely controls the domestic capital market for fixed-interest
securities. The system of controls is used to provide priority access
to the capital market for public and semipublic borrowers and for
private borrowers whose investment projects have been accorded a
high priority by official criteria. The Ministry of Finance prepares
annually a calendar for all public sector issues that will be offered
for subscription. This calendar is rarely modified during the year.
Private sector issues are supervised by the Banking Commission. The
Commission has the power to delay for three months a private sector
issue of which it does not approve. In practice such disputes do not
arise, since private firms accept the commission's recommendations
without challenge. Public sector issues dominate the volume of publicly marketed securities in Belgium, having averaged two-thirds or
more of total issues of fixed-interest securities in recent years.[14] Not
only the volume and timing of publicly marketed securities but also
their coupon yields are strongly influenced by official policy.

Various public and semipublic financial intermediaries are given
priority access to the bond market. The amounts they may borrow
as well as their lending policies are regulated by the Ministry of Finance and other relevant ministries. Among these official financial
intermediaries, the Municipal Credit Institution, the National Industrial Credit Company, the National Housing Company, and the
National Institute for Agricultural Credit are representative. By
offering medium- and long-term credit more cheaply and on better
terms than their respective clients can obtain in the regulated public
issues market, these institutions help to channel investment capital
into uses with high official priorities.

Private placements are relatively unimportant in the Belgian system. Those that do occur must fit into the highly regulated structure
of credit and capital markets that has been established by official
policy.

Access of nonresident borrowers to the Belgian capital market is
subject to approval by the Minister of Finance. This is rarely
granted.[15] But Belgian residents are free to buy foreign securities on
foreign markets. Individual Belgian investors have displayed a growing interest in foreign securities, including Eurobond issues but not
limited to these. This interest has been stimulated in part by higher

[14] European Communities Monetary Committee, *Policy on the Bond
Markets in the Countries of the EEC,* Brussels, October 1970, p. 66.
[15] Ibid., p. 31.

interest rates abroad and in part by a desire to evade high Belgian tax rates on interest and dividend income. Since there is no similar withholding tax on income from interest and dividends in Luxembourg, many Belgians have opened bank accounts in Luxembourg banks and entrusted securities to Luxembourg banks for custody and investment management. Despite measures to restrict the solicitation of Belgian investors for foreign securities, such investments constitute the chief gap in Belgian controls over capital flows. Foreign exchange used to purchase foreign securities must be purchased at the floating rate of the free market rather than at the official parity.

POLICY TOWARDS INTERNATIONAL CAPITAL MOVEMENTS

The domestic system of monetary instruments and credit controls in Belgium is supplemented by a system of foreign exchange controls administered by the Belgian-Luxembourg Foreign Exchange Institute (*Institut Belgo-Luxembourgeois du Change*) under the direct supervision of the Banque Nationale de Belgique. This system is used both to assist in the regulation of domestic liquidity and related credit conditions and, when necessary, to prevent an excessive inflow or outflow of foreign exchange through short-term capital movements. Since 1955, there have been two exchange markets in operation for spot transactions: the official market and the free market. Until May 10, 1971, the basic principles of operation were that any inpayment could be made on the regulated market and any outpayment on the free market. Certain outpayments, broadly speaking those arising from current account transactions, also were authorized for the official market. In the official market, central bank intervention kept the spot rate within prescribed bands around the official parity of the Belgian franc. The free market rate was permitted to rise against the franc when outpayments exceeded inpayments. When inpayments exceeded outpayments on the free market, the option of making inpayments through the official market put a floor under the free market rate at the support level of the official market.

This system was modified on May 10, 1971, following the floating of the German mark and the Dutch guilder. From that date, use of the official market has been restricted to specified current account transactions, whether they involve inpayments or outpayments. All other transactions in either direction must pass through the free market, in which the exchange rate is determined by the forces of supply and demand. Under this system, there is no predetermined floor or ceiling to the free market rate.[16]

---

[16] For details of the regulation, see "Decision du Conseil de l'Institut Belgo-Luxembourgeois du Change du 10 Mai 1971," in *Bulletin,* XLVI Année, vol. 1, no. 5 (May 1971): xxix–xxx.

Operation of such a system requires the establishing of criteria and rules for distinguishing types of transactions assignable to the respective markets and enforcement of such rules through an adequate inspection system. Exchange rate differentials that may arise between the two markets provide incentives for transactors to violate the rules of the system. Thus, a substantial administrative apparatus is required to guarantee the proper functioning of a two market system. In practice, leakages between the free and the regulated markets have occurred despite official surveillance. Such leakages tend to increase the larger the difference between the free and official exchange rates becomes and the longer such difference persists.

In addition to this system of exchange controls, the authorities have used other techniques to insulate domestic credit markets from external influences. The net foreign position of commercial banks has been subjected to officially determined limits, and the time period permitted for settlement of current account transactions has been regulated in an attempt to control commercial leads and lags. Banks have been prohibited from paying interest on nonresident, convertible demand deposits and from accepting time and notice deposits from nonresidents. These types of transactions provide channels for short-term capital transfers that are difficult to distinguish from legitimate current account transactions entitled to pass through the regulated exchange market. This fact may explain why they are the subject of special regulations.

BUDGETARY POLICY

Consideration of the role of the state budget completes this survey of the Belgian monetary and credit system. We have already seen that a variety of regulations and controls confers on the state and its official credit agencies the status of privileged borrowers in both money and capital markets. Moreover, through the agency of the Securities Stabilization Fund with its access to central bank credit, official policy has stabilized interest rates in these markets at low to moderate levels. In these circumstances, unless the state regulates its demands on the credit and financial markets so as to stay within the limits established by the flow of savings and the share of these allocated to the state by its system of priorities, an inflationary expansion in the money supply must occur.

For many years, preparation of the state budget in Belgium has been guided by the rule of thumb that government current consumption of goods and services, including social security, should be covered by tax levies, and that the government investment budget should be financed in the capital market. This rule may have diverted attention from the effects of the very size of the budget on aggregate demand and of the investment-linked deficit on interest rates and money supply, so that the compensatory role of the budget over the business cycle has been underutilized.[17] There has also been a tendency to increase extrabudget financing for certain projects such as highway construction so as to be able to reduce the size of the investment budget per se. There is little difference in the effects in the capital market of these alternative modes of budgeting the state's capital expenditures.

The restrictions that the law imposes on the ability of the central bank to purchase government debt and thus extend credit to the Treasury have occasionally led to the sale of Treasury obligations abroad to finance the government budget. The foreign exchange that the Treasury obtains in this fashion is then sold to the central bank in exchange for Belgian francs to finance domestic expenditures. This method increases the domestic money supply in the same way as net purchase of government securities by the central bank in open market operations. The accompanying capital inflow through the balance of payments is a side effect of this mode of government finance. The Treasury occasionally has used the proceeds of domestic taxes or bond sales to retire debt held abroad in order to reduce the domestic money supply to support a restrictive policy by the central bank.[18] To this extent, the mode of financing of the government budget may be said to have made a positive contribution to compensatory aggregate demand management.

LUXEMBOURG'S RELATIONSHIP TO THE BELGIAN FINANCIAL SYSTEM

No discussion of the Belgian monetary and financial system can omit reference to the monetary and economic union between Belgium and Luxembourg. By the same token, it is unrealistic to treat monetary and credit policy in Luxembourg separately from that of the major partner. Luxembourg is too small to be able to exist as an independent monetary and economic unit. The cost of economic independence would be prohibitive. Luxembourg's economic and monetary union with Belgium recognizes this fact.

Luxembourg has no central bank. Belgian currency circulates freely in Luxembourg and is estimated to constitute 98 per cent of

---

[17] In his study of Belgian fiscal policy, Bent Hansen concluded: "The recurrent 'budget crises' which have hamstrung the use of the budget for demand management purposes have rather had their origin in the fact that increased public borrowing in the narrow capital market tends to divert funds from private investment activities, and that rigorous provisions limit the possibilities of the central bank to extend loans to the government or to support the credit market," Bent Hansen, assisted by Wayne W. Snyder, *Fiscal Policy in Seven Countries, 1955–1965,* OECD, March 1969, p. 124.

[18] This practice stands in sharp contrast to that of the Netherlands, where the goal for capital flows through the balance of payments is one of monetary neutrality. Cf. chapter on the Netherlands.

the currency in circulation in Luxembourg.[19] An agreement between the two governments limits the amount of Luxembourg currency that the Luxembourg Ministry of Finance may issue. Foreign exchange reserves of Luxembourg are concentrated in the Banque Nationale de Belgique and administered jointly under the Belgian-Luxembourg Foreign Exchange Institute.

Luxembourg has a state banking system known as the State Savings Bank (*Caisse d'Epargne de l'Etat*). This is primarily a savings bank but does perform commercial banking functions also. Private banks tend to specialize in commercial banking, leaving savings banking and accompanying medium- and long-term lending, particularly mortgage lending, to the State Savings Bank.

The Commissioner for Control of Banks exercises supervisory authority over Luxembourg commercial banks, savings banks, and consumer credit institutions under authority delegated from the Ministry of Finance. His regulatory powers are limited essentially to those required to assure the safety and liquidity of banks in the interest of their depositors. The commissioner may also control consumer installment credit but requires the consent of 90 per cent of the banks and the approval of the Minister of Finance in doing so.

Luxembourg commercial banks are not entitled to rediscount at the Banque Nationale de Belgique or obtain advances from it. To obtain this privilege, they would have to fulfill certain conditions that they prefer not to meet. Their status is analagous to that of banks in the United States that are not members of the Federal Reserve System. Luxembourg banks do make use of the Belgian money market to adjust their liquidity positions. The primary source of monetary expansion in Luxembourg is foreign exchange earnings. The current account surplus has been persistent and substantial. It depends heavily on exports of the steel industry.

Short-term interest rates normally are somewhat lower in Luxembourg than in Belgium. Since various forms of credit rationing exist, market arbitrage does not remove these differences. There appear to be informal credit limits assigned by banks to Luxembourg firms with the approval of the Ministry of Finance. Interest rates on loans and deposits of commercial banks and also commissions of all sorts are agreed on among representatives of the commercial banks, also with the informal approval of the Ministry of Finance. Interlock among the directorates and lending committees of Belgian and Luxembourg banks assists the banks to resist customer efforts to shop for better lending terms.

The state is the primary borrower in the domestic capital market. Private banks, insurance companies, and pension funds all are required to invest a certain portion of their assets in state bonds. The State Savings Bank also lends to the state. The amount the state

[19] Norbert von Kunitzki, "Le systeme monetaire Luxembourgeois," *d'Letzeburger Land*, no. 27/2, July 1971.

budget may borrow from the State Savings Bank is limited to 500 million francs. There is a limit of 533 million francs on the amount that the Luxembourg budget may borrow from the Belgian central bank. The government's capacity effectively to use a compensatory budgetary policy in aggregate demand management is negligible owing to these limits, to the absence of a central bank able to assist in deficit financing by expanding the money supply, and above all to the extremely high degree of economic integration between the Luxembourg economy and its trading partners. Luxembourg is said to export 80 per cent of its domestic production and to import 80 per cent of the products it consumes.[20] Thus, the budget tax-expenditure multiplier is very low.

Luxembourg thus has no capacity for an independent monetary policy and very limited scope for an independent credit policy. Through mutual agreement these powers are exercised by the Belgian authorities within the framework of the Belgian-Luxembourg monetary and economic union.

EVALUATION AND COMMENTARY

The economic record of Belgium (and by implication of Luxembourg) in the past decade has combined a respectable rate of growth in real gross national product with moderate inflation and avoidance of any serious external imbalance in the balance of payments. Table 2.2 presents relevant statistics for money supply, real gross national product, and several measures of price changes. This favorable record owes little to monetary policy conducted by relying on the classic instruments of such policy — rediscount rate, cash reserve requirements, and open market operations — to influence the money supply and the cost and availability of credit in unregulated financial markets. These three market-oriented policy instruments have not played a principal role in monetary management; rather, the monetary authorities have relied increasingly on various forms of direct intervention and quantitative regulation to influence the amount, cost, and allocation of credit. Their techniques have included the placing of ceilings on bank lending, the establishment of quantitative limits to bank discounting at the central bank, the regulation of commercial bank lending and borrowing abroad, and the use of required liquid asset reserves to freeze banks into holdings of various rediscountable assets — commercial bills and government securities among them. Bank lending rates have been linked to the central bank's rediscount rate by tradition and official suggestion, and changes in bank deposits rates of interest have required approval by the central bank.

These "monetary" measures have been bolstered by the dominant

[20] Norbert von Kunitzki, "La Politique Monetaire," *d'Letzeburger Land*, no. 28/9, July 1971.

TABLE 2.2   Belgium: Money Supply, Real GNP,
            and Price Indexes (annual percentage changes)

Year	Money supply [a] (% change)	Real GNP [b] (% change)	GNP deflator [c] (% change)	Consumer prices [d] (% change)	Wholesale prices [e] (% change)
1960	1.89	5.49	0.94	....	....
1961	7.71	4.99	1.07	1.00	0.00
1962	7.20	5.64	1.15	1.35	0.98
1963	9.15	4.41	2.85	2.13	2.91
1964	7.05	6.84	4.66	4.17	4.71
1965	7.12	3.81	5.07	4.09	0.90
1966	6.62	2.94	4.60	4.17	2.67
1967	3.17	3.77	3.09	2.91	1.76
1968	7.41	3.56	2.37	2.70	0.88
1969	2.60	6.54	3.54	3.74	4.38
1970	8.33	....	....	3.91	5.04
Compound annual rate of growth					
	6.62	4.72	3.15	3.00	2.05

   [a] Currency, sight deposits, one-month deposits, and current accounts
with the BNB, OCP, Treasury. 1960–62 figures calculated from Institut
National de Statistique, Ministère des Affaires Economiques, *Annuaire
Statistique de la Belgique*, 1970, p. 461. 1963–70 figures calculated from
Bulletin de la Banque Nationale de Belgique, December 1971, p. 74.
   [b] Calculated from *Annuaire Statistique*, pp. 672–3.
   [c] 1960–63 figures calculated from real GNP figures and from *Annuaire
Statistique*, pp. 660–61. 1964–70 figures calculated from real GNP figures
and from *Bulletin*, p. 8.
   [d] 1961–65 figures calculated from *Annuaire Statistique*, pp. 555–56.
1966–70 figures calculated from *Bulletin*, p. 33.
   [e] Calculated from *Annuaire Statistique*, p. 559.

role of public organizations in financial intermediation. Among
these, the Securities Stabilization Fund, the Rediscount and Guarantee Institute, the General Savings and Pension Office, the Postal
Check Office, and the various public specialized credit institutions
are particularly important. Through this network of institutions, the
state exercises a strong influence on the allocation of credit to approved uses. Control of new bond issues on the capital market assures that the needs of priority public and semipublic borrowers will
take precedence over needs of private firms. Belgian firms are enticed
to undertake investments in accord with national priorities by low-
cost credits and interest subsidies.
   The Belgian two-tier foreign exchange market also deserves recognition as an important aspect of the authorities' system of financial
controls. By permitting the exchange rate for capital account transactions to respond to the market forces of supply and demand, the
authorities have greatly reduced the influence of disruptive short-

term capital movements on domestic credit markets. Thus, forces emanating from external money and capital markets have been less able to challenge and offset domestic policy measures in Belgium than in some other countries studied in this volume. The two-tier market should not be regarded as a panacea, however, since discrepancies between the exchange rate in the official market and in the free market offer incentives for evasion of the system and may at times pose significant enforcement problems.

The Belgian government has not placed large emphasis on prices and incomes policies in its approach to the control of inflation.[21] It has required prior notification of price increases and occasionally resorted to a price freeze for short periods. However, enforcement has not been vigorous.

Linkage to cost-of-living indexes of most wage contracts and of family allowances, unemployment compensation, and other social transfer payments are of interest. Such indexation often has been resisted in other countries as a built-in mechanism for accelerating an inflationary spiral. The Belgian experience shows that it need not function in this way. These aspects of the Belgian economic situation deserve further exploration in another study for their relevance to the Belgian record of moderate inflation in recent years.

In March 1972, a bill was presented to the Belgian Parliament proposing changes in existing legislation that were intended to strengthen the powers of the Banque Nationale de Belgique as the key monetary authority and to provide a more solid legal basis for certain techniques of monetary and credit policy that had been developed as expedients in recent years.[22] Since the bill resulted from extensive consultation among the relevant authorities and ministries, its passage in due course can be expected. A review of its principal features serves to indicate the direction in which monetary and credit techniques may develop in Belgium in the near future.

The main themes represented by the proposed changes are readily stated. The bill clarifies the respective roles of the central bank, the Banking Commission, the Ministry of Finance, and other ministries in initiating changes in monetary and credit policy. The central bank is to be empowered to take the initiative in requiring deposit banks, savings banks, and public financial intermediaries to observe various balance sheet ratios, to limit the volume of certain balance sheet items (for example, by loan ceilings), to place special non-interest-bearing deposits in Belgian francs or foreign exchange with the central bank, and to stipulate maximum interest rates payable on their deposits and other liabilities. The Banking Commission, the

[21] See, for example, OECD Economic Surveys, *Belgium-Luxembourg Economic Union*, June 1971, pp. 25–27.

[22] Projet de loi relatif au contrôle des changes, à la politique monetaire, et au statut des banques, des caisses d'épargne privées et de certains autres intermediaires financiers.

Ministry of Finance, and other appropriate ministries will retain their respective statutory roles in setting such requirements but will do so automatically at the initiative of the central bank. The Central Office for Small Savings, which has been the supervisory authority for private savings banks, will be dissolved and the Banking Commission will take over its functions. These provisions of the bill greatly strengthen the role of the central bank in initiating and co-ordinating measures of monetary and credit policy. They also extend the coverage of its actions from deposit banks to all of the important types of financial intermediaries. No restrictions are placed on the selective application of these measures to certain types of credit institutions.

The proposed bill also strengthens the powers of the Belgo-Luxembourg Foreign Exchange Institute to regulate short-term capital flows between the Belgian and foreign money markets. The Institute is given the authority to limit or prohibit the remuneration of non-resident deposits and placements in Belgian francs, or foreign currencies in banks and other financial intermediaries domiciled in Belgium, as well as deposits and placements in foreign currencies in Belgian banks and financial intermediaries by residents. The Institute can also levy a charge (for example, penalty interest) payable to the Treasury on such deposits and placements. Further, the bill provides the Institute with authority to limit the amount of borrowing in foreign currencies either from foreigners or from Belgians on the part of banks *and other enterprises* (for example, business firms). Likewise the Institute may limit lending to foreigners in Belgian francs by banks or other enterprises. It may also require stipulated portions of such lendings or borrowings as are permitted to be deposited in blocked, non-interest-bearing deposits at the central bank as a device to make the cost of such credits to the borrower more expensive. Finally, the Institute is permitted to be selective in applying these provisions.

The provisions of the bill if passed into law will certainly strengthen the authority of the central bank in implementing monetary and credit policy and of the Foreign Exchange Institute in regulating short-term international capital movements. The thrust of the measures proposed is toward greater direct intervention by the regulatory authorities in the management of banks and other credit institutions, more selective controls, and implied decreased reliance on the more general instruments of central bank policy such as the rediscount rate and open market policy. This emphasis on credit policy in contrast to general monetary policy is in accord with Belgian tradition.

3 France

The purpose of this chapter is to present French monetary and credit controls as a coherent system, to display the inner logic of this system, and to evaluate its implications for such policy objectives as economic growth, a stable price level, and a sustainable balance-of-payments situation. Despite its many elements in common with monetary and credit systems in other countries the French system is sufficiently different in the degree of direct administrative intervention by the authorities into credit affairs that any simple interpretation of policy actions by French authorities that relies on direct parallels to practice in other countries is likely to prove misleading. The effects of even such traditional central banking techniques as open market purchases and sales and alterations in the central bank rediscount rate cannot be understood in the French environment without a grasp of certain general features of French financial institutions. Moreover, in assessing the actions of the monetary authorities it is important to appreciate the priority that French authorities assign to selective credit policy as distinct from general monetary policy and the extent to which their system permits them to intervene by administrative measures into the free play of financial market forces.

The French approach to national monetary and credit policy is based upon a political consensus that asserts the need to control the financial system in the service of national economic goals. This consensus was formed during the years of occupation and resistance in the Second World War and appears to rest upon both a positive commitment to national economic planning and upon a critical view of the performance of banks and other financial institutions during certain episodes of pre-war French history.[1]

By way of orientation a brief and thus oversimplified statement of certain key features of the French system is helpful. First from 1945 to date the French system of monetary and credit controls has assigned a higher priority to the allocation of credit than to control of the money supply. Second, to encourage investment and to assist French export industries in meeting foreign competition the level of French interest rates has been deliberately kept at a level below that of market equilibrium throughout this period.[2] Third, speaking broadly, the *Banque de France* (central bank) has the responsibility for controlling the money supply and short-term credit; the Ministry of Economics and Finance exercises primary authority in the allocation of medium- and long-term credit.[3] The institutional base for control of the money supply and short-term credit is the banking system; that for control of medium- and long-term credit is the postal checking system, the network of Treasury local offices, the government budget, and the capital market, all of which are subject to control or influence by the Ministry of Economics and Finance either directly or via various intermediaries.

In the discussion that follows we develop these views in greater detail, examine the functioning and interaction of the systems for controlling money supply, short-term and longer-term credit, and consider their implications for objectives of French national economic policy.

MONEY SUPPLY AND SHORT-TERM CREDIT: THE INSTITUTIONAL BASE

In 1945, in a major step to establish government control over the financial system, the French Parliament nationalized the Banque de France and the then four principal commercial (or deposit) banks with nationwide branch systems. The same legislation established the National Credit Council (*Conseil National du Crédit*) as the focal point for formulation of national policy for monetary and short-term credit affairs and provided for broad representation of diverse economic interests among its membership, now 44 persons.[4]

[1] See P. Berger, "Le Contrôle du Crédit en France," *Revue Politique et Parlementaire*, December 1962, pp. 36–39; P. Besse, "Le Conseil National du Crédit," *Revue Economique*, no. 5 (September 1951), pp. 578–80.

[2] See P. Berger, "Les Taux d'Intérêt en France," *Moneta e Credito*, Banca Nazionale del Lavoro, December 1964, p. 8.

[3] F. Bloch-Lainè, "Pour une Réforme de l'Administration Economique," *Revue Economique*, November 1962, p. 877; P. Berger, *Monnaie et Marchés de Capitaux à Court Terme*, Centre d'Etudes Supérieures de Banque, Les Cours de Droit, Paris, 1965, pp. 104–9, 129–34.

[4] See "Law of December 2, 1945 Regarding the Nationalization of the Bank of France and the Large Banks and Regarding the Organization of

The chairman of the National Credit Council is the Minister of Economics and Finance, and the vice-chairman and customary acting chairman is the governor of the Banque de France. Other members represent the interests of labor, management, agriculture and certain government ministries and departments concerned with economic affairs. The director of the Treasury is a nonvoting member but functions as the principal representative of the government in the deliberations of the Council.

The line of policy implementation passes from the Council through the Banque de France and the Banking Control Commission to the Professional Association for Banks (*Association Professionnelle des Banques*) or alternatively to the Association of Financial Enterprises and Institutions (*Association Professionnelle des Etablissements Financiers*) for certain nonbank financial firms. It is the responsibility of these professional associations to see to it that their members are informed of the decisions of the National Credit Council as well as all banking regulations and mutual agreements concerning professional practice.

In French law "All enterprises or institutions whose customary business is to accept from the public, in the form of deposits or otherwise, funds which they use for their own account in discount, credit or financial transactions shall be regarded as banks."[5] All such banks must be registered with the National Credit Council under one of three categories depending on their type of banking business. The categories are deposit banks (*banques de dépôts*), business banks (*banques d'affaires*), and banks for medium- and long-term credit (*banques de crédit à moyen et à long terme*). Certain banks with special legal status are not required to register since they are controlled under other legislation. These include the popular banks, savings banks, and agricultural and professional credit associations.

The deposit banks accept sight and time deposits, make short- and medium-term loans (mostly by discounting bills), underwrite and deal in securities, and carry on a general banking business. Until January 1966, the deposit banks were prohibited from accepting savings deposits with terms above two years and the business banks could accept deposits with terms under two years only from a very limited clientele. The deposit banks can now accept deposits of any maturity, and the business banks can accept deposits at sight,

---

Credit," in *Central Banking Legislation, A Collection of Central Bank, Monetary and Banking Laws*, vol. 2, *Europe,* ed. Hans Aufricht, International Monetary Fund, 1967, pp. 199–211; and Décret, No. 67-748 du 30 Août 1967, in Conseil National du Crédit, *Vingt-Deuxième Rapport Annuel, Année 1967*, Annexe A, p. 17.

[5] See "The Law of June 13, 1941, Relative to Regulation of the Banking Profession," Art. 1, in Aufricht, p. 211.

TABLE 3.1   France: Credits and Loans to the French Economy
             from Various Sources (end of 1969)

Source	Billion francs	Billion francs
1. Bank credit		F 213.07[a]
Registered banks	(162.36)[b]	
of which nationalized banks (91.0)[d]		
Popular banks	(11.16)[b]	
Agricultural credit intermediaries	(37.85)[b]	
Banque Francaise du Commerce Ext.	(1.70)[b]	
2. Specialized financial intermediaries and the Treasury		165.74
3. Financial establishments		18.55
Based on bank credit	(11.49)[b]	
Capital and reserves	(6.43)[c]	
Discrepancy	(0.63)	
4. Banque de France (includes only direct loans)		0.15
Total		F 397.51

Note: Loans to regional and local public collectivities are not included in this table.

[a] All figures in this column are from Conseil National du Crédit, *Vingt-Quatrième Rapport Annuel, Année 1969,* Annexe 78, p. 214.

[b] Ibid., Annexe 1, p. 55.

[c] *Vingt-Quatrième Rapport Annuel, Année 1969,* p. 124.

[d] Estimated from diverse balance sheet data for Crédit Lyonnais, Banque Nationale de Paris and Société Générale, in *Polks World Bank Dictionary,* 152nd ed., September 1970.

or short-term, from anyone but they still serve a limited and traditional clientele of large firms and old families. The banks for medium- and long-term investment make investments whose maturity must exceed two years and in practice typically exceeds five years.

At the end of 1969, there were 191 deposit banks of various descriptions (including 7 discount houses), 18 business banks, and 28 banks for medium- and long-term investments.[6] At year-end 1969, total credit outstanding by these registered banks was F 162.36 billion, of which the three nationalized deposit banks accounted for about F 91 billion, or 56 per cent, as shown in Table 3.1.

Regulatory decisions of the authorities (in this case the National Credit Council, the Banque de France, and the Banking Control Commission) reach the registered banks through the Professional

[6] See Conseil National du Crédit, *Vingt-Quatrième Rapport Annuel, Année 1969,* p. 120.

Association of Banks, in which membership is obligatory for each registered bank. Government authority over the nationalized banks is also expressed in the form of government ownership of their shares and appointment of their boards of directors. These boards must represent a broad range of economic interests. Appointment to the board is by or with the approval of the Minister of Economics and Finance. He must also approve the selection of the chairman and the general manager. Operating officers of these banks hold their appointments on indefinite tenure and may be removed by the authorities for cause, including failure to implement directives from the authorities. In addition, the Banking Control Commission appoints a permanent government auditor (*censeur*) for each of the nationalized banks, who has access to all meetings and records of these banks and the duty to report to the commission. The Law of 1945 provides for nationalization of additional deposit banks should their characteristics (e.g., size and branch structure) become similar to the existing nationalized banks.

Operating control over those business banks whose balance-sheet together with off-balance-sheet liabilities exceed F 20 million takes the form of a government commissioner appointed by the Minister of Economics and Finance and assisted by a control committee of three members chosen to represent labor, business, and government interests. The government commissioner attends all meetings of the bank's board of directors and has a "veto over any decision contrary to the national interest which is taken by the board of directors, by one of its committees, or by the general meeting [of stockholders]. . . . He may present to the board of directors any measures which seem to him to be in the general interest and, in particular, those which conform to the wishes or decisions of the National Credit Council." [7] A commissioner can also be named to those banks or financial establishments over which these business banks may possess or acquire control.

The authority of the National Credit Council extends also to firms and individuals whose financial business does not fit the category of registered banks but which are engaged in brokerage, short- or medium-term credit transactions and exchange transactions; or discounting, accepting as collateral, or cashing commercial paper, checks, or government securities.[8] At the end of 1969 there were 446 such firms [9] with only F 18.55 billion in credit extended of which almost two-thirds or F 11.49 billion represented credit they had received in turn from banks, as shown in Table 3.1. Decisions of the National Credit Council concerning the activities of these firms

[7] See "Law of December 2, 1945," Title IV, Art. 11, in Aufricht, p. 203.
[8] See "The Law of June 13, 1941, Relative to Regulation of the Banking Profession," Art. 27 (2) in Aufricht, p. 218.
[9] *Vingt-Quatrième Rapport Annuel, Année 1969*, p. 123.

and individuals are transmitted via the Banking Control Commission and the Professional Association of Financial Enterprises and Institutions.

The Banque de France has the key functional position in this entire regulatory structure for money and short-term credit.[10] This is evident from the role of the governor of the Banque de France as vice-chairman and customary acting chairman of the National Credit Council and as permanent chairman of the Banking Control Commission. Moreover the technical and professional skills he brings to these positions assure that his advice and recommendations will be accorded special weight in the decisions of these bodies.

A variety of establishments of semipublic character engage in banking and credit of a kind not dissimilar to that of the registered banks. These include popular banks specializing in banking for individuals and smaller enterprises, institutions for agricultural credit (*caisses de crédit agricole*) and for mutual credit, and the French Bank for Foreign Commerce (*Banque Française du Commerce Extérieur*). All these are under the direct control of government authority and are generally required by their respective authorities to observe the regulations and instructions ordered for the registered banks. Their contribution to credit outstanding at the end of 1969 also can be seen in Table 3.1.

MEDIUM-TERM AND LONG-TERM CREDIT: ALLOCATION AND CONTROL

The French government has the dominant voice in the allocation and control of medium- and long-term credit.[11] The primary locus of government authority over such credit is the Ministry of Economics and Finance, but policy is strongly influenced by the *Commissariat Général du Plan* and to a lesser degree by discretion left to various public and semipublic financial intermediaries with assigned roles in credit allocation. The means available to the government to control the allocation of medium- and longer-term credit include the tax, subsidy and loan program of the government budget; obligatory redeposit with the Treasury of the liquid resources of the organs of local and regional government and the postal checking system; policy control over the investment-allocation of savings that flow to savings banks via centralization of such funds in the public *Caisse des Dépôts et Consignations;* and control of access to the capital market. These domestic controls have been supplemented by exchange controls over capital movements between France and foreign countries that have varied in intensity in recent years and are currently both comprehensive and rigorous.

---

[10] P. Berger, *Monnaie et Marchés de Capitaux à Court Terme*, pp. 104–9.
[11] J. Dony, A. Giovaninetti, B. Tibi, *L'Etat et le Financement des Investissements Privés* (Paris: Editions Berger-Levrault, 1969), pp. 90–99.

Direct investment aid from the state treasury is channeled through the Fund for Economic and Social Development (*Fonds de Développement Economique et Social*) and may be in the form of grants or loans.[12] The FESD was created from the fusion of diverse state funds and stands at the center of financial procedures for granting state aid. Its board of directors unites the highest officials of the administration and of the various specialized financial establishments. The board approves annually the investment program of nationalized industries (e.g. gas, electricity, coal, aircraft, railroad) which are financed by a combination of state and private capital. The board also coordinates and encourages investment in other industries in accordance with the national development plan.

State intervention in the allocation of investment funds occurs at a level once removed from the direct procedures of FESD via a variety of public and semipublic institutions chief among which are the *Caisse des Dépôts et Consignations*, the *Crédit National* (long-term credits to private industry and commerce), the *Crédit Foncier* (war damage, construction, mortgage credit), and the *Caisse Nationale des Marchés de l'État* (mutual credit for professions, medium-term credit for public enterprises). The Crédit National and Crédit Foncier operate either by granting loans or by signing their approval of medium-term loans granted by the banking system thus making these bank loans eligible for rediscount at the Banque de France. They obtain funds for direct loans by issuing their bonds on the capital market or by rediscounting with the Caisse des Dépôts.

As the major channel through which private savings reach the money and capital markets the Caisse des Dépôts et Consignations is the dominant financial intermediary in the French financial system.[13] Its resources come primarily from the network of public and mutual savings banks which are legally obligated to redeposit their funds with it.[14] In addition it holds the liquid funds of the social security system. Prior to 1945 the resources of the CDC were largely absorbed in financing long-term government debt. Inflation since 1945 has greatly reduced the share of such debt in the assets of CDC. Currently its major lending commitments are to finance housing construction and the construction needs of local governments. It also lends to public and mixed-ownership industrial firms and purchases their bonds or, occasionally, stocks. Another major role of the CDC is loans to and rediscounting for financial institutions such as the Crédit National and the Crédit Foncier. Until recently, the approval of the CDC has been required on all bank-initiated medium-term loans eligible for rediscount at the Banque de France.

[12] Ibid., pp. 95–102.
[13] Ibid.
[14] Until 1967, insurance companies and pension funds were required to deposit their liquid funds with the CDC. Since 1967, they have been permitted to place them in the money market. This is a change from the closed Treasury circuit in favor of the banking system.

Neither the Treasury nor any of its so-called "correspondants" just discussed maintains deposits in the deposit banks. Instead deposits of liquid funds are made with the Banque de France either directly by the institution (Treasury or CDC) or indirectly through prior deposit with the Treasury (as in the case of local authorities and of the giro payments system operated by the Post and Telegraph System). This fact together with the guidance of credit flows moving through the system according to criteria derivative from national economic policy gives rise to the phenomenon of the "Treasury circuit" with implications both for monetary policy and for credit policy.[15]

Net drains from the commercial banking system into the Treasury circuit occur whenever depositors in banks make payments into accounts in the postal giro system, pay taxes, purchase newly issued government debt, or place savings in savings banks. Most such funds are promptly returned to circulation by government disbursements, investment expenditures by loan recipients, and in other ways. But the banking system can lose liquidity on balance owing to timing lags, a decision by Treasury *correspondants* to increase their liquid balances, or a permanent shift in savings or payments habits of the population toward the Treasury circuit. Any net drain on banking liquidity into the Treasury circuit must be settled in the form of a transfer of deposit claims on the books of the Banque de France, i.e., in central bank money. This, then, is an aspect of the Treasury circuit with implications for monetary policy.

Implications of the Treasury circuit for credit policy and for the interaction of credit policy with monetary policy (e.g., rediscounting of medium-term loans by the central bank) are far more profound. Provisions for the rediscounting of medium-term loans by registered banks at the CDC, the Crédit Foncier, the Crédit National, and at the Banque de France are among the major gaps in the central bank's controls over the money supply.

Allocation of credit to the economy by the Treasury and other institutions constituting the Treasury circuit is intended to serve national goals as defined in French national economic plans. The volume of such credit outstanding at the end of 1969 is shown in Table 3.1 as F 165.74 billion. This sum, which exceeds that of the registered banks, is understated by the omission from the table of loans to local public collectivities. A balance sheet for the CDC shows these in the amount of F 37 billion as of September 30, 1969.[16]

Credit through the Treasury circuit customarily is offered to

[15] F. Bloch-Lainè, P. de Vogüe, "Le phénomène du circuit," in *Le Trésor Public* et le Mouvement Général des Fonds (Paris: Presses Universitaires de France, 1960), pp. 271–83; P. Berger, *Monnaie et Marchés de Capitaux à Court Terme*, pp. 129–34; M. Walther, "Problèms de Trésorie Rencontrés par les Banques Françaises," *Revue de Science Financière*, April–June 1965, pp. 244–45.
[16] *Journal Officiel de la République Française*, January 8, 1970, p. 352.

eligible borrowers at interest rates below those prevailing in the banking circuit. Moreover, the interest rates as well as the volume of funds allocated through the Treasury circuit are less variable in response to credit and business conditions than through the banking circuit.[17] The supply of funds through the Treasury circuit has been guaranteed in part by the government's administrative controls over savings flows; in part through the use of tax differentials to favor deposits and debt sales by the Treasury and its *correspondants;* and in part by enlisting monetary expansion via rediscounting with the Banque de France as an ultimate source of funds for the Treasury circuit and its clients should other sources prove inadequate.

It is these two forms of interlock between monetary and credit policy and between the banking system and the Treasury circuit that make it impossible to understand French monetary and central banking policy without attention to credit policy, the role of the Treasury and its *correspondants*, and to the responsibilities of the central bank in the realm of credit policy. The implications of these interrelationships will be developed more fully in the discussion that follows of the central bank's responsibility for monetary policy.

GENERAL INSTRUMENTS OF MONETARY AND CREDIT POLICY

In France, as in other countries, the money supply may be defined as currency in circulation plus demand deposits and, according to one's purpose, time and savings deposits. In any such system the ultimate reserves of the banking system are currency and claims against the central bank. By regulating the terms of access by the banking system to claims against the central bank, the latter influences commercial bank behavior and thus the money supply.

In the French system as elsewhere the supply of claims against the central bank that is available to the banking system depends not only on actions by the monetary authorities but also upon the demand of the public for currency; the condition of the government budget with respect to balance or imbalance between revenues and expenditures; the implications of this for government finance and debt management; and upon the balance of payments as this gives rise to a net inflow or outflow of foreign exchange. The following discussion focuses on the instruments and policies of the central bank, but will refer briefly on occasion to these other influences when they are particularly relevant.

The general (i.e., nonselective) instruments of central bank policy usually are taken to the rediscounting, open market operations, and minimum reserve requirements. This general usage is followed here.

---

[17] S. Guillaumont-Jeanneney, *Politique Monétaire et Croissance Economique en France, 1950–1966,* Librairie Armand Colin et Fondation Nationale des Sciences Politiques, 1969, pp. 118–21.

However, as will become clear, both rediscounting and minimum (asset) reserve requirements have been and are used by the Banque de France for selective ends.

One fact is central to an understanding of the varied approaches of the Banque de France to the regulation of the French money supply. At no time since the end of the Second World War has the rediscount rate (or more properly, the array of rediscount rates) charged by the Banque de France been high enough to prevent the demand for credit in the economy from causing too rapid an expansion in the money supply for reasonable stability in the general price level.[18] Deprived of the interest rate as an adequate price-rationing device for control of the money supply, the Banque de France has had to rely on a variety of expedients such as asset reserve ratios, ceilings on primary rediscount lines, changed definitions and procedures for prior approval of paper eligible for rediscount, and imposition of ceilings on the granting of credit by banks and other financial institutions. Moreover, the existence of privileged categories of paper eligible for rediscount "above ceiling" (*hors plafond*), such as credits for medium-term equipment loans and export credit, has always provided the banking system and the economy with channels by which to vitiate measures by the Banque de France to restrict monetary expansion. Only credit ceilings are free of this defect. But they have other severe disadvantages.

Rediscount Policy

Rediscounting has been the principal channel through which the Banque de France regulates bank liquidity, although recent reforms have increased the relative importance of open market purchases and sales in making short-term adjustments in bank liquidity.[19] Discount facilities at the Banque de France are available by law to "any member of the public," but in practice only discounts for registered banks and the public and semipublic financial institutions mentioned above are quantitatively important. Each bank is assigned individually a discount limit (its *plafond de réescompte*) up to which it may discount at the Banque de France at the basic discount rate. On occasion the authorities have reduced these rediscount ceilings across the board, for example in 1951 and 1956, and most recently in October 1970. Supplementary and temporary accommodation has been available under various arrangements at rates above the basic discount rate. Following the disorders of May–June 1968, these ceilings were

---

[18] On this point, see R. Marjolin, J. Sadrin, O. Wormser, *Rapport Demandé, par Décision en Date du 6 Décembre, 1968* (Paris: April 6, 1969), pp. 4, 9; P. Berger, "Les Taux d'Intérêt en France," p. 8; *Les Instruments de la Politique Monétaire en France* (Document rédigé a l'intention du Comité Monétaire de la Communauté Economique Européenne), Banque de France, October 1968, p. 30.

[19] *Les Instruments,* pp. 32–35, 44–46.

temporarily raised by 20 per cent across the board to aid in the economic recovery. At the end of October 1968 they reverted to their previous level.

Since 1951, supplementary and temporary accommodation (*en pension,* or "under repurchase agreement") has been available at rates above the basic rediscount rate. Until December 1967, this was largely through the rediscount channel, in two steps: the so-called hell and superhell rates. Since December 1967, the Banque de France has made such credit available only through open market purchases on repurchase agreements (*en pension*) and at a rate of interest 2.5 per cent above the basic rediscount rate. This "superhell" channel has been used very little because the central bank prefers the open market channel at variable rates close to the rediscount rate.

Properly drawn commercial bills are eligible for rediscount. In addition, a variety of credit instruments are accorded the privilege of being discountable at the basic rate but in excess of a bank's discount ceiling (*hors plafond*). These include medium-term loans to finance housing, industrial equipment and exports, and grain storage bills. To be discountable, the medium-term credits require the endorsement of one of the specialized financial institutions (e.g., Crédit National, Crédit Foncier, Caisse des Dépôts) and the *prior approval* of the Banque de France. Most medium-term credits that are discounted at the *Banque de France* have first been discounted at one of the public institutions such as the Crédit National, Crédit Foncier, or the Caisse des Dépôts. For tap Treasury bills [available for purchase on demand] (*bons du Tresor sur formule*) there has been a privileged discount rate below even the basic discount rate.

The privilege accorded to banks of rediscounting medium-term credits for housing and industrial equipment, export credits, and grain storage bills above the banks' individually assigned discount ceilings has its rationale in credit policy considerations. These are preferred credit categories which the government wishes to encourage the banks to support. In practice these privileged categories have become the avenue for bank rediscounting that has been excessive in its effect on the liquidity of the banking system and on the money supply within the limits of interest rate policy that the authorities have been willing to enforce. In short, the authorities have been unwilling to rely sufficiently on price rationing of central bank credit to check the inflationary expansion of commercial banks' loans and deposits supported by rediscount credit at the central bank. To restrict the volume of such credit instruments eligible for rediscount the authorities have resorted to two additional types of nonprice rationing. They have limited the central bank's obligation to accept Treasury debt instruments and medium-term credits for rediscount except by prior agreement; and they have introduced asset-reserve requirements to freeze bank holdings of both government and private paper that would otherwise have been eligible for rediscount.

Under present policy *medium-term credits* are eligible for discount when they carry three signatures and are presented to the central bank by the intermediary of one of the specialized public or semi-public institutions. In practice one of these institutions provides the third signature. Their approval is given only if the basic credit meets criteria of national policy with respect to facilitating purchase of industrial equipment or a program of modernization. Note that eligibility for rediscount is determined on a case-by-case basis, normally by review at the time the commercial bank is making the basic loan.[20] Although the criteria by which a credit may be endorsed for rediscount have varied from time to time to allow for changing credit conditions, the overall volume of such paper presented for discount has remained excessive from the viewpoint of monetary stability.

Prior to 1958 the Banque de France had to accept Treasury bills and notes under three months maturity for discount at a fixed rate without discretion. From 1958 it was relieved of this obligation and from December 1960 the discounting of such short-term public bills was made subject to prior agreement. By this time, however, the low rate of interest on such bills sold to the banks on tap, the freezing of banks into holdings of such bills by means of the Treasury floor (see below), and the more balanced state of the national budget had greatly reduced the significance of Treasury bills held by the banks as rediscountable paper. Since 1969 the Banque de France acquires these Treasury obligations through open market channels and at variable interest charges of its own selection depending on policy considerations. Treasury obligations may also be used by banks to collateralize "advances" from the Banque de France at a rate 1.5 per cent above the basic rediscount rate.

Reserve Ratios

Since 1945 French banks have been subject to three different reserve requirements in the form of required minimum ratios between specified assets and specified liabilities. The first of these, the Treasury "floor" (*plancher*) came into existence on October 1, 1948 and required the banks to retain at least 95 per cent of their portfolios of government obligations on hand as of September 30, 1948 and to invest in such obligations 20 per cent of any increase in deposits above their level on that benchmark date.[21] The purpose of the floor was to prevent the monetization of government debt at a time when the government budget still was running substantial deficits, a monetization the banks had been able to cause by discounting Treasury notes and bills at the central bank or letting them mature without renewal. The floor also provided funds for the Treasury at rates some 2 per cent below prevailing market rates of interest. In more recent years fol-

[20] Ibid., pp. 54–55.
[21] P. Berger, "Le Contrôle du Crédit en France," pp. 43–44.

lowing the introduction of the bank liquidity coefficient (*coefficient de trésorerie*) and the improvement of government finances with more balanced budgets, the Treasury floor has been progressively reduced until removed altogether in 1967.

A second liquid asset ratio or bank liquidity coefficient (*coefficient de trésorerie*) was introduced in October 1960 with effect from January 1961.[22] The primary purpose of this coefficient was to reduce the volume of medium-term credits eligible for rediscount that the banks could actually use to borrow at the central bank. The bank liquidity coefficient specified a minimum ratio between certain of the bank's liquid assets and their deposit liabilities. The liquid assets eligible to satisfy the requirement were of two kinds: (1) cash assets, including vault cash, demand claims against the Treasury, the postal checking system and the Banque de France; and (2) a second category, composed of rediscountable medium-term credits, grain storage bills, and rediscountable export credits. Treasury notes and bills held to satisfy the Treasury floor requirement also counted toward the bank liquidity requirement. Thus the coefficient acted to freeze the banks into a portion of their stock of liquid assets that they might otherwise have presented for rediscount.

Introduced at 30 per cent of deposits in January 1961, the bank liquidity coefficient was progressively raised until it reached 36 per cent in May 1963 at which level it remained until January 1966 when it was reduced to 35 per cent. On occasion it was also varied downward to aid the Banque de France in relieving month-end tightness in the money market.

In January 1967 the French monetary authorities introduced for the first time a system of required minimum reserves in the form of non-interest-bearing deposits at the Banque de France.[23] On this occasion both the Treasury floor and the bank liquidity coefficient were canceled and their place taken by a so-called coefficient of retention (*coefficient de retenue*), which specifies a "minimum portfolio of rediscountable bills representing medium-term credit" fixed as a percentage of banks' deposits.[24] Once again the purpose has been to freeze in bank portfolios a portion of existing bills eligible for rediscount and thus to limit rediscounting above ceilings for discounts at the basic discount rate. The definition of the new coefficient is such that two categories of bills formerly covered by the bank liquidity coefficient have regained unrestricted rediscountability above discount ceilings. These are short-term export credits (under two years, or more recently under 18 months) and grain storage bills guaranteed by the Office of Cereals.

When introduced the coefficient of retention was regarded as transi-

[22] *Les Instruments;* pp. 38–39.
[23] Ibid., pp. 38–43.
[24] Ibid., pp. 46–48.

tional between the asset-reserve requirement of the *coefficient de trésorerie* and the newly established system of minimum required reserves in the form of deposits with the Banque de France. Apparently the authorities expected the latter reserve requirement to be so effective as to make the asset-reserve requirement redundant. Experience has demonstrated otherwise.[25] After lowering the coefficient of retention successively from 20 per cent in January, 1967 at time of introduction, to 13 per cent in July 1968, the authorities have had to raise the coefficient on three occasions, most recently in April 1970, at which time it was set at 16 per cent.

The shortcomings of the system of minimum cash reserves (deposits at the Banque de France) are inherent in the French system of monetary and credit controls. Such reserves, like open market operations, are effective restraints on bank-credit expansion only if the banks are prevented by cost considerations or administrative denial from offsetting an increase in minimum required reserves or open market sales by recourse to further rediscounting of eligible paper. In the French system the rediscount rate is maintained at too low a level to have this effect and privileged channels for rediscounting remain open in the service of national priority uses of credit. Thus an increase in required reserves simply results in an offsetting increase in rediscounting so long as the banks have eligible paper to spare. The role of the coefficient of retention is to freeze the excess stock of such paper into bank portfolios while permitting *currently created*, discount-eligible credits to enjoy their privileged status. The objective is to allocate credit to priority uses at favorable interest rates.

Effective April 1, 1971, French banks are required to hold minimum obligatory cash reserves, defined as a percentage of their credits as well as of their deposits. The stated rationale for a separate reserve requirement against bank credit is that this will give the authorities more direct influence on credit expansion regarded as a process responsible for money creation.[26]

Open Market Policy

In France, the short-term money market in which the Banque de France intervenes with open market operations is restricted to banks, financial establishments, public and semipublic financial intermediaries, and certain insurance companies and pension funds.[27] Thus it is nearly analogous to the federal funds market in the United States. Operations of the Banque de France in the money market are limited by decision of the Banque's general council to Treasury notes, "mobilization bills" (i.e., a short-term bill drawn in favor of a banker and

[25] Banque de France, *Compte Rendu des Opérations*, Exercise 1969, Edition Provisoire. (Paris, June 1970), p. 33.

[26] Conseil National du Crédit, *Vingt-Cinquième Rapport Annuel, Année 1970*, Edition Provisoire, pp. 1–14.

[27] *Les Instruments*, pp. 48–52; Marjolin, Sadrin, Wormser, pp. 79–80.

secured by other liquid bills) that the Banque de France has approved for rediscounting at time of issue, bills guaranteed unconditionally by the Caisse National des Marchés de l'Etat, and sight bills issued by the National Society for Railroads. When the supply of such bills is inadequate for open market operations, the Banque de France *on its own initiative* will accept commercial bills at a higher rate of discount. Thus, during 1968 and 1969 when bank liquidity was drained both by a massive outflow of foreign exchange and by a substantial increase in the public's demand for currency, open market purchases (*en pension*) were broadened to include both commercial bills and even some paper technically ineligible for rediscount. Since 1968, the Banque de France has sought successfully to enlarge the role of open market operations in extending credit to the banking system. A principal reason for this emphasis has been the desire of the Banque de France to achieve greater interest rate flexibility in its credit operations than rediscounting practice (with its privileged categories) makes possible. The Banque de France intervenes in the market at rates set by the governor in the light of policy considerations. These rates may vary from day to day. The influence of the Eurocurrency market on short-term international capital flows has been a principal force stimulating the adoption of more flexible rate policy in the French money market.

DIRECT AND SELECTIVE INSTRUMENTS
OF MONETARY AND CREDIT POLICY

The monetary and credit authorities in France have utilized in recent years a variety of direct and selective policy instruments to supplement the more general instruments just discussed. These include control of deposit and lending rates set by banks and other financial firms, regulation of interest rates on government securities, annual and month-by-month controls on the maximum permissible rate of expansion in bank credit, direct administrative review of bank discounts and loans for larger borrowers, control of security issues of borrowers in the capital market, control of installment credit terms and of maximum loan-to-capital ratios for installment lenders, a variety of controls on international capital movements, and general price controls. In addition, the public and semipublic financial intermediaries such as the Caisse des Dépôts et Consignations, the Crédit Foncier, the Crédit National are subject to direct administrative control with respect to their lending, discounting, and endorsement policies.

Perhaps the most precise of these direct controls is that exercised by the Banque de France over bank credits whose eligibility for subsequent rediscounting the bank wishes to establish.[28] To establish

[28] *Les Instruments,* pp. 52–55.

such eligibility, the lending bank must submit full credit information on the loan and borrower to the Banque de France for review and approval *at the time the loan is made*. If the Banque de France does not find these aspects of the loan in conformity with its established policies, it will refuse its approval for rediscount. Ordinarily the lending bank will not make a loan to which the central bank has taken exception. In addition to such review, until June 1969 *any* bank credit extended to a firm that brought the total such credit by one or several banks beyond F 10 million could not be granted without the *prior approval* of the Banque de France.[29] In June 1970, the requirement of prior approval was suspended and replaced by a system of ex post reporting for loans to enterprises that bring the total credit to the enterprise to an amount in excess of 25 million francs. These measures permit the Banque de France to exercise a rather detailed direct supervision over the amount and terms for bank credit to major borrowers and to enforce its conformity to national policy. As a further control the banks are required to report monthly to the central bank's *Service Central des Risques* total short-term credits outstanding to a firm or individual in excess of F 100,000.[30] Banks are still required to be able to justify on request of the Banque de France any credit subject to this reporting. Such a census is very helpful to the National Credit Council in observing the responsiveness of credit flows to national policy objectives. Eighty-five per cent of bank credit is subject to reporting and review at the present time.

A second important direct control is regulation of the maximum rate of bank credit expansion.[31] This measure was first introduced in February 1958 and later suspended. It was reactivated in September 1963 and remained in force until June 1965 when it was again suspended. Reactivated again in November 1968 credit ceilings remained in force until late October 1970 when they were suspended once again. In setting ceiling rates for bank credit expansion the Banque de France has sometimes exempted the high-priority categories of export, medium-term investment, and construction credits from the ceilings and on other occasion has permitted these categories to expand at higher rates than bank credit generally.[32]

Regulation of lending and borrowing rates of interest is another direct control actively employed by the authorities. Virtually all key interest rates on bank deposits and loans, on short- and medium-term credit through banks and other financial institutions, in the money

[29] Ibid.

[30] Ibid.; Conseil National du Crédit, *Vingt et Unième Rapport Annuel, Année 1966*, pp. 34–36.

[31] *Les Instruments*, pp. 56–57. A decree of the Ministry of Economics and Finance dated 5 February 1970 formally extended to the specialized banks the authority of the Banque de France in regulating credit expansion previously limited to the "registered banks."

[32] *Compte Rendu des Opérations*, p. 35.

and government securities markets, rates paid on various forms of saving, and interest rates on loans to priority national uses of credit made by the public and semipublic financial intermediaries are subject to regulation either formally or informally. The only major exception to such control is occasioned by the need to pay interest on large savings deposit balances (over F 100,000), which are sufficiently competitive with Eurodollar rates to prevent the outflow of foreign exchange to the international money market through commercial leads and lags and other loopholes in exchange controls. Interest rates on time deposits and nonnegotiable certificates of deposit for maturities in excess of one year also have been exempted from ceilings in an effort to entice savers to make longer-term commitments.

Interest rates on bank credit are not formally controlled but the nationalized banks receive administrative guidance in setting rates and all three nationalized banks use an identical and mutually agreed rate schedule. To influence bank lending terms the Banque de France has provided rediscounts at more than a dozen different rates, when the basic, privileged, and penalty rates are counted. Schedules of various allowable bank fees and charges are set by the National Credit Council. Changes in the *basic* rediscount rate have been accompanied by suggestions to the nationalized banks that they alter their customer rates by lesser or greater amounts. These suggestions are always followed. The Banque de France with the aid of the public and semipublic financial intermediaries reviews lending terms on all credits whose eligibility for rediscount depends on their prior approval and will refuse this approval if the *terms* are not to its liking.

The money market is a kind of annex to rediscounting, and its rate is determined by the rate at which the Banque de France participates in the market. But here interaction with the Eurodollar market limits the full freedom of action of the French authorities. Interest rates on Treasury bills, notes, and bonds are set by the Treasury at time of issue. Tap Treasury obligations, regardless of maturity, are redeemable at the central bank beginning three months after issue at a slight penalty in realized interest. Registered banks are forbidden to discount Treasury notes for their customers at other than authorized rates specified in a maturity schedule. Thus the rates on government debt are regulated.

The lending and deposit rates of savings banks, popular banks, agricultural banks and mutual credit associations are subject to control by appropriate authorities such as the Ministry of Economics and Finance, and the Ministry of Agriculture and are ordinarily adjusted in conformity with policy action by the National Credit Council and the Banque de France.

On the basis of this review one may conclude that every important interest rate in France is subject to a very substantial measure of direct government influence or even outright control. Clearly this is only possible because of the comprehensive breadth of the system of

credit controls as outlined in the foregoing discussion. This system
includes control of access to the capital market and, since September
1968, comprehensive foreign exchange controls.

EVALUATION AND COMMENTARY

The French system of monetary controls is contained within a broader
framework of credit controls operated in the service of national economic goals. The system of credit controls is comprehensive. Flows of
credit through the commercial, savings, agricultural, and popular
banks, the postal checking system, financial intermediaries, the
money and capital markets and the government budget are regulated
as to terms, conditions, purpose, and in certain instances, even specific borrower, in the service of national goals. A succession of national economic plans has expressed these goals, which have included modernization of the technical and organizational structure
of industry, further industrialization, modernization of agriculture,
construction of housing, expansion and modernization of transportation and public utilities, and encouragement of exports to achieve a
favorable current-account balance in international transactions.

Throughout the years since 1945 successive French governments
have been strongly committed to a low interest rate policy. The rationale for this policy is that it encourages investment required for
the success of the national economic plans, and by keeping interest
costs low, contributes to the price competitiveness of French exports
in international markets.[33] To safeguard the benefits of a steady
supply of credit at low interest rates to high priority uses, the Ministry of Economics and Finance has supervised a Treasury circuit to
gather and disburse funds and the Banque de France has provided
privileged access to rediscount facilities for paper related to export
financing, construction, and medium-term business investment.

These features of the French system of monetary and credit controls have modified substantially the significance of traditional instruments of central bank policy: changes in rediscount rate and
reserve requirements, and the use of open market policy. The rediscount channel normally accounts for the major portion of central
bank credit to the French banking system. Moreover the banks are
permanently indebted to the central bank and this indebtedness has
increased steadily year after year. Potentially therefore, a rise in the
rediscount rate could exert a potent force on the cost of bank credit.
But this force has been blunted in its impact on the banks and on the
cost of credit in the economy by the existence of the privileged categories for rediscounting and the Treasury circuit.

On occasion a rise in the basic discount rate has not been ac-

[33] Dony, Giovaninetti, Tibi, pp. 297–98; P. Berger, "Les Taux d'Intérêt
en France," p. 8.

companied by a change in the lower rates for privileged categories. Even when these special rates were changed they remained below the basic rate. As a result a rise in the basic rediscount rate typically has had only a very attenuated effect on the actual cost of rediscounting subsequent to the rise.[34] Open market operations traditionally have been of very limited importance in the French system and have accounted for an almost insignificant portion of total central bank credit. Thus a rise in the Banque de France's intervention rate on the money market has affected a minor portion of central bank credit and, moreover, has tended to divert borrowing to the privileged rediscount categories. A similar difficulty has hampered the effectiveness of reserve requirements in that an increase in reserve requirements has tended to be offset by an increase in rediscounting.

The essential difficulty with all three of these traditional instruments of central banking policy has been the opposition to their effectiveness posed by the government's commitment to low interest rates and preferred credit categories as a means for allocating real resources to priority uses. Not only have the traditional instruments of monetary policy been restrained in application by considerations of credit policy, but a substantial portion of the total flow of credit in the economy has been sheltered from their influence by the operation of the privileged Treasury circuit to be discussed below.

Recourse by banks to the privileged rediscount categories has prevented the Banque de France from controlling the money supply. Regardless of efforts by the Banque de France to control the money supply by traditional instruments, the privileged rediscount channels have allowed the money supply to expand in response to the presentation for rediscount of the privileged types of credit paper.[35] There is no necessary relationship between the volume of such paper created and presented to the central bank which leads to growth in the money supply and the needs of the growing French economy for additional money. The situation is analogous to that under the commercial bills doctrine adopted as a guide to discounting by other central banks at an earlier time.

Most of the nontraditional instruments employed by the Banque de France have had their origin in attempts to control the expansion of bank credit and money supply without resort to adequate increases in the level of interest rates. The three successive asset reserve requirements imposed on banks, namely the floor (*plancher*) for holdings of Treasury notes, the bank liquidity coefficient (*coefficient de trésorerie*) and the current coefficient for retention of medium-term rediscountable paper (*portefeuille minimum d'éffets représentatifs de crédits à moyen terme*) have aimed at freezing a portion of the existing stock of rediscountable assets in bank portfolios so as to slow

[34] Marjolin, Sadrin, Wormser, p. 69.
[35] Ibid., pp. 70–71.

down monetary expansion. So long as credit policy dominates monetary policy, application of such asset reserves will almost certainly be among the improvisations needed by the Banque de France in its attempts to fulfill its assigned tasks.

In a system of comparatively free credit markets all interest rates move upward when the central bank slows the rate of growth in the money supply relative to that in the real magnitudes of the economy. This response is muted in the French economy owing to restraints exerted through administrative controls rather than through market processes. A prime example of this is the use of ceilings on the rate of bank credit expansion. Such ceilings restrain both the supply of bank credit and the demand by banks for central bank credit. In a free market situation such ceilings on bank credit would be accompanied by a rise in interest rates charged by banks to their customers. In the French system this is prevented by administrative suggestions and informal but powerful understandings among officials of the appropriate government ministries, the National Credit Council, the Banque de France, the financial intermediaries and secondary discount institutions, bank officials, and others.

Since 1945 the government has had all the legal authority it needs over the banking and credit establishments and institutions to make its suggestions and directives prevail: witness the nationalized status of the principal branch banks. The stock in these banks is held by the government so that within reason their profits are no constraint on national credit policy. Moreover their managers and directors hold office at the pleasure of the government and can be removed for failing to follow directives from the authorities. These and other sanctions guarantee their compliance with national policy. Thus, credit ceilings and interest rate controls have been combined to restrain credit while maintaining a relatively low level of interest rates. Here again these devices are likely to remain as persistent features of the French monetary and credit system so long as credit policy continues to dominate monetary policy. The credit ceilings may be suspended from time to time when conditions permit and interest controls can be latent when relaxed credit conditions are possible.

International capital flows have posed problems for the French system of monetary and credit controls, as they do for most countries. But the implications for France are different from those for a country which has no carefully formulated national policy for credit allocation. For France a major capital inflow may pose problems not only because it expands the money supply and thus may add to domestic inflation, but also because it may bypass the carefully designed system of credit controls. Thus money obtained from a capital inflow may be spent for investment purposes other than those of high national priority since it is not subject to initial credit review. Moreover, if the authorities find it necessary to offset the inflationary thrust of capital imports by tightening credit at home, they may actually have to reduce the flow of credit to categories which they would prefer to the use made of the capital import.

Given the credit allocation and real investment objectives of the French authorities, one can imagine that they would prefer comprehensive foreign-exchange controls to an open frontier were it not for the substantial reciprocal benefits of the latter. Indeed, a recent careful review of the legislation and regulations which replaced long-standing exchange controls in 1966 concludes:

> Reaction to these new regulations was enthusiastic: government officials announced that a new era of economic freedom in international relations had begun, and various commentators concurred. But while it is true that the new regulations largely abolish control of foreign exchange as such, there has been no substantial liberalization of governmental control over investments by foreigners in France. Indeed, under the new regulations investments are submitted to control procedures which in certain circumstances, are more rigorous than antecedent measures.[36]

Thus, practice with respect to foreign investments appears to have followed the logic of the system of credit controls even during the short interval (1966–68) in which the French system of foreign-exchange controls was temporarily suspended.

Since the reestablishment of exchange controls in France in 1968, control over all forms of capital flows has been gradually strengthened by the adoption of successively more stringent measures. Most recently, in response to international monetary turbulence during 1971, a dual market for foreign exchange was organized in France. One section constitutes the official market based on the official parity of the franc and providing for transactions in imports, exports, and other narrowly defined current account items. All other transactions must take place through the financial franc market, in which the exchange rate is permitted to fluctuate in response to market forces of supply and demand. In addition, a variety of other regulations were temporarily imposed on banks, business firms, and individuals to tighten further the authorities' control over capital flows. Most of these supplementary regulations subsequently were lifted.

Thus far we have described the French system of monetary and credit controls and considered some of its important implications, particularly for the interpretation of French monetary policy. The system is not without some important defects. The most obvious one is that the system as operated is biased towards inflation. Under this system, it has been impossible for the Banque de France to control the money supply. Table 3.2 presents data on changes in money supply, real gross national product, and two measures of price developments for years since 1960. For the actual growth in the money

[36] Charles Torem and W. L. Craig, "Control of Foreign Investment in France," *Michigan Law Review*, vol. 66, no. 4 (February 1968): 670.

TABLE 3.2   France: Money Supply, Real GNP,
and Price Indexes (annual percentage changes)

Year	Money supply [a] (% change)	Real GNP [b] (% change)	GNP deflator [c] (% change)	Wholesale prices [d] (% change)
1960	10.6	7.1	3.27	....
1961	8.9	5.4	3.31	2.06
1962	11.8	6.8	4.71	2.73
1963	12.2	5.8	6.10	3.66
1964	10.9	6.6	3.98	1.58
1965	7.2	4.7	2.45	1.51
1966	8.7	5.6	2.94	2.23
1967	7.9	4.7	2.80	− 0.83
1968	9.6	4.8	4.60	1.47
1969	16.2	7.9	6.95	8.55
Compound Annual Rate of Growth				
	10.55	5.80	4.20	2.52

[a] Notes, coins, and sight deposits, Conseil National du Crédit, *Vingt-Quatrième Rapport Annuel, Année 1970*, Annexes, p. 125.
[b] Calculated from data in Institut National de la Statistique et des Etudes Economiques, *Annuaire Statistique de la France, 1970–71*, p. 641.
[c] Calculated from data in *Annuaire Statistique*, p. 641, on current and real GNP.
[d] Calculated from data in *Annuaire Statistique*, p. 521.

supply to be so adjusted to growth in real economic magnitudes as to achieve price stability would be purely fortuitous and is most unlikely. The prospect of continuous inflation carries implications for the rate of voluntary saving in the French economy and for the persistent reappearance of balance-of-payments deficits leading to the need for periodic devaluations. Only if the outside world inflates at an equal or faster rate will periodic devaluations prove unnecessary.

The problem of inadequate saving in the French economy is recognized as a central one by French officials and economists. To speak of inadequate saving implies some stipulated investment goals and a desire to avoid or at least restrain inflation. The French economic plans confirm both objectives. French economic analysis, both official and private, views both business and household saving as inadequate. The French have business saving in mind when they refer to the low proportion of firms' capital investment programs contributed by their retained earnings. This problem is partly a matter of tax policy but more importantly of cost inflation pressing against price controls and squeezing business profits.[37] There is a tendency among French

[37] Marjolin, Sadrin, Wormser, p. 9.

authors to look toward foreign competition as an explanation for low profit margins, but this neglects the contribution of domestic cost inflation and price controls.[38]

The detrimental influence of inflation on the amount of saving done by households and on their choice of assets is recognized to the point of lamentation in French official and private writings. After fifty years of almost uninterrupted inflation, household savings habits have become adjusted to the shrinking value of fixed-income assets so that long-term bonds, whether state or private, are regarded as unattractive unless indexed. Since 1958, issue of indexed bonds has been forbidden. Stocks are not very attractive given the narrow profit margins of firms, the paucity of information made available to the public by French firms, and the high cost of capital market transactions. Interest paid on savings deposits, even though accorded favorable tax treatment, often has been set so low as to imply a zero or negative real yield after allowance for price inflation. For all these reasons, household savings have been low in proportion to income, have normally not been invested in longer-term financial assets but have sought out short-term liquid forms that could be quickly converted into land, consumer goods, precious metals, and similar real assets should inflation appear to be getting out of hand.

Savings habits of this kind formed over half a century do not alter quickly during short episodes of price stability. Neither do they respond readily to the enticement of moderate increases in interest rates paid to savers. Despite this fact, an effort has been made since 1967 to encourage increased saving by households and to allocate a larger share of such saving to the banking system. Steps have included permitting deposit banks to compete for savings deposits, higher interest ceilings on savings and time deposits, and more even tax treatment among the various forms of deposit-savings and between these and Treasury notes and bills.

In view of the attention accorded to the problem of increasing saving and the recent measures intended to stimulate such increase, it is ironic that the monetary and credit system contains a built-in inflationary mechanism which constantly reinforces the seasoned skepticism of savers by generating further inflation. To seek a solution to the problem of inflation by trying to encourage saving without first putting an end to excessive monetary expansion is a strategy that appears certain to fail.

Another defect of the present system is the damage it does to the flexibility and efficiency of financial institutions. Required asset ratios reduce the flexibility of bank portfolio management. Ceiling rates of credit expansion freeze the relative size of financial firms, and protect inefficient firms from the competition of more efficient firms, thus tending to prevent cost reduction in the financial industry. Administra-

---

[38] S. Guillaumont-Jeanneney, p. 151.

tive controls on the volume of credit coupled with interest rate ceilings force lenders to choose among borrowers on grounds other than price and usually result in discrimination against smaller and newer customers. All these are commonly recognized and regretted evils of the present French system.[39]

There can be little doubt that the French system of monetary and credit controls succeeds in allocating credit approximately as the authorities intend. But does this allocation of credit have a similar effect on real resource allocation? Explicit quantitative evidence on this point is almost impossible to obtain. Reasoning from the nature of the system of credit controls, however, one can say that it is so comprehensive as to leave no important gaps through which credit may flow to enable borrowers to acquire money to frustrate the will of the authorities. Only retained earnings might do this, but they are so low that the authorities seek ways to increase them. Thus the substitution of alternative channels for those regulated or blocked by the authorities, which is a common defect of less comprehensive systems of credit control, does not seem to be a shortcoming chargeable to the French system.

A major theme of this discussion has been the French dilemma of reconciling the requirements of noninflationary monetary policy with those of a comprehensive system for credit allocation in the service of high-priority national economic goals. It is our view that these goals are incompatible under the present French system.

This dilemma is emphasized in the report of a recent high-level commission appointed by the Council of Ministers to study the money market and recommend reforms.[40] There is no space here to consider this interesting report in detail. But we shall mention several of its key recommendations. First, it seeks an end to the system of preferential discount rates as soon as alternative arrangements can be worked out. Second, it recommends replacement of rediscounting by open market operations as the major channel for providing central bank credit to the banking system. Third, it calls for opening of the closed [Treasury] financial circuit to the forces of market competition accompanied by a greater role for the registered banks as intermediaries between savings and longer-term investments. This last pair of recommendations has the dual objective of replacing administrative with market decisions and of reducing the banks' motivation for rediscounting at the central bank.

If implemented, these recommendations would free the Banque de France to control the money supply and conduct a noninflationary monetary policy. But success in such a policy would almost certainly require a substantial increase in the interest rate charged by the Banque de France for its credit whether made available through re-

[39] *Compte Rendu des Opérations*, pp. 33–34, 68.
[40] Marjolin, Sadrin, Wormser, *passim*.

discount or open market channel. This would raise the general level of interest rates throughout the economy. The monetary and price level effects of this increase in interest levels would be entirely salutary. It is a gross fallacy to regard a low level of interest rates as desirable to keep down costs and prices. Just the opposite is true if at the low interest level excessive monetary expansion produces price inflation, as in the French case. Thus the basic rationale for the French policy of low interest rates, i.e., to avoid cost increases that contribute to domestic inflation and thus to aid the competitiveness of French goods in international markets, is seriously in error.[41]

The report is much less satisfactory in its implications for credit allocation to high-priority national objectives. Its basic recommendation in this area amounts to the suspension of administrative intervention so that decentralized (though guided) market processes may undertake the task. It recognizes that under these circumstances different borrowers would be accommodated at different rates of interest than under the present system.[42] This result is not likely to appeal to that substantial segment of public and official opinion that distrusts the power and influence of private financial institutions and private financial markets in national economic affairs.[43]

Since the publication of this report in 1968, the Banque de France has made progress in modifying the French system in the directions that the report recommends. The number of privileged rediscount categories has been reduced and their rates of interest moved closer to the basic rate of rediscount. The role of the open market in the extension of central bank credit has been increased relative to that of rediscounting. The share of the open market channel rose from 15 per cent in 1967 to 38 per cent at the end of 1970. In July of 1971, this share soared to 81 per cent.[44] Moreover during 1969, under the influence of high rates of interest in the Eurocurrency market, the discount rate of the Banque de France reached 8 per cent and its money market intervention rate rose at one point to 10⅝ per cent. There has also been some relaxation in the closed Treasury circuit. Credit ceilings have been suspended.

It is not clear how far these changes in the system will go nor to what degree they are permanent. For example, the sharp rise in the role of the open market channel for central bank credit during 1971 is due in large part to temporary measures to reduce the attraction of

---

[41] The *Report* acknowledges that low interest rates on export credit have not played a decisive role as concerns the price-competitiveness of French exports and have impaired the effectiveness of measures intended to stabilize credit and prices. Marjolin, Sadrin, Wormser, p. 104.

[42] Ibid., p. 14

[43] For an example, see Dony, Giovaninetti, Tibi, pp. 129–31.

[44] Conseil National du Crédit, *Vingt Cinquième Rapport Annuel, Année 1970*, Edition Provisoire, Annexe 3, p. 14 and *Statistiques Mensuelles Provisoires, Mois de Juin*, 1971, p. 3.

the French money market for nonresident short-term capital. Despite exchange controls, funds move between the Eurocurrency market and the French money market when the interest rate differential becomes sufficiently attractive. To discourage the inflow of these funds, the Banque de France has set its money market intervention rate below its discount rate, thus abandoning the traditional relationship between these two rates. Since bank rates on customer loans conventionally move with the discount rate rather than the open market rate, the Banque de France by moving these rates differently has partially insulated the domestic credit markets from its policy in the money market. Thus, current reliance on the open market channel cannot be taken as unambiguous evidence of a basic change in policy in favor of reliance on price rationing of central bank credit. Moreover, authority to reimpose credit ceilings remains in reserve. The authorities continue to influence the cost and availability of credit by administrative and selective means. The Treasury circuit continues to function. Finally, the tradition of credit control by qualitative and selective measures still has strong support in some official quarters.

Whether the job of real resource allocation would be better done simply by allowing private credit markets to work is debatable under present French circumstances. This does not mean that the present system must be retained. If national policy calls for official intervention in the economy to secure an allocation of real resources different from what would emerge from the play of private market forces, there are alternatives to a system of credit controls. The task could be assigned to the budgetary system with an appropriate set of taxes and subsidies to redistribute purchasing power from low- to high-priority economic purposes. This would free credit policy from the task of altering real resource allocation, for which the credit system is ill suited, and would free monetary policy from the restraints imposed on it by credit policy.

Whether the French electorate would support a government that openly adopted such a budgetary policy is not clear. Moreover, there is the possibility that an increased rate of taxation would be offset by a reduction in saving and thus not achieve its objective of restricting consumption. Some problems may also arise concerning the use of subsidies, from the perspective of the international agreements to which France is a party.[45] But only greater reliance on budgetary policy to reallocate real resources in line with official priorities will remove the inconsistency between the requirements of monetary policy and those of credit policy that constitutes the dilemma of the present French system.

[45] *Compte Rendu des Opérations,* p. 28; Dony, Giovaninetti, Tibi, p. 22.

4 The Federal Republic of Germany

From the perspective of international comparisons, the German approach to monetary and credit policy is distinctive for its emphasis on policy instruments that work through market processes rather than administrative controls. Moreover, tne German record of price stability, high employment, economic growth, and balance-of-payments surplus has been impressive in recent years, so that the economic goals toward which monetary policy usually seeks to contribute have been achieved reasonably well. In our consideration of how German monetary and credit policy works, we shall assess the factors that have contributed to its comparative success. Among those factors that appear to be significant are the wide variety of financial institutions treated as banks for purposes of regulation by the *Deutsche Bundesbank* and the Federal Banking Supervisory Office; the restricted nature of the money market; the key role of commercial banks in investment banking and the market for new issues; the relatively small size of the government debt; widespread social awareness of the ravages of inflation and resulting popular support for anti-inflationary policy; and increasingly effective coordination of fiscal policy with monetary policy since passage in 1967 of the Law to Promote Economic Stability and Growth.

FINANCIAL STRUCTURE AND REGULATION

Under the banking law of the Federal Republic of Germany, any credit institution that performs banking functions is classified as a bank for regulatory purposes. Banking functions are defined to include deposit, loan and discount, purchase, sale, administration and safekeeping of securities for others, acceptance and guarantee business, and transfer and clearings business. Institutions other than commercial banks that are subject to central bank regulation for purposes of monetary policy and to supervision by the Federal Banking Supervisory Office include savings banks and their central giro institutions, mortgage banks, industrial and agricultural credit cooperatives and their central institutions, and hire purchase finance houses. The postal check and Postal Savings Bank offices also are classified for regulatory supervision as banks.

Among the important credit institutions not classified as banks and thus not subject to reserve requirements as an instrument of monetary policy are the insurance companies, social insurance institutions, and the Federal Office for Labor. However, under the Law to Promote Economic Stability and Growth of 1967, the latter two organizations may be required to invest substantial amounts of their funds in money market paper (mobilization and liquidity paper) offered by the Bundesbank as a form of open market operation to absorb bank liquidity for purposes of monetary control. Moreover, insurance companies, although they are important in the capital market, do not play a major role in short-term credit. Accordingly, no significant credit institution escapes direct or indirect central bank influence on its liquidity position.

With the exceptions just noted, all credit institutions regarded as banks in the broad sense are subject to regulations concerning licensing, capital requirements, liquidity ratios, and minimum reserve requirements. For many years prior to 1967, the Federal Banking Supervisory Office in consultation with the Bundesbank regulated maximum interest rates payable on deposits and chargeable on loans by credit institutions. Since April 1, 1967, these interest rate regulations have no longer been in force. As "banks," all these diverse credit institutions have access to discounts and advances from the Bundesbank and can if they wish engage in open market transactions in securities with the central bank. (No more than 80 had done so by 1971.) Thus, they are participants in the "money market," in the German usage of the term.

Central and commercial banking structure in the Federal Republic of Germany achieved its present form in 1957 with the establishment of the Deutsche Bundesbank as the central bank, with its head office in Frankfurt and principal branch offices in each of the 11 states, or *Lander* (including Berlin and the Saar), followed by the mergers of certain commercial banks to reconstitute the "big three" commercial banks of national importance; the whole process was completed in 1958.[1] At the end of 1969, there were 9,536 credit institutions (excluding building and loan associations and postal check and

---

[1] The "big three" are the Deutsche Bank, the Dresdner Bank, and the Commerzbank.

postal savings bank offices) in the federal area of which only 315 were classified as commercial banks. The big three accounted for 2,479 out of 4,708 commercial bank offices. At the end of 1968, the big three held 43 per cent of total assets of all commercial banks. In addition to the big three, there were 114 regional and local banks, 23 foreign banks, and 172 private bankers (sole proprietorships or personal partnerships).[2] Other credit institutions included 851 savings banks with 14,704 branches, 13 central giro institutions, 8,004 credit cooperatives and their 18 central institutions, 48 mortgage banks, 191 installment sales finance houses, and a miscellany of 79 other credit institutions (investment companies, security depositories, guarantee banks, and other specialized banks). Two aspects of this system are noteworthy. One is the wide variety of credit institutions subject to supervision as banks. The other is the dominant role of the big three banks within the commercial banking category. The importance of the big three is heightened by their key position in the investment banking and international banking fields. The key position of the big three commercial banks has been subject to increasing challenge by the growth in importance of savings banks and their central giro institutions in the past decade. These banks have diversified increasingly to become full service banks and have steadily gained in relative importance even in fields traditionally identified with commercial banking. For example, the savings banks improved their position in short-term lending to residents from 14 per cent of the total in 1962 to almost 20 per cent at the end of 1970. Their central giro institutions have made a significant penetration into the business of lending to foreign nonbanks, having increased their share of this business from 8 per cent at the end of 1967 to 21 per cent at the end of 1970.

THE INSTRUMENTS OF MONETARY POLICY

In German usage, "monetary" policy is essentially central bank policy. The influence of the government budget and debt management on interest rates and the money supply, as well as interest rate regulation by the Federal Banking Supervisory Office in years prior to 1967, is not considered monetary policy in the strict sense of German usage. Nevertheless, the Bundesbank has had consultative influence in these areas closely related to its responsibilities for monetary policy,

[2] Data on number and types of credit institutions from Table 21, "Number of Banks and their Branches," Statistical Section, p. 37*, *Monthly Report of the Deutsche Bundesbank,* August 1970. Data on share of "big three" banks in total commercial bank assets from *Monthly Report of the Deutsche Bundesbank,* April 1969, p. 7. Data on savings banks and their central giro institutions from "Trends in the Business of the Banking Groups 1960 to 1970" in *Monthly Report of the Deutsche Bundesbank,* April 1971, pp. 32–33.

and the Law to Promote Economic Stability and Growth, passed in 1967, has helped to coordinate the monetary aspects of fiscal policy with Bundesbank policy, as we shall see below.

Bundesbank policy decisions are the province of the Central Bank Council, which consists of the president and vice-president of the Bundesbank, other members of the directorate, who must be professionally qualified, and the presidents of the Bundesbank's main branches in the 11 Lander, or states, of the federal republic. The branches are subordinate in policy matters to the Deutsche Bundesbank in a manner comparable to the relation between regional Federal Reserve banks and the board of governors of the Federal Reserve system in the United States. In a legal sense, the Deutsche Bundesbank is among the more independent central banks in the world. Its relationship to the federal government is specified in its fundamental law as follows:

> The Deutsche Bundesbank shall be obliged insofar as is consistent with its functions to support the general economic policy of the Federal Government. In the exercise of the powers conferred on it under this Law it shall not be subject to instructions from the Federal Government.[3]

Practically, the ability of the Bundesbank to exert an independent influence on policy depends on the professional competence it brings to its task and on its ability to develop public understanding and support for its policy measures. In practice, there can be little doubt that the Bundesbank has exerted more independent influence on macroeconomic policy than most other central banks in Western Europe.

In recent years, the Deutsche Bundesbank has relied on four principal policy instruments: discount policy, minimum reserve policy, open market purchases and sales of securities, and a variety of measures to influence short-term international capital movements.

Discount Policy
Credit institutions may borrow from the central bank by discounting eligible bills of exchange and foreign currency bills and checks. Some 2,000 important credit institutions have discount quotas. Other institutions (for example, savings banks and credit cooperatives) may borrow indirectly via their central institutions. Eligible bills include a variety of instruments such as regular commercial bills, installment sales financing bills, building bills, and export financing bills. Limited discountability is accorded to prime bankers' acceptances, promissory notes of the import and storage agencies, and several other specific types of bills. The discount rate is set at the discretion of the Deutsche Bundesbank. Each credit institution is as-

---

[3] *Central Banking Legislation*, vol. 2, *Europe*, ed. Hans Aufricht, International Monetary Fund, 1967, "Deutsche Bundesbank Law, 1957," Art. 12, p. 255.

signed a discount quota that is determined in relation to its capital and surplus and its type of business. These quotas are not public information but are known to the individual institutions concerned. The discount quota may never be exceeded even temporarily.

A credit institution that has exhausted its rediscount quota may have recourse to advances or loans of not more than three months maturity, using securities as collateral. This is known as Lombard credit. There are no fixed limits to Lombard credit, but the Bundesbank has proposed the guide that Lombard credit should not exceed 20 per cent of an institution's rediscount quota. Moreover, the central bank reserves the right to decide on the amount advanced in the light of the general credit situation and the individual circumstances of the borrower, with special emphasis on the principle that the need for additional liquidity should be of short duration. Usually the rate on advances has been 1 per cent above the discount rate, although differentials of as little as 0.5 per cent and as much as 3 per cent have been used on some occasions. In the summer of 1969, the Bundesbank for a short time introduced a system of progressively higher "penalty" rates for successive "steps" in borrowing by means of advances but abolished this system soon afterwards. The graded steps were based on average borrowings in relation to a bank's capital resources.

Rediscount quotas are variable at central bank discretion and have been varied as a counter-cyclical device and also to correct for secular growth in capital and surplus of credit institutions. Cuts in rediscount quotas are in percentage terms and apply to all credit institutions with quotas. On occasion, in an effort to stem the inflow of short-term capital from abroad, the Bundesbank has reduced rediscount quotas for any credit institution by the amount that its foreign borrowing exceeded the average of such borrowing in a defined base period. Certain paper for import, export, and transit financing is exempt from the rediscount ceilings. The Bundesbank has occasionally refused to discount bills relating to certain classes of business such as installment buying, interim finance for building projects, and bank acceptances; an exception was made for bank acceptances that were clearly intended only to provide short-term finance for specific transactions.

Minimum Reserve Requirements

A wide variety of credit institutions are subject to minimum reserve requirements that must be met by holding interest-free clearing balances with the central bank. Exempt from such requirements are building and loan societies, social insurance institutions, and mortgage banks (since 1965, but only for one calendar year at a time) whose balance sheet shows "funds available at long term (including bonds in circulation) amounting to at least 90 per cent of the volume of business." Minimum reserve requirements are calculated on a monthly formula and are differentiated by three types of deposit (sight, time, and savings), by size of institution, and by whether there is a branch of the central bank close at hand (in which case they are higher). Special provisions sometimes apply to nonresident deposits.

The Bundesbank has the authority to vary the percentage reserve requirements from zero up to their permissible maxima: 30 per cent for sight deposits, 20 per cent for time deposits, 10 per cent for savings deposits, and 100 per cent for nonresident deposits. Adjustments to reserve requirements usually are made in terms of percentage changes that apply across the board to all credit institutions subject to reserve requirements. Liabilities subject to reserve requirements include all those to nonbanks, to other credit institutions not subject to reserve requirements, and to banks in foreign countries. When credit institutions "take loans" (borrow) with maturities less than four years, these obligations are subject to minimum reserve requirements. "Loans taken" are interpreted to include registered bonds and, unless they are part of an aggregate issue, order instruments. Liabilities under repurchase agreements also are subject to reserve requirements. The Bundesbank may fix different reserve ratios on identical obligations of different institutions but has not done so. Reserve deficiencies are assessed a penalty charge that is usually 3 per cent above the current rate on advances.

On fairly numerous occasions in recent years, especially from 1968 on, the Bundesbank has applied higher reserve ratios against the deposit liabilities of German credit institutions to *nonresidents* than against deposit obligations to residents. The purpose of this differential treatment has been to reduce the inflow of short-term capital from abroad attracted either by high domestic interest rates during periods of tight money or by anticipated speculative gains arising from expected revaluation of the mark.

In attempts to reduce or prevent such capital inflows, the Bundesbank has employed both higher average reserve requirements on bank liabilities to nonresidents and special requirements on increments to such liabilities above levels at defined base periods. The latter on occasion have reached 100 per cent. For example, from December 1, 1968, until November 6, 1969 (shortly following revaluation of the Deutsche mark on October 24, 1969), a 100 per cent reserve was required on all increments to foreign liabilities of banks above a specified benchmark date, at first November 15, 1968, later changed to either April 15 or April 30, 1969. At first this special reserve was subject to the qualification that it should not raise a bank's average reserve ratio for residents and nonresidents together above the limits of 30 per cent for sight liabilities, 20 per cent for time liabilities and 10 per cent for savings deposits. Effective in September 1969, the special requirements on nonresident liabilities were freed from this limitation, so that the Bundesbank now has full discretion in setting required reserve ratios for nonresident liabilities. We shall return briefly to this matter in our discussion below of measures to deal with international capital flows.

Open Market Operations

Open market operations are very different in the German setting from those in the United States; the German operations have a much more limited significance, and are best viewed as an extension of central bank discount policy. The Deutsche Bundesbank is empowered to buy and sell discountable bills, Treasury bills, bonds and debt certificates issued by the federal government, one of its special funds, or a Land, and other bonds quoted on the stock exchange. Most open market dealings, however, are in the form of special issues of Treasury bills and notes deliberately created to serve the purpose of open market operations. There are two such forms: mobilization paper and liquidity paper.

As an aspect of the currency reform in Germany following the economic chaos at the end of World War II, the national debt was repudiated and became worthless. Resulting gaps in the asset structure of credit institutions and the central bank were filled by "equalization claims" against the federal government. To provide the central bank with securities that could be bought and sold to alter commercial bank liquidity, provision was made for the exchange of equalization claims held by the central bank for mobilization paper in the form of a special issue of Treasury bills. The amount authorized was DM 8.1 billion.[4]

With the growth in the German economy and the increase in liquidity of the financial system in recent years, this amount became inadequate. In 1967, the Law to Promote Economic Stability and Growth amended the Bundesbank law by inserting Section 42a to provide for the issue of "liquidity paper" by the federal government to supplement the resources of the Bundesbank in its open market policy. To quote the amendment:

Sec. 42a (1) When the mobilization papers have been placed in circulation by the German Bundesbank up to the nominal value of the equalization claim, the Federal Government shall transfer to the Bank on demand Treasury bills or non-interest bearing [i.e. discount] Treasury bonds, with the denominations and terms to be determined by the Bank, (liquidity paper) up to a maximum of eight billion Deutsche Marks. (2) The nominal value of the negotiated liquidity paper shall be entered by the Deutsche Bundesbank in a special account. The money in this special account may only be used for the redemption of such liquidity paper as has become due or has been repurchased by the Deutsche Bundesbank prior to maturity.[5]

[4] European Economic Community, *The Instruments of Monetary Policy in the Countries of the European Economic Community,* 1962, p. 80.
[5] *Law to Promote Economic Stability and Growth,* June 8, 1967, Section 42(1) and 42(2).

Under these provisions, the Bundesbank obtains Treasury bills or discount notes that it can sell to credit institutions or nonbanks to absorb cash or claims against the central bank when it seeks to tighten credit in the economy. Moreover, the initial counterbalancing liability of the Bundesbank takes the form of a blocked special account rather than an increase in the balance of the federal government at the Bundesbank. By this latter measure, the initial issue of the liquidity paper does not add to the money supply, so that its subsequent sale to the banking system reduces the liquid claims of the banks against the central bank.

Thus, one part of the explanation for the restricted nature of open market operations by the Bundesbank derives from the limited size and distribution of suitable marketable securities in the form of government debt. There is another aspect of financial organization and practice in Germany that also serves to restrict the scope and effectiveness of open market measures. Traditionally the Bundesbank has limited its open market operations to dealings with credit institutions, and in practice more specifically to the larger commercial banks and the central institutions of the savings banks and credit cooperatives. Although the Bundesbank has the authority to engage in open market transactions with nonbanks (that is, noncredit institutions) such as industrial corporations, insurance companies, private pension funds, and individuals, its practice has been not to do so.

Doubtless the tradition of relying on discounting and reserve requirements as principal policy instruments partially accounts for this self-imposed restriction on the Bundesbank's freedom of action. But there was also a more specific rationale arising from the fact that the bank supervisory authorities in consultation with the central bank had for about thirty years, until 1967, regulated maximum rates of interest that credit institutions could charge on loans or pay on deposits. Under such restrictions on rates of interest, the credit institutions would not have been able to bid competitively with deposit interest against terms offered to their deposit customers on open market paper by the Bundesbank. To avoid this situation, the Bundesbank refrained from selling such paper to the customers of credit institutions and was thus limited to offering it for sale to commercial banks and other credit institutions at terms that they might or might not regard as attractive when compared with customer loans. The resulting situation has been described as follows:

It is a special feature of open-market operations in the Federal Republic that dealings in money-market securities take place only between the Bundesbank on the one hand and credit institutions and certain public authorities (e.g. Federal Postal Administration, Social Insurance Institutions) on the other. It is in practice impossible for business undertakings or private individuals to acquire Treasury bills, Treasury bonds or other money-market securities at the selling prices fixed by the Bundesbank. The Bundesbank sells them only to the above-mentioned groups, while the banks can sell them to non-bank customers only within the limits laid down in the *Habenzinsabkommen* (agreement on deposit interest rates); moreover the banks have very little interest in business of this sort because it would lead to withdrawals from deposits.[6]

In 1967, the order regulating maximum interest rates on deposits and loans was revoked.[7] But not until 1971 did the Bundesbank begin actively to contemplate offering open market paper to business firms and the general public. Moreover, its open market offers of this kind in 1971 were in insignificant quantities and at rates that were not competitive. In most instances, these offers did not result in actual sales to nonbanks. Either the business firms lacked interest or banks overbid by raising the interest rate paid on the specific deposits they would have lost had the sale been completed. The net result has been to preserve the limited scope of the Bundesbank's open market instrument.

The underlying rationale for the banks' behavior in these instances is revealing. It is advantageous for the banks to purchase open market paper, or to permit their customers to purchase it only when their customer loan demand leaves them with excess reserves. In the absence of excess reserves, a purchase of open market paper either by banks or by their customers will force a multiple contraction of customer loans to restore the required minimum reserve position with the Bundesbank. The multiple by which deposits and loans must contract in these circumstances depends on the current level of the required reserve ratio. Thus, on specific or isolated transactions affecting their reserve positions via their customers' accounts, the banks can afford to pay substantially higher rates of interest on deposits to deter their customers from using these deposits to acquire mobilization or liquidity paper from the Bundesbank. However, should these higher deposit rates on individual transactions become generalized through competition to the entire deposit structure, it would no longer pay the banks to overbid in this fashion.[8] In this latter case, the cost of overbidding would be a general rise in deposit interest rates and presumably in loan rates as well. This should be exactly the result sought by the Bundesbank through its open market policy.

The interesting question is why the rise in deposit rates produced by the practice of overbidding does not become general. For any specific bank faced by a potential loss of customer deposits to the Bundesbank because of open market sales, the reserves lost to the Bundesbank can be replaced more cheaply by bidding deposits away from another bank at a slight increase in interest offered than by overbidding the rate on open market paper. For overbidding to suc-

---

[6] *The Instruments of Monetary Policy*, 1962, pp. 83–85.

[7] *Report of the Deutsche Bundesbank for the Year 1966*, p. 15.

[8] For a precise analysis of these two cases, see the mathematical appendix to this chapter.

ceed in preventing a generalized rise in deposit rates, the spread of such interbank competition for deposits must be avoided by the banks through a sense of communality of interest. The conditions necessary for such group discipline to succeed are those of concentrated markets and price leadership. These conditions are present in the German banking industry. Even under these conditions, however, overbidding would fail as a strategy if customers contemplating open market purchases did not discuss their intentions with their banks before acting so as to give the banks the opportunity to make a counter offer. The ability of the banks to retain the initiative in open market transactions with the Bundesbank strongly suggests that bank group discipline is strong and that oligopolistic modes of behavior exert an important influence in German credit markets.

Interest Rate Regulation

From the banking crisis of 1931 until 1967, creditor (deposit) and debtor (loan and overdraft) rates of interest of credit institutions were regulated in Germany. Such regulation was a governmental rather than a central bank function. From 1945 until 1961, it was exercised by the Lander bank supervisory authorities. From 1961 to its termination in 1967, the control of interest rates was the responsibility of the Federal Banking Supervisory Office under authority delegated from the Ministry of Economics. The central bank's role was consultative rather than executive. Thus, interest rate regulation was not an instrument of monetary policy in the strict sense prior to its suspension in 1967. Nevertheless, in the years 1965 and 1966 and to a lesser extent even earlier, the power to regulate interest rates was used experimentally to support goals of monetary policy; therefore, German experience with this control is worth examining.

The initial purpose of interest rate regulation in Germany in the 1930's was twofold: to protect borrowers from exorbitant interest charges and to prevent credit institutions from engaging in cutthroat competition for deposits that might lead to deterioration of risk standards in asset management. These objectives were thought to be served by setting *maximum* rates of interest that credit institutions could pay on deposits or receive on loans. (We note in passing the difference between this practice and that of the English banking cartel that set *minimum* rates on loans and maximum rates on deposits.) In postwar years of inflationary pressure, the equity and bank supervision aspects of interest rate regulation were supplemented by increased use of rate regulation to serve goals of monetary policy.

An important landmark of interest rate regulation was the "Order Concerning the Terms on Which Credit Institutions May Grant Credits and Receive Deposits," which came into force on March 1, 1965, and was revoked without successor effective April 1, 1967. Since the provisions, effects, and defects of this order provide a good illustration of German experience with interest rate regulation, and since it is the most recent German experience available, we shall confine our attention to it in preference to a more historical discussion.[9]

Prior to promulgation of the interest rate order in 1965, there were extensive consultations among representatives of departments of the federal government, the Bundesbank, and credit associations, and academic economists. The academic economists and representatives of the federal government sought an end to interest rate regulation, whereas representatives of credit associations and the Bundesbank sought its continuance and strengthening. Those who favored abandonment of regulation did so on grounds of its inconsistency with free markets. Representatives of the credit associations apparently feared the effects of decontrol on their respective competitive positions and on their cartel relation to their depositors and borrowers. Representatives from the Bundesbank appear to have emphasized continued control of lending rates as a device for more certain transmission of central bank discount policy to the credit markets.

Disregarding refinements, we may say that the order fixed maximum rates for loans, credit commissions, overdraft commissions, and turnover commissions on credits to nonbanks for periods of less than four years. *The order linked these to the central bank discount rate by fixed but nonidentical differentials.* Various lending rates were specifically exempt from the scope of the order, such as interbank (that is, inter-credit-institution) transactions, credits with maturities of more than four years or subject to regular redemption extending more than four years, credits granted to the Reconstruction Loan Corporation or to building and loan associations, and small personal loans and installment loans that were separately regulated.

Maximum creditor interest rates were established separately for sight deposits, notice deposits and time deposits (with maxima increasing by maturity classes), and savings deposits. Separate maximum rates were set for savings deposits of less than and more than 12 months and for corporate versus other savers on deposits of less than 12 months. These maximum *deposit* rates were not linked to the central bank discount rate but typically were separately adjusted by amendments to the interest rate order by the Federal Banking Supervisory Office. Other provisions of the order tightened the definition of obligations to which such maximum creditor rates applied in an effort to prevent evasion of the regulation under the pressure of competition for deposits. To this end the order provided that credit institutions, in principle, had to treat as deposits any money that was received from a nonbank without a written loan contract and without

[9] Details in the next several paragraphs concerning the interest rate order are based on an article "Regulation of the Terms for Banking Business under Article 23 of the Banking Law (Interest Rate Order)," in *Monthly Report of the Deutsche Bundesbank,* March 1965, pp. 3–6.

normal banking security. The order applied also to deposits in foreign currency to prevent evasion through choice of currency units.

Effective April 1, 1967, the interest rate order was revoked. The 1966 *Annual Report* of the Deutsche Bundesbank contains this illuminating commentary on the revocation:

> One important reason for the complete liberalizing of bank interest rates, after more than 35 years of official regulation, was that even after the various partial liberalizations, the observance of the Interest Rate Order could be verified only with difficulty and could not be enforced at all. At all events numerous "legal" subterfuges enabled the larger and more adroit employers of money to obtain higher rates of interest, although often only at the cost of accepting complicated technical forms like transactions under repurchase agreement and other devices. The official fixing of interest rates also became increasingly questionable the more the course of the "free" rates made it obvious that the hard and fast interest rate structure needed major alterations (for instance through wider spreading of interest rates according to maturities), although without the authorities having any firm guidance as to how great these alterations were to be. Finally, however, it was to be expected that "genuine" interest rates, fully conforming to the market, would guide the markets for credit with more efficiency than governmentally regulated rates, the justification for which lay, at least partly, in the fact that they often diverged from the "equilibrium rate" for the various kinds of deposits.[10]

Thus, difficulties of enforcement and lack of adequate criteria to guide the authorities in setting deposit and lending rates led to the end of interest rate regulation, at least for the present.[11] Clearly, the monetary authorities who had argued for continued control at the time of the interest rate order in 1964 had become disenchanted during the two years of its application. Moreover, the need for interest rate ceilings to discourage inflationary inflows of foreign short-term capital during the credit squeeze had ended with the onset of a German recession and the appearance of a deficit in the German balance of payments. The authorities do not appear to have attempted to influence the domestic *incidence* of their restrictive monetary policy by direct interest rate controls. Rather their purposes appear to have been (1) to reduce capital inflows from abroad by preventing domestic deposit and lending rates from rising, thus forcing greater reliance on credit rationing by nonprice means; and (2) to limit interest rate competition for deposits among credit institutions to reduce the efficiency of their performance as intermediaries in raising the velocity of money.

New Powers under the Stabilization Law

With the passage on June 8, 1967, of the Law to Promote Economic Stability and Growth, the federal government, and to a more limited

---

[10] *Report of the Deutsche Bundesbank for the Year 1966*, p. 15.

[11] An exception is interest on bank liabilities to nonresidents, which continues subject to regulation as conditions indicate.

extent the Bundesbank, acquired new powers to conduct macro-economic policy. The basic purpose of this law clearly is to make budgetary policy more readily responsive to the need for economic stabilization and to strengthen central bank policy by giving it, in close cooperation with the federal government, a more firm control over the domestic determinants of liquidity. To this end the law provides for adjustments to governmental spending through an *equalization reserve*, or the accelerated repayment of government loans from the Bundesbank, measures to limit or suspend government borrowing, authority to raise or lower income and corporate taxes within limits, the issue of liquidity paper to supplement the supply of open market paper available to the Bundesbank, and authority to require social security insurance institutions and the Federal Office for Labor to invest in Bundesbank mobilization and liquidity papers. Most of these measures must be initiated by the Minister of Economics and validated within six weeks by parliamentary endorsement. The law increased the authority of the central government in economic policy, but only modestly increased the authority of the central bank. The Bundesbank has the initiative for requesting the issue of liquidity paper and for requiring investment in such paper by retirement and unemployment funds. There is provision for consultation between the government and the Bundesbank on other measures.

The basic thrust of all these measures is to strengthen the co-ordination of federal and Lander governments' budgetary and fiscal policy with monetary policy and to add to the effectiveness of central bank measures in controlling liquidity in the economy. The under-lying rationale for the measures contained in the law may be said to derive from monetary-policy as well as from fiscal-policy considerations. Measures to reduce or increase the flow of government spending are tied to dispositions that alter basic liquidity in the banking system. For example, a reduction in government spending is implemented by means of a transfer of funds to an equalization reserve in the form of a blocked account at the Bundesbank. Such a reduction in spending may be accompanied under the law by an increase in taxes. The transfer of funds to such a blocked account reduces the reserve accounts of credit institutions at the Bundesbank and effectively drains liquidity from the "banking" system. Restrictions on or suspension of borrowing in the capital market by federal, Lander, and local governments are intended to relieve excessive downward pressure on prices of outstanding government and industrial bonds when the Bundesbank is restricting liquidity through its traditional techniques. The purpose is to avoid having to create money in the process of supporting an overburdened bond market depressed by new government financing during a period of monetary stringency produced by the Bundesbank.

Other measures such as provision for the issue of liquidity papers and authority to require investment in Bundesbank open market paper by social security funds strengthen the capacity of the Bundesbank to absorb liquidity from the "banking" system by means of open market operations. The social security institutions are among the few types of financial institutions (although they are oriented primarily toward the capital market) exempt from reserve requirements regulated by the Bundesbank. The new law permits the Bundesbank via government order to modify their liquidity directly by requiring them to invest in mobilization and liquidity paper. Thus, in each case the measures enumerated have a direct effect on the liquidity of the "banking" system. Even the fiscal measures focused on government spending and borrowing are tied to monetary policy through their deliberate link to Bundesbank-blocked accounts and thus to liquidity effects on the banking system. These measures have certainly strengthened the effectiveness of monetary policy even though for most of them the Bundesbank's role is consultative rather than executive.

Measures to Influence International Flows of Short-Term Capital

Flows of short-term capital between the Federal Republic of Germany and other countries are largely free of exchange controls in the form of licensing requirements or quantitative restrictions. In this sense, the German capital market is one of the freest and least controlled in the world. This circumstance, together with German participation in the Bretton Woods–International Monetary Fund system of exchange rates held by mutual agreement within narrow bands around stipulated parities, results in a familiar interdependence of German money and capital markets and those of other countries. Capital movements into or out of Germany in response both to interest rate differentials between the German and foreign money and capital markets and to speculation on possible changes in the exchange parity of the Deutsche mark have exerted powerful effects on the liquidity of the monetary system and on the interest cost and availability of borrowed funds in Germany. These effects have not always been in the direction sought by the Bundesbank for domestic economic stabilization nor welcomed from the perspective of international monetary cooperation. Therefore, while avoiding exchange controls and interference with current account transactions, as well as any *direct* regulation of capital flows, the Deutsche Bundesbank has evolved several techniques for indirectly influencing these flows. These techniques are part of the battery of instruments used by the Bundesbank to modify domestic monetary conditions.

The principal techniques used by the Bundesbank to influence international capital flows have been these: (1) offer of especially favorable rates for the repurchase of foreign currency, usually dollars, in the forward exchange market combined with a sale on the spot market; this is the so-called swap policy of the Bundesbank; (2) special reserve requirements on deposits of nonresidents in German credit institutions; (3) prohibition of interest payments on deposits of nonresidents and regulation of such substitute transactions as the sale (accompanied by agreement to repurchase) of Treasury bills or other fixed-interest obligations to nonresidents. Prior to 1967, for a time, the Bundesbank made the holding of foreign assets more attractive to banks by permitting the offset of such assets against liabilities to nonresidents before determining minimum reserves required against the latter. These various measures have in common their application to credit institutions as distinct from other business firms and individuals as well as their mode of operation, which is to influence the profitability of lending and borrowing transactions between German credit institutions and nonresidents while avoiding outright prohibition of such transactions.[12]

The swap technique takes advantage of the need of German credit institutions, principally the big three commercial banks but also others, to reconvert foreign currency loans into German marks at their maturity. The cost of such conversion depends on the effective exchange rate between the mark and the other currency. This spot exchange rate can vary within limits prescribed in the International Monetary Fund agreement and thus involves some uncertainty. Moreover, there is always the hypothetical possibility of a major change in parity during the life of the loan. Thus, while credit institutions can choose to subject their loans to this risk by carrying an "uncovered position," they usually prefer to cover by executing a sale against marks in the forward market of the foreign currency they will receive when the loan matures.

There is a private international market for forward exchange where such a covering transaction can be executed at the time the initial loan is made. The exchange rates in this forward market vary, for complex reasons, with market forces of supply and demand. It is when they have been unfavorable in the sense of lowering the profit on foreign short-term assets the holding of which the Bundesbank wished to encourage that the latter has offered credit institutions its own more favorable swap terms on such transactions. By means of such swap terms, the Bundesbank can alter the assured profitability of foreign short-term assets and thus influence their volume. The effect is not unlike a subsidy whose size can be altered to increase or decrease the volume of such assets.

In recent years, the Bundesbank has made active use of swaps to encourage German banks to invest funds abroad to offset heavy inflows of foreign "hot money" during periods of heightened specula-

---

[12] Since 1964, there has been a 25 per cent coupon tax on DM-denominated fixed interest securities issued in Germany and purchased by nonresidents. Though not an instrument of monetary policy, this tax does operate to direct capital inflows from the German domestic bond market to foreign markets so far as net coupon yield is important in investor calculations.

tion on the revaluation of the Deutsche mark (for example, prior to its revaluation on October 24, 1969). On occasion the Bundesbank has had to stipulate rather precisely the conditions to be observed before a bank could qualify for official swap assistance, in particular the nature of the foreign asset to be purchased, usually United States Treasury bills, and absence of matching foreign borrowing by the bank. Before such stipulation, some German banks had devised ingenious "recycling" schemes to profit from the spread between official swap rates and private market rates for forward cover, in a manner indicated by the following quotation:

> In view of the relatively wide difference between the swap rates charged by the Bundesbank and those of the free market, it was profitable, for example, to borrow dollars abroad, to have the exchange rate of these dollar borrowings guaranteed by a forward cover transaction at market rates, to exchange the borrowed dollars for Deutsche marks from the Bundesbank and to reinvest these dollars abroad, the foreign exchange cover being effective this time at the rates of the Bundesbank. By means of such transactions it was possible without using own liquid funds to achieve a profit approximately corresponding to the difference between the forward discount rates charged by the market and those charged by the Bundesbank. Although formally the criterion of money exports was fulfilled in these transactions, it was a matter of not actually exporting funds available within this country but of investing funds which previously had been borrowed abroad.[13]

The official swap procedure is not employed continuously by the Bundesbank but only during those periods when it regards domestic liquidity as excessive for stabilization purposes or when it is cooperating with foreign central banks experiencing excessive capital outflows for speculative reasons. In their effects on domestic liquidity, swap operations produce results comparable to open market operations. Money invested abroad by the banks can be and is repatriated to swell domestic liquidity when German banks run short of reserves under the pressure of expanding domestic credit demands. Thus, liquidity invested abroad is never firmly under Bundesbank control and may be repatriated when least desired from the perspective of official policy, though not from the perspective of the banks as private, profit-making firms. Official swaps have been most actively used during episodes of unusual speculative activity, when investor behavior has not responded to more moderate measures such as higher reserve requirements or prohibition of interest payments on nonresident deposits.

When neither internal nor external monetary conditions are causing the monetary authorities any special concern, reserve requirements for nonresident deposits may be identical to those for similar

[13] *Monthly Report of the Deutsche Bundesbank,* June 1969, footnote, p. 42.

types of resident deposits. However, during the decade of the 1960's, conditions were rarely normal for long, and the Bundesbank has used a variety of special reserve requirements on nonresident deposits. These have included higher average reserve ratios, still higher marginal reserve ratios applied to increases in nonresident deposits over some benchmark period, and 100 per cent reserve requirements on such increments, intended to offset completely the increase in domestic liquidity caused by a deposit inflow from abroad. When they were first applied, these higher reserve requirements were subject to the limitation that they should not push a credit institution's total reserve obligations above the amount that would have been required, had legally authorized maximum ratios been applied to the institution's *domestic* deposit obligations. However, this ceiling was removed by legislation during the summer of 1969. The effect of these special reserve requirements is to reduce the profit margins on foreign borrowing undertaken by German banks to offset a domestic liquidity squeeze.

Current account transactions between Germany and other countries are free from exchange regulation. An important gap thus exists in the effectiveness of special reserve requirements as a barrier to the inflow of deposit funds from abroad. German business firms (nonbanks) and individuals may borrow abroad, convert the foreign currency proceeds of their loans into Deutsche marks with the aid of their banks, and place these as resident deposits with their banks. On the same rationale, the mark deposits of the German subsidiary of a foreign firm are legally classified as resident deposits and exempt from the special reserve requirements applied to nonresident deposits. German credit institutions are free to pay interest on the resulting resident deposits. Large sums of foreign short-term capital have entered the German banking system through these channels, particularly during periods of speculation on revaluation of the Deutsche mark such as those in 1969 and 1971. Together with shifts in foreign trade financing and commercial leads and lags in settlement terms in foreign trade, these channels weaken the effectiveness of central bank measures to prevent inflows of foreign capital from offsetting domestic tight-credit policy.

These various techniques proved to be inadequate to limit the inflow of foreign short-term capital motivated by interest rate differentials and by mounting speculation on the revaluation of the Deutsche mark in the spring of 1971. On May 10, 1971, the convertibility of the Deutsche mark was suspended and its foreign exchange value permitted to rise in response to market forces. By floating the Deutsche mark in this manner, the German authorities effectively shut off the inflow of funds from abroad and regained control over the sources of liquidity in the German economy. This float continued until the agreement among the principal industrial powers on December 18, 1971, on a new set of multilateral exchange rates.

The government, in the light of its experience with uncontrolled corporate borrowing abroad in the period preceding the floating of the Deutsche mark, has requested and received legislative authority to require firms to deposit a portion of such borrowed funds in blocked deposit accounts at the Bundesbank. By sterilizing a portion of borrowed funds in this manner, the government will be able in the future to alter the effective cost of borrowing abroad and thus to regulate such borrowing more effectively in the interest of domestic policy considerations.

The Bundesbank has also tightened its regulations governing reserve requirements that apply when German banks borrow abroad to relend abroad in the performance of interest arbitrage transactions between foreign credit markets or in the Eurodollar market. Since October 21, 1970, such borrowings are exempt from reserve requirements provided only that they are expressed in a foreign currency, are passed on without delay in the same currency, and are not associated with a Bundesbank swap transaction. The latter proviso is intended to prevent the recycling strategy.

The remaining device used on various occasions by the authorities to limit short-term capital inflows from abroad has been to prohibit (except by special license) the payment of interest on nonresident deposits and also the sale on repurchase agreement to nonresidents of Treasury bills and other short-term money market paper, a sale that might serve as a substitute for deposit interest. Savings accounts of individuals always have been exempt from this prohibition. This prohibition was a governmental regulation rather than a Bundesbank one. It was in force from June 4, 1960, to December 10, 1969, by which time speculation-induced capital inflows into Germany had abated.[14] It was reintroduced in 1971 under the speculative pressures of that year.

THEORETICAL UNDERPINNINGS OF GERMAN MONETARY POLICY

The theoretical concepts that guide German monetary policy have not been set out systematically by official spokesmen but must be inferred from policy-oriented discussions in the monthly and annual reports of the Deutsche Bundesbank and from the policy measures developed and used in different situations by the German government and the Bundesbank. Moreover, the academic economic literature does not represent an alternative source to which one may turn for vigorous theoretical discussion of monetary and related macroeconomic policy issues. Most of the standard academic dis-

[14] For initial date, see International Monetary Fund *Annual Report on Exchange Restrictions, 1961*, p. 138. For terminal date, see *Report of the Deutsche Bundesbank for the Year 1969*, p. 118.

cussions of monetary policy focus their attention on the ability of the central bank to influence the liquidity of commercial banks and other financial institutions and thus interest rates and the availability of credit. They do not present more extensive models that incorporate the interaction between the monetary and real variables in a macroeconomic system nor do they investigate intensively the forces that modify economic behavior of financial institutions, firms, and households.[15] Thus, what follows is more an impressionistic sketch of German monetary theory as applied to policy concerns than a well-documented synthesis of existing writings by German authors.

The monetary authorities organize their policy discussions in terms that may be described generally as those of the neoclassical, post-Keynesian synthesis. That is to say, the authorities think in terms of the main flows such as consumption, investment, saving, government expenditure, and net exports, which constitute the important uses and dispositions of gross national product, and of the manner in which these are influenced by monetary and budgetary policy, tax incentives, domestic versus foreign price levels, and other familiar economic forces.[16]

There are, however, important differences in emphasis between the policy-oriented theoretical views of the German authorities and those of their opposite numbers in such countries as the United States, the United Kingdom, and Sweden, who employ rather similar frameworks to analyze the determinants of aggregate demand. The German authorities have tended to accord greater relative importance to monetary than to fiscal policy. Within the realm of monetary policy broadly defined, they have attached greater significance to measures to influence the "liquidity" of banks and other financial institutions than to control of the money supply (in the narrow usage of the term), and greater significance to "credit" policy than to "monetary" policy. In their concern for the liquidity of the credit system and thus of the economy, the German authorities hold a view not unlike that of the monetarist economists in the United States, but with the emphasis on the stock of liquid assets available to a broader spectrum of financial institutions, rather than on the cash and commercial bank liabilities that constitute the money supply. However, the German authorities view the ramifications of a change in liquidity in terms of a Keynesian-type macroeconomic model, with emphasis on

[15] For standard works in this area by German authors, see Rudolf Stucken, *Deutsche Geld- und Kreditpolitik, 1914–1963*, 3. (Tuebingen: Auflage, J. C. B. Mohr (Paul Siebeck), 1964); and Otto Veit, *Gundriss der Wehrungspolitik* (Frankfurt: Fritz Knapp Verlag, 1961). Also G. Schmölders, "The Liquidity Theory of Money," *Kyklos* 13, fasc. (1960): 346–60.

[16] For a policy discussion that is revealing of the theoretical views of the Deutsche Bundesbank, see *Report of the Deutsche Bundesbank for the Year 1967*, pp. 1–33.

changes in entrepreneurial expectations and investment behavior induced by changes in credit terms rather than the more direct link
between stock of money and aggregate demand that is characteristic
of the quantity theory, in even its modern versions.

In its analysis of bank (that is, credit institution) liquidity, the
Bundesbank incorporates the standard factors that change the volume
of claims against the central bank in most modern monetary systems.[17] Principal among these are changes in cash in circulation, in
deposits of governmental organs at the central bank, in open market
purchases and sales with nonbanks and in long-term bonds, and in
foreign exchange flows between Germany and other countries. The
Bundesbank regards changes in discounts and advances and in open
market purchases and sales with credit institutions not as a determi-
nant of liquidity changes but as a consequence. This view attributes
initiative in these two areas to the credit institutions, albeit on terms
set by the Bundesbank. In its analysis, the Bundesbank considers
changes in reserve requirements as relevant with respect to the excess liquidity position of credit institutions.

It is principally "the banks' free liquid reserves" and to a much
lesser degree the excess reserves (that is, banks' balances with the
Bundesbank minus reserve requirements) to which the Bundesbank
gives special attention in its liquidity analysis. Free liquid reserves
are defined to include potential claims against the Bundesbank in
view of credit institutions' unutilized capacity to discount, obtain
advances, sell open market paper to the Bundesbank, or repatriate
liquid assets held abroad. The rationale for this treatment turns on
asserted unwillingness or inability of the Bundesbank to refuse to
honor requests for reserves (that is, deposit claims against itself)
when approached through these channels. Excess reserves usually are
zero since they are readily converted by credit institutions into open
market paper or foreign money market assets.

The Bundesbank's theoretical views are clarified by relating to its
liquidity analysis its further concern for what it calls "monetary capital formation." The Bundesbank defines as monetary capital all deposits in credit institutions whose maturity exceeds three months.
Essentially, therefore, monetary capital matches rather closely the
concept of time and savings accounts with the indicated maturity.
The Bundesbank regards the increase or formation of monetary capital as a desirable phenomenon from the point of view of restricting
the growth of the money supply. The rationale for this is that monetary capital represents assets that are comparatively firmly held by
their saver-owners and that replace shorter-term and more liquid deposits (that is, money stock) on the balance sheets of credit institutions. Thus an expansion of bank liquidity and bank credit that may

---

[17] See "Notes on the Bundesbank's Liquidity Analysis" in *Monthly Report of the Deutsche Bundesbank*, April 1970, pp. 26 ff.

be potentially inflationary can be neutralized in its effect on the money supply to the extent that monetary capital formation occurs. Another facet of Bundesbank concern with the volume and form of saving is the effect it has on the performance of the capital market. This aspect is discussed in the section entitled "evaluation and commentary."

Although there are Keynesian elements in the macroeconomic framework that guides monetary policy in Germany, the views of the monetary authorities are distinctly *not* neo-Keynesian in their evaluation of the relative importance of "credit" policy and fiscal policy. Here it is necessary to keep terminological usage straight. When the German authorities speak of *fiscal policy*, they mean *governmental budget policy inclusive not only of tax and expenditure measures but also of government debt policy and the effects of government finance on the liquidity position of credit institutions and the economy.*

Until the passage of the Law for Economic Stability and Growth in 1967, compensatory budgetary policy to aid monetary policy in aggregate demand management could not be said to have been systematically practiced in federal Germany. Indeed, the Bundesbank often deplored the lack of coordination of fiscal and monetary policy during the decade prior to 1967. The law of 1967 greatly strengthened the power of the central government to modify budget policy at federal, Lander, and local levels in a compensatory manner. Moreover, provisions of the law of 1967 (see section, this chapter, on new powers) reveal an acute awareness of the monetary, or "credit," effects as well as the income effects of fiscal policy. For example, as an aspect of restrictive policy, deliberately created government surpluses are to be transferred to a blocked account at the Bundesbank, thus reducing bank liquidity. For expansionary purposes the process is reversed. This emphasis on the monetary or credit aspects of budget policy as well as its income effects distinguishes the theoretical views of the German authorities sharply from those of the neo-Keynesians.

EVALUATION AND COMMENTARY

The most generally accepted goals of national economic policy are high employment, economic growth, price stability, and cyclical equilibrium on balance of payments with the rest of the world. Not infrequently there is the further balance-of-payments goal of basic equilibrium accompanied by a current account surplus. Judged by these criteria, the economic performance of the Federal Republic of Germany in the past two decades has been exceptional. (See Table 4.1 for money supply, real GNP, and various price indexes.) Unquestionably numerous factors other than monetary policy have contributed to this performance. Among these are a skilled labor force substantially underemployed at the beginning; the availability for

TABLE 4.1   Germany: Money Supply, Real GNP,
              and Price Indexes (annual percentage changes)

Year	Money supply [a] (% change)	Real GNP [b] 1962 prices (% change)	GNP deflator [c] (% change)	Retail prices [d] (% change)	Whole-sale prices [e] (% change)	Export prices [f] (% change)
1960	7.28	....	....	....	....	....
1961	13.89	5.42	4.36	0.00	0.20	−0.30
1962	8.77	4.01	4.09	1.98	1.11	0.10
1963	7.10	3.44	3.08	1.45	0.60	0.10
1964	7.78	6.65	2.77	1.05	0.19	2.39
1965	7.50	5.58	3.58	1.98	2.08	2.24
1966	1.39	2.90	3.57	2.04	1.06	2.09
1967	10.42	−0.27	1.07	0.45	−0.48	−0.09
1968	6.30	7.24	1.60	0.00	−6.04	−1.03
1969	6.37	8.10	3.46	1.35	2.45	5.19
1970	8.84	4.86	7.41	3.48	5.60	4.76
1960–70	8.70	4.77	3.49	1.37	0.67	1.52

[a] Demand deposits and currency, calculated from *Monthly Report* of the Deutsche Bundesbank, July 1971, pp. 23–25.

[b] Calculated from Statistisches Bundesamt, Wiesbaden, *Statistisches Jahrbuch für die Bundesrepublik Deutschland,* 1971, p. 504.

[c] Calculated from real GNP and GNP at current prices series, in *Statistisches Jahrbuch,* p. 504.

[d] Calculated from *Statistisches Jahrbuch,* 1970, p. 427.

[e] 1961–63 figures calculated from data in *Statistisches Jahrbuch,* 1968, p. 428. 1964–70 figures calculated from data in *Statistisches Jahrbuch,* 1970/71, p. 439.

[f] 1961–62 figures calculated from data in *Statistisches Jahrbuch,* 1968, pp. 438–39. 1963–69 figures calculated from data in *Statistisches Jahrbuch,* 1970, pp. 421–22. 1970 figure calculated from data in *Statistisches Jahrbuch,* 1970/71, pp. 448–49.

many years of an abundant additional supply of labor emigrating from East Germany and drawn from foreign countries such as Italy and Yugoslavia, where employment opportunities were inadequate; and a tradition of hard work and thrift that stimulated labor productivity and a high rate of personal saving and may have restrained labor unions in the past in their quest for higher wages as a means to higher real incomes.

In a measure these factors also have contributed to the relative success of monetary policy in Germany, as reflected in the moderate rate of inflation, by making possible the application of monetary restraint under circumstances in which the inflation-unemployment trade-off was less difficult or the balance of payments less a restraint on economic growth than frequently is the case. Moreover, public experience with the ravages of runaway inflation twice since 1918 has resulted in wide popular support for the goal of price stability and thus for central bank action to moderate if not prevent inflation.

In our evaluation, having recognized these factors, we shall keep them in the background to concentrate instead on matters more directly related to the ability of the central bank to influence the monetary and financial climate of the German economy. In particular we shall explore certain problem areas drawn from recent experience including coordination of fiscal with monetary policy, the adequacy of Bundesbank policy instruments to control liquidity in the economy, and international capital flows. We shall evaluate also the extent to which the organization of financial institutions and markets and certain established financial procedures and practices aid or hinder the accomplishment of central bank objectives.

Powers conferred on the federal government and to a lesser degree on the Bundesbank by the Law for Economic Stability and Growth of 1967 have increased the ability of these organizations to coordinate fiscal with monetary policy. The law permits the federal government to vary federal expenditures and taxes within limits on short notice, and provides for restriction or suspension of government borrowing at all levels of government and for obligatory transfer of federal and Lander surpluses to sterilized "equalization fund" accounts at the Bundesbank, thus draining private liquidity without adding to spendable government balances. The law requires that federal budget management shall be based on a financial plan covering a five-year period, to be revised annually. Federal expenditures, taxes, and deficit financing are to be planned with due regard for overall economic potential. While this latter provision stresses the income effects of the budget, other provisions of the law are directed to its monetary effects. The law appears well designed to permit the authorities to achieve better coordination between monetary policy and fiscal policy in the future.

The Bundesbank has a comprehensive array of *market-oriented* policy instruments to implement domestic monetary policy. By its reserve and rediscount policies supplemented by newly strengthened capabilities for open market operations and by its new authority via government order to specify limited investments of social insurance institutions in open market paper, the Bundesbank can influence directly the liquidity of a wide range of credit institutions.

International capital flows, however, continue to challenge the capacity of the Bundesbank to control monetary and credit conditions in the German economy. Even in this area the capabilities of the Bundesbank have been strengthened recently, although some gaps remain and are likely to persist. By its authority to raise reserve requirements on nonresident deposits in credit institutions to 100 per cent when necessary, the Bundesbank is able to neutralize completely the effects on domestic liquidity of inflows of short-term capital from abroad that take the form of credit institutions' deposit or borrowing obligations to nonresidents. Moreover, when this reserve requirement is set at less than 100 per cent, it can reduce or eliminate the profitability of such deposits to credit institutions unless they receive them at no interest cost. Foreigners speculating on revaluation of the mark sometimes have transferred deposits to German banks even when payment of interest was prohibited. Such prohibition of interest, exercised by the federal government in consultation with the Bundesbank, is another deterrent to attracting short-term capital from abroad. The Bundesbank also employs its swap policy to encourage German banks to acquire foreign short-term assets in preference to domestic money market or longer-term financial assets when it regards domestic liquidity as excessive. This policy of agreeing to repurchase foreign currencies at favorable rates of exchange relative to those in the private forward exchange market so as to increase the effective rate of return on investment in foreign assets does not prevent the repatriation of foreign assets by credit institutions that are under pressure from customers who seek credit accommodation. Thus foreign assets, other than minimum working balances maintained abroad, may be regarded by commercial banks as substitutes for holdings of domestic open market or mobilization paper but not as substitutes for customer loans.

Borrowing abroad by resident individuals and nonfinancial firms has constituted a large breach in the defenses that the Bundesbank has been able to use against excessive inflows of foreign short-term capital. Individuals and nonfinancial firms are free to borrow abroad and to convert the loan proceeds to Deutsche marks. Moreover, German subsidiaries of foreign firms are treated as residents from the standpoint of interest-rate and reserve-requirement controls on their deposits in German banks. When interest rates in Germany exceed those abroad or when speculative sentiment is aroused, very large amounts of foreign short-term capital have flowed into Germany through these unregulated channels. Such loans permit their recipients to avoid paying the higher interest rates occasioned by Bundesbank policies to tighten credit on domestic credit markets. Moreover, such inflows increase the volume of resident deposits in German credit institutions and thus add to the liquidity of these institutions when Bundesbank policy may be seeking to reduce such liquidity. German banks may even encourage enterprises to borrow abroad by offering attractive interest on the resulting deposits as a means of offsetting a domestic liquidity squeeze. Massive inflows of foreign short-term capital through these channels contributed decisively to the decision to float the Deutsche mark on May 10, 1971.

As a counter strategy the authorities have attempted to compensate for the increase in liquidity produced by such flows by raising reserve requirements on both resident and nonresident deposits and by using other general policy instruments such as rediscount and advance rates and open market sales to tighten domestic liquidity. These measures have proven to be inadequate. Accordingly, in February 1972, the authorities introduced a new technique to help regulate short-term capital inflows from abroad. By order of the federal government, borrowing abroad by nonbanks may be subject to a non-interest-bearing cash deposit requirement to be held as a special deposit at the Deutsche Bundesbank. The requirement applies to borrowings by nonbanks in excess of two million Deutsche marks. The federal government (not the Bundesbank) may require cash deposits up to 50 per cent of the amounts borrowed abroad. A variety of exceptions or exemptions exist, including liabilities arising from customary payment periods for imports or from the acceptance of customary advance payments in export transactions.[18] The effect of the measure when used is to increase the effective interest cost on foreign borrowings by nonbanks and thus to reduce their attractiveness.

Beyond such modifications in policy instruments, the German monetary authorities have shown an alert concern over more fundamental and longer-term solutions to the problems posed by international capital flows. In particular, they favored the revaluation of the mark in October 1969 and the general realignment of exchange parities in December 1971 to correct what they had come to regard as a fundamental disequilibrium in the balance of payments of Germany and other countries. In addition, they have taken an active part in international discussions of possibilities for greater flexibility in official exchange parities and their adjustment under the IMF system. Moreover, their desire to improve their capacity to cope with the problems posed by short-term international capital flows while simultaneously maintaining fixed parities within the European Common Market has stimulated their interest in the proposals for monetary union among the member states of the European Economic Community.

In the past few years the German monetary authorities have substantially strengthened their capacity to control domestic sources of change in liquidity. With the adoption of the cash deposit scheme, they may have developed reasonably effective policy measures to neutralize and offset changes in domestic liquidity caused by international capital flows. With rare exceptions, such as the prohibition of interest payments on nonresident deposits during certain periods, the German methods produce their results by modifying the profitability of different courses of action for lenders, investors, and credit institutions rather than by substituting official for private decisions.

---

[18] For further details, see *Monthly Report of the Deutsche Bundesbank,* March 1972, pp. 5–7.

Thus the German controls work through changing the environment for market decisions rather than through direct controls such as ceilings on loans, maximum interest rates, and control of foreign exchange.

When assessed by the criteria of economic growth, high employment, and price stability, the German record in the decade 1960–70 is exceptional. The authorities have also shown a growing determination to cope with persistent surpluses in the balance of payments by their willingness to revalue the Deutsche mark and by measures to strengthen their capacity to control short-term capital flows. The German record has been one of a high degree of effectiveness in monetary policy that, until the Law for Economic Stability and Growth of 1967, received little assistance from fiscal policy in the management of aggregate demand.

A principal question remaining is, Has financial organization and practice in Germany contributed to the effectiveness of monetary policy. The interaction among structural aspects of a financial system, officially variable rules such as those governing tax rates, rediscount rates, and reserve requirements, legal controls over the assets in which a particular financial institution may invest, and the domains respectively of private and official decision making are complex and have not been the subject of much systematic study. The German case, however, is suggestive in this regard. Certain features stand out.

Traditionally, the commercial banking system in Germany has been highly concentrated, having been dominated by three main commercial banking organizations. In recent years this degree of concentration has lessened somewhat with the rise to prominence in commercial banking of several central giro institutions, as the savings banks have diversified into all-purpose banks. Despite this development, the degree of concentration remains substantial. This concentration is enhanced by legal arrangements permissive of interlocking stock ownership as well as of a principal role for banks in voting stock placed with them by customers for safekeeping in security deposits. Commercial and investment banking are carried on within the same banking organization with the result that the big three commercial banks and a few other big credit institutions perform a crucial role in the issue of new securities, both shares and bonds. The amount of government debt outstanding, though rising, remains low in comparison with many other industrialized countries when it is viewed in relation to national income or per capita of population. The role of institutional investors such as insurance companies and pension funds in the long-term capital market is less important than in countries like the United States and the United Kingdom. This is due in part to the extensive coverage of the government system of old-age benefits and in part to the asset preferences exhibited by savers who prefer to hold the shorter-maturity obligations of commercial banks, savings banks, and building and loan associations. In such a system, the opportunities for frustration of restrictive credit policy by disintermediation via the capital market are less than, for example, in the United States. Another consequence is the unusual dependence of the capital market on the banking system and savings institutions, a dependence reflected in the marked responsiveness of long-term interest rates to changes in money market conditions produced by monetary policy.

The money market itself is restricted in scope with nonbank firms and individuals barred in practice from direct participation. Despite some recent increase in Bundesbank willingness to include these firms and individuals in its open market transactions, the older, established tradition of their nonparticipation prevails. In the years since the monetary reform of 1948, German business firms have been unusually dependent on the banking system and other credit institutions for their financing. This reflects in part the high cost of capital market borrowing owing to issue costs and taxes, and in part the small capital and reserve base of German enterprises following the monetary reform. The closed nature of the money market removes the possibility for nonbank firms to bypass the banks through the money market, so this alternative also is absent. This combination of circumstances suggests that central bank measures to tighten or ease the liquidity of credit institutions may be transmitted to business firms more directly and promptly than is the case in countries with more diverse alternative channels for credit flows between borrowers and ultimate lenders.

These features of the German credit and financial system confer a key role on credit institutions, especially commercial banks, in the credit intermediation process. Moreover, the relative importance of commercial banking in credit intermediation increases rather than decreases when the Bundesbank tightens credit significantly by using its most powerful instrument, an increase in reserve requirements. To understand how this happens, it is necessary to examine the relationship of the credit institutions to the bond market.

The principal borrowers in the bond market normally are mortgage banks, federal, Lander, and local authorities, governmental special funds such as the Equalization of Burdens Fund, and the federal railways and the federal postal administration. Principal lenders in the bond market include the savings banks and their central giro institutions, social insurance institutions, private insurance companies, nonbank businesses and individuals, and to a lesser extent, commercial banks. When the Bundesbank raises reserve requirements, this immediately reduces the supply of funds to the bond market via commercial banks and via savings banks and their central giro institutions by diverting some of these flows to increase the reserve balances of these institutions at the central bank. Commercial banks as well as the savings banks that also accept demand deposits and make commercial loans normally protect their ability to make loans to customers by reducing bond purchases to meet the additional required reserves and to make additional customer loans. These responses are sufficient to cause a rise in interest rates and a decline in prices in the bond market.

At this point, a secondary expectations effect begins to operate to reduce demand for bonds by social insurance institutions, insurance companies, and nonbank firms and individuals whose capacity to purchase bonds has not been directly reduced by the increase in reserve requirements. These potential purchasers, fearing capital losses on bonds, tend to divert their demand toward fixed-yield assets, whose capital value does not fluctuate in organized markets. For individuals, the most readily available assets that meet this specification are the time and savings deposit obligations of commercial banks and other credit institutions. For institutional investors and nonbank businesses, two such assets are supplied by the commercial banks, mortgage banks, and business borrowers. These are repurchase agreements and loans against borrowers' notes. Thus, the supply of funds to the bond market declines and that to banks and other credit institutions increases as credit tightens.

At this point, yet another feature of the German system comes into play to facilitate the ability of the central bank to tighten credit while avoiding undesirable risk of precipitating insolvency and failure for business firms and credit institutions. Both repurchase agreements and loans against borrowers' notes are forms of registered bonds as distinct from bearer bonds. Medium- and longer-term registered bonds also exist. Registered bonds are not traded in organized markets and thus do not have recognized market prices. Therefore, credit and financial institutions are permitted to carry their holdings of these bonds in their balance sheets at par rather than market value. When interest rates rise so that even registered bonds are worth less than their par values, their institutional holders need not suffer visible capital losses so long as their need for liquidity does not force them to sell. Futhermore, the necessity to sell registered bonds at a capital loss even under strong pressure of need for cash liquidity is obviated by the practice of using repurchase agreements to transfer securities to another holder without an actual sale taking place.

The scope of the repurchase agreement is suggested in this definition developed by the Bundesbank to guide credit institutions in reporting such agreements in a special survey:

> All agreements under which assets (e.g. bills of exchange, securities, loans granted) are transferred to another party (creditor) against payment of a certain sum, with the proviso that they be repurchased at a date laid down in advance, or to be appointed by the creditor, against payment of the sum received or of another sum agreed on in advance. The report

shall also include those transactions under which issuing institutions transfer bonds of their own issue for certain periods under an obligation to repurchase.[19]

By a repurchase agreement the banks can arrange *effective* maturities and yields to suit the buyer's terms regardless of the terms specified in the underlying security contract. They have also sought a device to make such instruments transferable before their maturity:

> By issuing "bearer certificates" a number of banks are trying to re-establish the advantage of greater transferability inherent in bearer securities as compared with registered bonds and unbonded loans. In these certificates, which are attached to the securities, the issuing institution undertakes to repurchase the security from its holder before maturity at a fixed rate. By this means a formally long-term security becomes, for all practical purposes, a medium- or even short-term security not only for the initial purchaser, but virtually for any buyer.[20]

By the device of the repurchase agreement, explicit capital losses are minimized during a period when monetary policy causes a sharp rise in interest rates. A borrower who wishes to exchange an existing registered bond for cash need not sell it in the market at a reduced price, thereby incurring a capital loss; he can offer it under a repurchase agreement at a rate of interest and for a maturity specified in the repurchase agreement to match current market terms. In effect, this replaces a potential capital loss by its equivalent in higher current interest costs for the maturity period of the repurchase agreement. Moreover, the purchaser, as in the case of social insurance institutions, obtains an asset whose price is stable rather than fluctuating in the market. Neither party, therefore, is exposed to overt capital loss such as might lead to technical bankruptcy.

Loans against borrowers' notes also are classified as registered bonds rather than bearer bonds, are not traded in organized markets, and thus do not undergo visible changes in capital value when the level of interest rates changes. These loans are issued for large sums as borrowing instruments of business firms. The big commercial banks play a central role in the issue and placement of both repurchase agreements and loans against borrowers' notes. They also issue repurchase agreements as their own obligations in an endeavor to find cash to make additional customer loans.

These practices and behavior patterns have the effect of decreasing the role of the open capital market and increasing that of the banks and of direct placements assisted by the banks when interest rates

---

[19] "The Credit Institutions Transactions under Repurchase Agreements," *Monthly Report of the Deutsche Bundesbank*, November 1965, p. 3. On this subject, see also "Security Transactions under Repurchase Agreements and Bond Market," *Monthly Report of the Deutsche Bundesbank*, July 1967, pp. 7–12.

[20] *Monthly Report of the Deutsche Bundesbank*, November 1965, p. 10.

rise in response to restrictive monetary policy of the Bundesbank. *Thus, under German conditions, bank intermediation increases and open market intermediation decreases during a credit squeeze. Moreover, overt capital losses and solvency effects of a liquidity squeeze are reduced and interest rate and availability effects enhanced by the role of registered bonds and repurchase agreements combined with the increased importance of bank-customer relationships during a credit squeeze. The way the German financial system responds to changes in central bank policy appears to reinforce the effectiveness of that policy while minimizing its disadvantages as compared with alternative arrangements to be found in some other countries, such as the United States and the United Kingdom.*

To conclude, the relative success of the German monetary authorities in implementing an anticyclical monetary policy can be explained in part by favorable financial structure and practices; in part by favorable public attitudes towards thrift, liquidity preference, and price stability; and in part by factors that have contributed toward real growth of the German economy. These favorable factors have supported the Deutsche Bundesbank's concern for price stability and have diminished its inhibitions concerning capital losses and insolvency effects of tight money. Recent developments have enhanced the ability of the monetary authorities to control disequilibrating short-term capital flows from abroad, but these international influences remain as important challenges to the autonomy of the German authorities. Their longer-range approach to this problem emphasizes monetary cooperation within the European Economic Community, together with the possibility for greater flexibility of exchange parities between the Community currencies and the dollar. Finally, the Law for Economic Stability and Growth of 1967 provides the means for greater coordination between budgetary and monetary policies in aggregate demand management and closes some loopholes in the ability of the Bundesbank to control the domestic sources of liquidity. Only the recent marked increases in money wages raise doubts about the domestic environment for German monetary policy and its effectiveness in the foreseeable future.

Mathematical Appendix

Let

$$r = \text{minimum required reserve ratio}$$
$$R = \text{volume of minimum required reserves}$$
$$L = \text{bank loans}$$
$$D = \text{bank deposits}$$
$$i_d = \text{deposit rate of interest}$$

i_l = loan rate of interest
Δ = first difference operator
P = bank profits.

Then for minimum required reserves, we have

$$R = rD.$$

On the assumption of no excess reserves,

$$D = \frac{R}{r}.$$

Simplify the analysis by assuming no bank costs other than costs of funds. Ignore bank liabilities other than deposits and bank assets other than loans and required reserves. Then the balance sheet identity is

$$L + R = D,$$

and

$$L = D - R = D - rD = D(1 - r) = \frac{R}{r}\,(1 - r).$$

Bank costs are

$$i_d D = i_d \left(\frac{R}{r}\right),$$

on the assumption of competitive markets (no discrimination among depositors).

Bank revenues are

$$i_l L = i_l \frac{R}{r}(1 - r).$$

Bank profits are

$$
\begin{aligned}
P &\equiv i_l L - i_d D \\
&= i_l \frac{R}{r}(1 - r) - i_d \left(\frac{R}{r}\right) \\
&= \frac{R}{r}\Big[i_l(1 - r) - i_d\Big].
\end{aligned}
$$

The break-even relation between deposit and loan rates of interest occurs when

$$i_l(1 - r) - i_d = 0,$$

that is, when

$$i_d = i_l(1 - r).$$

Thus, if i_d represents the competitive cost of funds, the maximum i_d that banks can afford to pay is

$$i_d = i_l\,(1 - r).$$

For a minimum required reserve ratio of 10 per cent, this expression becomes

$$i_d = 0.9i_l.$$

Consider, now, central bank open market sales of securities to bank customers such as to produce a decline in bank deposits ΔD. Within our assumptions, this will force a reduction of loans, expressed by

$$\Delta L = \frac{\Delta D}{r}(1 - r),$$

since $\Delta D = \Delta R$, and there are no excess reserves. Thus the revenue lost through the loss of reserves can be expressed as

$$i_l \, \Delta L = i_l \left[\frac{\Delta D}{r}(1 - r) \right].$$

We may assume that the interest yield on the open market securities offered by the central bank will be close to the deposit rate of interest, and so we may approximate customer revenue from purchase of the open market securities by $i_d \, \Delta D$.

This magnitude $i_d \, \Delta D$ approximates (understates slightly) the opportunity cost the bank faces in retaining the deposit on the assumption that this is an isolated transaction, whose effects do not become generalized to the entire market and thus to all deposit funds.

Then the relation between the bank's potential loss of revenue and the opportunity cost (in an isolated transaction that does not alter the rate paid on all deposits) may be expressed as

$$i_l \left[\frac{\Delta D}{r}(1 - r) \right] - i_d \Delta D.$$

For this isolated transaction, the break-even relation between i_l *and* i_d becomes

$$i_d = i_l \left(\frac{1 - r}{r} \right).$$

Suppose, for example, that the minimum required reserve ratio r is 10 per cent. Then on such an isolated transaction

$$i_d = i_l \left(\frac{0.90}{0.10} \right) = 9i_l.$$

This is 10 times as large as our previous result.

Clearly, therefore, banks will find it profitable to overbid the rate offered by the central bank on open market securities to retain deposits, reserves and loans, provided that interbank competition for deposits that raises i_d generally can be avoided. This requires price discrimination among deposit customers. Note that by paying premium deposit rates to a customer who contemplates purchase of open market securities a bank avoids entirely the loss of revenues that such a customer purchase would entail.

5 Italy

Since the Second World War, the primary goal of economic policy in Italy has been modernization and development of the Italian economy. Industrialization, technological modernization of industrial plant and equipment, development of electrical and petroleum sources of power, improvement of roads, railroads, airlines, port facilities and shipping, improved farming methods, regional economic development, and broader provision for education and health services and for old age pensions have preoccupied economic policy makers in Italian government, both national and local.

To understand the techniques and priorities of Italian monetary and credit policy, it is essential to keep in mind the goal of economic development. In Italy, economic development with its implications for deliberate modernization and for changes in economic structure replaces the familiar macroeconomic policy objective of economic growth. As a consequence, the monetary authorities in Italy have been concerned not only with the *volume* of credit but also with its *allocation* to support investments linked to high national priorities. Allocative objectives help to explain the persistent policy of maintaining low and stable interest rates in the medium- and long-term bond market, as well as regulations limiting the maturity and rate of interest of time deposits that commercial banks may offer to savers in competition for funds with the capital market. Permission for commercial and savings banks to substitute specified types of bonds and mortgages for cash deposits and Treasury bills in meeting obligatory reserve requirements at the central bank likewise is intended to help in keeping down long-term rates of interest.

Commitments made by the national budget and by special credit institutions to provide loans and interest rate subsidies to investment projects having high priorities in an economic development sense have resulted in pressures on the *Banca d'Italia* to acquire both Treasury bills and medium- and long-term bonds in quantities that have been excessive by the criterion of monetary stability. Attempts of the monetary authorities to acquire more scope for discretionary monetary policy in meeting these pressures have motivated two reforms of the money market during the 1960's, with attendant consequences for Treasury bill financing and for central bank discount, minimum obligatory reserve, and open market policies. These developments also have been in the nature of responses to problems derivative from the drive for economic development.

Innovations by the Italian authorities in the use of incentives and controls to influence the net foreign position of Italian commercial banks have been stimulated by the rigidity within the Italian system of the conventional central bank instruments to control the money supply: the discount rate, reserve requirements, and open market operations. Foreign exchange regulations governing capital movements between the Italian money and capital markets and their foreign counterparts derive their basic rationale from efforts by the authorities to channel Italian savings into priority domestic investments. The Banca d'Italia also controls new issues of both stocks and bonds in the capital market in accordance with priorities established by the Interministerial Committee for Credit and Savings.

In subsequent sections of this chapter we shall review the institutional structure of the Italian financial system. Then we shall discuss the principal instruments and controls of monetary and credit policy and examine the manner in which they complement each other in the coherent system that the authorities have fashioned to direct credit flows. After briefly treating the theoretical framework for monetary policy in Italy, we conclude with an evaluation and commentary.

FINANCIAL STRUCTURE AND REGULATION

In Italy the power of the government to regulate the activities of credit institutions in the public interest is comprehensive. This power is exercised by the Interministerial Committee for Credit and Savings, created by law in 1947.[1] The committee is presided over by the Minister of the Treasury and has as additional members the ministers of Public Works, Budget, Agriculture and Forestry, Industry and Commerce, and Foreign Trade, and the Minister for Enterprises with State Participation. The Italian central bank, the Banca d'Italia, is the

[1] "The Decree on the Interministerial Committee for Credit and Savings, 1947," in *Central Banking Legislation*, vol. 2, *Europe*, ed. Hans Aufricht, International Monetary Fund, Washington, D.C., 1967, pp. 453–55.

executive agent for decisions of the Interministerial Committee. The governor of the Banca d'Italia participates in the meetings of the committee. The committee delegates much of its operational authority to the Banca d'Italia, but the latter is clearly subordinate to the committee and specifically to supervision by the Minister of the Treasury. The committee is charged with the duty "to supervise, at the highest level, the safeguarding of savings, the carrying on of credit activities, and exchange matters." [2] Moreover, the committee is the final authority for powers of regulation conferred under the Banking Law of 1936.

The Banking Law of 1936 provides that

All business enterprises that accept deposits from the public and grant credit, whether constituted under public law or private law, shall be subject to the control of a government agency [now the Banca d'Italia] . . .

The terms "bank," "banking," "savings bank," "credit," "savings," and the like may under no circumstances be used in the title of institutions, bodies, or enterprises which are not subject to the control of the Bank of Italy and which consequently have not received its authorization.[3]

The banking law lists the following types of credit institutions that are subject to supervision by the Banca d'Italia: credit institutions incorporated under public law and banks of national interest (these two groups constitute the principal commercial banks); banks and credit institutions in general, however constituted, including people's cooperative banks, which accept sight or short-term deposits from the public, on savings account, on current account, or in any form and denomination whatever; savings banks, pawnshops; farmers' and artisans' cooperatives; and branch offices of foreign credit institutions.[4] Institutions of the types enumerated may not be established without authorization by the Banca d'Italia. They are subject to inspection by examiners from the Banca d'Italia. Moreover, under authority derivative from the Interministerial Committee for Credit and Savings, the Banca d'Italia can regulate the rates of interest payable or charged by banks to customers and the terms applicable to deposit and current account transactions; regulate commissions chargeable for various banking services; and set rules governing liquid asset and investment ratios and the allocation of investments to different economic sectors; and it has the power "to determine the maximum limits of the credits that may be granted and to establish regulations and time limits for reducing these maxima in the case of proven excesses." [5]

[2] Ibid., Art. 1.
[3] "The Banking Law, 1936," Art. 2, in Aufricht, p. 449.
[4] "The Banking Law, 1936," Art. 5, in Aufricht, p. 450.
[5] "The Banking Law, 1936," in Aufricht, pp. 447, 451.

In addition to these extensive powers over credit institutions, the Banca d'Italia also regulates issues on the capital market:

Any issue of shares, bonds, Treasury bills, or transferable securities of any kind, whether this is to be effected through enterprises subject to the Bank of Italy's control or whether the intention is to place transferable securities on the market in the stock exchanges of the Republic, is subject to authorization by the Bank of Italy.[6]

The Banca d'Italia uses these powers of supervision over new issues on the capital market to ensure that new issues conform to public policy in regard to their purpose, amount, timing, and terms, including coupon rate of interest and maturity.

In addition to the credit institutions enumerated above, over 15,000 branches of the post office offer savings account services to individuals. Post office savings are turned over to an agency of the Treasury known as the Fund for Deposits and Loans (*Cassa Depositi e Prestiti*) and used to make medium- and long-term loans in accordance with public priorities.

The primary sources of medium- and long-term loans, however, are the so-called special credit institutions.[7] These are essentially financial intermediaries that specialize in transferring savings into medium- and long-term investments. They are active in industrial, real estate, and agricultural credit, in financing of exports, and as channels through which state funds are funneled to priority borrowers via loans and interest rate subsidies. They also serve as agencies of the Treasury in issuing bonds for railroads and to finance investment in state-owned industry, public utilities, and important highway systems.

The special credit institutions had their origin in the early 1930's, when the prototype *Institute Mobiliare Italiano* was set up by the state with capital subscribed by public bodies to relieve insolvent commercial banks from long-term loans that had become frozen during the international liquidity crisis of 1931. Other special credit institutions have been organized over the years, specializing in various sectors of the economy, with capital stock largely subscribed by the state. Some special credit institutions are organized as "special sections" of big banks, to concentrate on medium- and long-term credit. Others are affiliated with banking groups, and still others have no specific banking connections.

The principal sources of funds lent out by the special credit institutions are bond issues sold to private investors and companies, insurance companies and social insurance funds, commercial banks and other credit institutions, and the Central Post Office Savings Fund. However, they also obtain funds through accepting longer-term (over

[6] "The Banking Law," 1936, Art. 2, in Aufricht, p. 449.

[7] For discussion of these institutions and their activities, see Banco di Roma, *The Italian Banking System*, 2nd ed. (Rome: 1969), chaps. 4 and 5, pp. 55–87.

18 months) time deposits and issuing interest-bearing certificates, grants from the state budget, and loans from domestic and foreign commercial banks, and by borrowing in the Eurobond market.

An indication of the relative importance of these various classes of banks and financial institutions is provided by Table 5.1 which shows the assets of various types of banks and of the principal classes of special credit institutions. There are six banks incorporated under public law. These are the *Banco di Napoli, Banco di Sicilia, Banca Nazionale del Lavoro, Instituto Bancario S. Paolo di Torino, Monte dei Paschi di Diena,* and *Banco di Sardegna.*[8] These accounted for 24.1 per cent of the assets of regular credit institutions as of December 31, 1969. In national geographic coverage and comprehensive array of commercial banking services, the Banca Nazionale del Lavoro is the most important of the six publicly owned banks.

TABLE 5.1   Italy: Assets of Banks and Other Credit
Institutions in Italy (December 31, 1969)

	Billion lire	*Percentage*
A. Banks incorporated under public law [a]	12,368.5	24.1
B. Banks of national interest	11,497.3	22.4
C. Ordinary credit banks	10,722.9	20.9
D. People's cooperative banks	4,825.9	9.3
E. Savings banks and first-class pawn banks	11,955.0	23.3
Total, banks	51,369.8	100.0
F. Special credit institutes	22,134.6 [b]	
Industrial 15,270.8 [c]		
Real estate 4,979.0 [d]		
Agriculture 1,231.4 [e]		

Source: Banca d'Italia, *Bollettino,* April 1970.
[a] A–E, p. 230.
[b] p. 259.
[c] p. 260.
[d] p. 266.
[e] p. 268.

There are three banks of national interest, so named for their nationwide branch systems and comprehensive banking services. These are the *Banca Commerciale Italiana, Banco di Roma,* and *Credito Italiano.* In character they are similar to the Banca Nazionale del Lavoro. Although these banks are incorporated under private law, they are controlled by the public Institute for Industrial Reconstruc-

[8] For a discussion of banking structure in Italy and related aspects of bank markets and bank competition, see David A. Alhadeff, *Competition and Controls in Banking* (Berkeley and Los Angeles: University of California Press, 1968), part 1, "Italy," pp. 1–98.

tion, which owns 80 per cent or more of the stock of each.[9] Thus, for all practical purposes the banks of national interest are as subject to public control as the banks incorporated under public law. The three banks of national interest accounted for 22.4 per cent of total bank assets at the end of 1969.

The nine principal banks in the first two categories held 46.5 per cent of the assets of commercial banks proper on December 31, 1969. Thus, the concentration of banking in major banks is less in Italy than in France, Germany, Belgium, and the Netherlands. Nevertheless, Italian commercial banking is substantially more concentrated than commercial banking in the United States.

Assets of the special credit institutions at year-end 1969 totaled 22,134.6 billion lire, an amount 43 per cent as large as that of regular credit institutions and almost equal to that of the nine major banks. Comparable asset figures are not given in the *Bollettino* of the Banca d'Italia for the Central Post Office Savings Fund. However, at year-end 1969, the postal administration had 6,248.0 billion lire in deposits, compared with 9,399.0 billion lire in deposits with savings banks and first-class pawn banks, and a total of 34,330.0 billion lire in deposits at all regular credit institutions on that date.[10] Accordingly, the Central Post Office Savings Fund provides the authorities with a significant volume of investment funds subject to direct public control as they are invested through the Cassa Depositi e Prestiti.

What emerges from this survey of Italian banking and credit institutions is the picture of a system over which the public authorities have the legal authority to exercise very complete control in determining the cost and availability of both short-term and long-term credit. Public ownership of major banks, extensive supervisory powers over private credit institutions, control of new issues on the capital market, an array of special credit institutions for long-term investment in the main sectors of the economy, which are for the most part publicly owned and with investments subject to public policy through the Interministerial Committee for Credit and Savings — these are the instrumentalities available to the authorities to guide and control credit flows.

To these domestic powers must be added the system of exchange controls administered by the Italian Exchange Office (*Ufficio Italiano dei Cambi*) under instructions from the Ministry of Foreign Trade. In recent years, this system has been used primarily to control capital movements between Italy and foreign countries. Current account transactions are relatively unencumbered with controls. However, authority for more stringent controls on both current and capital account transactions is available under existing legislation. If circumstance should require more stringent controls, they doubtless would be ap-

[9] R. S. Sayers, ed. *Banking in Western Europe* (London: Oxford University Press, 1962) p. 133.
[10] Banca d'Italia, *Bollettino,* April 1970, pp. 221, 223.

plied. Thus, the authorities are in a strong position to influence credit flows between Italy and foreign countries as well as within domestic credit markets.

THE INSTRUMENTS OF MONETARY POLICY

From our brief survey of financial organization and regulation in Italy, it is clear that the authorities are concerned not only with the level of overall aggregate demand but also with its composition. In particular, they have sought to increase the proportion of income saved and to direct this into investments regarded as having high priority in Italian economic development. It is these objectives of composition and incidence that require the authorities to be concerned not only with monetary policy but also with credit policy. In the Italian context, the distinction between *general* monetary policy and *selective* credit policy is of practical as well as theoretical significance.

Under proper circumstances the classic instruments of monetary policy, which include discount policy, variable obligatory reserve requirements, and open market purchases and sales of securities by the central bank, can powerfully influence aggregate demand. But the selective, or incidence, effects of these general instruments are less predictable and are not readily controlled by adjustments in the classic instruments themselves. Thus, in Italian practice the traditional instruments have been supplemented by various rules, regulations, and institutional reforms that have been intended to modify the cost and availability of credit and the pattern of credit flows in the economy.

Understanding Italian monetary policy is best accomplished by beginning with the traditional instruments and gradually broadening our account to include credit policies and institutional reforms in the money and capital markets and to a lesser extent in banking. National budgetary policy and foreign exchange policy and techniques are relevant to our central theme of monetary and credit policy. Only when viewed in this broad perspective does the rationale for Italian monetary and credit policy become clear.

The degree of independence of the Banca d'Italia affects central bank policy. In matters of money, credit, and foreign exchange policy the Banca d'Italia is subordinate on the policy-making level to the Interministerial Committee for Credit and Savings. No doubt the technical expertise of the Banca d'Italia influences policy decisions of the Interministerial Committee through the participation of the governor of the bank in meetings of the committee. However, the board of directors of the Banca d'Italia is specifically prohibited by law from intervening in policy matters assigned to the Interministerial Committee.[11] These include safeguarding savings, the carrying on of credit activities, and exchange matters. Thus, the Banca d'Italia is primarily

---

[11] "The Banking Law, 1936," Art. 22, in Aufricht, p. 442.

an executive agency for the policies decided by the Interministerial Committee, that is, by the primary economic ministers of the government. It is presumably impossible for the Banca d'Italia to take an independent line in monetary and credit policy from that established by the government through the Interministerial Committee.

Discount Policy

Under its statute dating from 1936, the Banca d'Italia is entitled to discount eligible paper and to make secured advances to the various types of credit institutions subject to its supervision. These include commercial banks, cooperative banks, savings banks, and pawn banks. It may also discount paper for the special credit institutions. In practice, however, the Banca d'Italia makes discounts and advances only to some twenty-five of the big commercial banks. Paper eligible for discount includes bills of exchange and payment orders. Treasury bills, grain storage bills, and certain warehouse warrants. Securities and other assets may be pledged to secure advances. At the end of 1969, there was roughly twice as much central bank credit extended to credit institutions by way of advances as by rediscounting, owing to the greater technical simplicity of secured advances.

Credit by means of rediscounting or advances is extended for a maximum duration of four months and is regarded as a temporary accommodation. The amount of credit made available to any credit institution is determined by administrative rationing, usually in relation to the institution's own capital-to-deposit ratio. There are, however, no fixed rules to limit central bank discretion.

Until 1969, variations in the interest rate for discounts and advances were extremely rare. Between 1947 and 1969, the rate changed only five times and never exceeded 3.75 per cent. In 1967, the Banca d'Italia inaugurated a system of fixed-term advances to supplement the existing arrangements for rediscounts and variable-term advances. Some banks borrowed under the new system with greater frequency than the authorities approved. To discourage repeated borrowings by the same institution, the Banca d'Italia introduced in March of 1969 a system of incremental interest-rate charges as mild penalties for successive borrowings. For each new resort by a bank to central bank advances, the base charge of 3.50 per cent was raised 0.5 per cent until it reached a maximum of 5.00 per cent.[12]

Later in 1969 and in early 1970, changes were made to increase the cost of rediscounting. The basic rediscount rate was raised to 4.00 per cent, and a surcharge of 1.50 per cent was added for any bank whose rediscounting (other than by grain storage bills) in the preceding calendar half-year had exceeded 5 per cent of its obligatory reserves constituted in the middle of the half-year. Grain storage and certain

[12] Banca d'Italia, *Report for the Year 1969* (abridged version in English), (this and like reports hereafter cited as e.g. *Report,* 1969), pp. 83–84.

other agrarian bills were exempt from the increase in rediscount rate and continued to be rediscounted at 3.50 per cent. The surcharge of 1.50 per cent was automatic for operations of registered central credit institutions.[13]

Accompanying these changes in rates on discounts and advances were parallel changes in the rate on Treasury bills and on minimum rates for bank loans. The relationships among these rates is an important aspect of credit policy. Even following these increases the rates charged by the Banca d'Italia remained well below rates on bank loans or in the international money markets. *Thus, administrative rationing rather than price rationing persists as the basic policy of the Banca d'Italia for controlling the volume of discounts and advances to credit institutions.* No data are published concerning the quantitative limits for rediscounts and advances available to the twenty-five major banks to whom this privilege is extended. However, officials of the Banca d'Italia state that these limits are adjusted with sufficient frequency and vigor to make the rediscount channel an active policy instrument of the central bank despite the stability of interest rates on discounts and advances. This preference for administrative rather than price controls is part of a more general policy extending to other instruments as well. This will become clear as we proceed.

Minimum Reserve Requirements

To understand the role of obligatory minimum reserve requirements in Italy, it is essential to see them as part of a system designed to allocate credit and not simply as one of several central bank instruments to control the money supply. From the latter perspective, the actual formula for calculation of minimum required reserves and the variety of forms in which reserves may be held are unnecessarily complex and cumbersome. It is the allocative goal that provides their rationale.

Minimum reserve requirements are defined differently for three categories of credit institutions: commercial banks (including cooperatives), savings banks and pawnbrokers, and farmers' and artisans' cooperatives. The simplest reserve requirements are those for farmers' and artisans' cooperatives. Since 1932, these have been required to invest a prescribed percentage of deposits in government bonds or bonds of the special credit institutions and to deposit them with the Banca d'Italia or other authorized depositories. Initially 10 per cent, the required reserve ratio was raised to 20 per cent in 1955 and remains at that level.[14]

Obligatory minimum reserve requirements for commercial banks were first introduced in Italy in 1947. Legislative authority for these

[13] Ibid.
[14] European Economic Community, *The Instruments of Monetary Policy in the Countries of the European Economic Community*, Publishing Services of the European Communities, 1962, p. 170.

requirements was found in the Banking Law of 1926, which empowered the central bank to require commercial banks to invest prescribed amounts in government securities to be deposited with the central bank or to hold cash reserves in interest-bearing blocked accounts at the central bank. The initial purpose of these provisions was to protect depositors from bank insolvency. Thus, the law linked the obligatory reserves to the excess of banks' deposits over their net capital resources.

Upon its introduction in 1947, the minimum reserve ratio was defined as 20 per cent of the amount by which the commercial banks' deposits exceeded ten times their net capital resources, subject, however, to an upper limit of 15 per cent of their deposits as of the end of September 1947. For any growth in deposits after October 1, 1947, the required reserve was set at 40 per cent of the increase, again subject to a maximum overall required reserve of 25 per cent of deposits. For most commercial banks these provisions resulted in an effective minimum reserve ratio of 25 per cent.[15] This effective minimum reserve ratio remained unchanged from 1947 until December 1, 1962, at which time it was reduced to 22.5 per cent, where it has remained since.[16] This reduction occurred in the context of general reforms of the money market. A minimum reserve ratio that has changed only once in twenty-four years certainly cannot be considered an instrument of general monetary policy, and is not so considered by the Banca d'Italia.

When obligatory minimum reserves for commercial banks were first introduced in 1947, the banks were permitted to meet the requirement either by depositing government securities with the Banca d'Italia or holding cash in interest-bearing deposits with the central bank. The commercial banks could choose freely between these two forms of reserves in any combination of the two. Moreover, they were permitted a wide choice among securities to be held for reserve purposes, since Treasury bills, medium- and long-term government bonds and government-guaranteed securities all were eligible. Beginning in 1953, only cash and Treasury bills could be held to satisfy minimum reserve requirements, still in freely variable proportions.[17] On December 1, 1962, the Banca d'Italia stipulated that the portion of the required reserve held in cash must not fall below 10 per cent of the excess of deposits over capital.[18] In view of the minimum overall reserve requirement of 22.5 per cent, this stipulation, which remains in effect, means in practice that the cash component in obligatory reserves may not fall below 44 per cent of the total.

Until 1965, the minimum reserve requirement applied uniformly to

---

[15] Ibid.

[16] Banca d'Italia, *Report,* 1962, p. 67.

[17] Bank for International Settlements, *Eight European Central Banks,* (New York: Frederick A. Praeger, 1963), p. 220.

[18] Banca d'Italia, *Report,* 1962, p. 68.

all types of commercial bank deposits. In addition, banks were required to hold reserves against cashier's checks outstanding. In Italy, these circulate widely as means of payment. Beginning in 1953, 100 per cent reserves in the form of Treasury bills were required against circulating cashier's checks. On January 1, 1963, banks were given permission to use bonds and shares as backing for cashier's checks.[19] Then, beginning in October 1965 they were permitted to hold agricultural and other mortgage bonds to meet additions to required reserves caused by increases in time and savings deposits. Use of these longer-term securities was restricted to no more than 12.5 per cent of any such increase in time and savings deposits.[20] In 1967, securities intended to finance school buildings and bonds issued by the Credit Consortium for Public Works (CREDIOP) issued on behalf of the Treasury were made eligible to meet additional reserve requirements resulting from growth in time and savings deposits. The authorities' rationale for thus broadening the list of eligible securities was to encourage banks to supply funds to the capital market and thus "to assist in the absorption of fixed interest securities at stable prices." [21]

For savings banks and pawnbrokers, the reserve requirement established in 1947 was 20 per cent of any increase in deposits that occurred after October 1, 1947. These minimum reserves were to be held in the form of agricultural and other mortgage bonds and other long-term securities.[22] The reform of reserve requirements in 1962 applied the 10 per cent minimum cash ratio to savings banks and pawnbrokers because they were gradually diversifying into commercial banking activities.[23] In 1965, however, this cash requirement was cancelled, so that in recent years savings banks and pawnbrokers have met their minimum reserve requirements almost exclusively by holding eligible longer-term securities, upon which the yield is higher than on Treasury bills or cash deposits at the central bank.[24] Here again, the intent of the authorities has been to increase the demand for longer term securities in the capital markets.

Despite the fixity of the obligatory minimum reserve ratio, this instrument is not without some flexibility as a general instrument of monetary policy in Italy. By permitting changes in the composition of obligatory minimum reserves, the authorities can alter the effective minimum reserve ratio in a manner comparable with a change in the required ratio itself. When the banks are permitted to substitute long-term bonds for cash deposits or Treasury bills, this is equivalent to a decrease in the obligatory liquid-asset reserve ratio. Moreover, by changing the rate of interest paid to banks on cash reserve deposits

[19] Banca d'Italia, *Report*, 1962, p. 71.
[20] Banca d'Italia, *Report*, 1965, p. 85.
[21] Banca d'Italia, *Report*, 1967, p. 104.
[22] European Economic Community, p. 170.
[23] Banca d'Italia, *Report*, 1962, p. 67.
[24] Banca d'Italia, *Report*, 1966, p. 144.

or by permitting banks to substitute higher-yielding long-term bonds for more liquid assets at lower yields, the authorities can alter the incremental cost of loanable funds to the banking system. Such an alteration may then influence the banks to change interest charges and volume of their loans to customers.[25] Of course, designation of the specific earning assets that may be substituted for cash or Treasury bills is intended to influence credit allocation.

The full significance of the use made by the authorities of reserve requirements cannot be appreciated until they are viewed as part of a broader system of controls. Preparation for such an overview requires familiarity with several other components of the system. One important aspect involves the techniques of open market operations.

Open Market Operations

By purchasing and selling securities in the open market, a central bank alters the supply of reserve or base money in the hands of the commercial banks and the public and thus influences the money supply and credit terms. A typical objective of open market operations, therefore, is to alter the liquidity of the commercial banking system so as to increase the effectiveness of the central bank's reserve requirements and discount policy. Customarily the open market instrument chosen by the central bank is Treasury bills because the market for these usually is broader than for longer-term government securities or for most private securities. This means that central bank transactions of a given volume to alter bank liquidity can be carried out in the market for Treasury bills with less disturbance to market yields and prices than on other security markets. Moreover, the breadth of the Treasury bill market is facilitated by the absence of credit risk.

The Italian central bank has not employed open market operations as a primary policy instrument. Moreover, its use of open market operations has been confined primarily to price support (that is, pegging) operations in the market for long-term government bonds and bonds of special credit institutions rather than to purchases and sales of Treasury bills.

The chief reason for both these aspects of the open market policy of the Banca d'Italia is the constraint that the concern of the Italian monetary authorities for credit allocation imposes on the goal of quantitative control of the monetary base and money supply. A second and related reason is the highly restricted nature of the Italian money market. This is almost exclusively an interbank market, and it has been heavily controlled by the authorities throughout its entire history. To develop these views we shall begin with a discussion of the Italian money market. Subsequently we shall discuss open market

[25] Francesco Masera, *La Riserva Obbligatoria Nel Sistema Instituzionale Italiano*, Banca d'Italia, pp. 40–58.

operations to peg the price of long-term government securities, their rationale, and their effects.

The Money Market and Treasury Bills. Regulation of the money market is an aspect of the authorities' approach to the control of short-term credit; in general it includes regulation of interest rates payable by banks on deposits, control of interest rates on outstanding Treasury bills, regulation of bank commissions and minimum rates charged on customer loans, regulation of net foreign borrowing and lending by the commercial banks, and a variety of other, related measures.

From 1947 until 1962, the Treasury issued bills on tap at the fixed rate of 3.5 per cent.[26] The eligibility of Treasury bills to meet commercial bank obligatory reserve requirements, coupled with the Banca d'Italia's support for new issues when needed, guaranteed a minimum stock demand for these bills at their fixed yield. On the other hand, any surplus liquidity experienced by the commercial banks was readily invested in tap issues of Treasury bills, whose supply was perfectly elastic at the quoted yield. The result was a fully pegged rate for the yield on Treasury bills, a situation that completely precluded the Banca d'Italia's using the Treasury bill market for open market policy.

In 1962, the tap issue of Treasury bills was discontinued as one aspect of an important reform of the money market. Statements made by the authorities at the time of this reform present a variety of motives. The basic policy goal appears to have been to create a money market in which Treasury bills could be traded at variable yields so as to permit the authorities to vary short-term interest rates and thus influence both the supply of funds to the capital market and short-term capital flows between the Italian and foreign money markets. At the time of the reform, the Italian balance of payments was in considerable surplus, and commercial banks were purchasing what the authorities regarded as an excessive volume of tap Treasury bills. Moreover, the abundant liquidity in commercial banks did not seem to improve the supply of funds in the capital market. Prior to the reform the Banca d'Italia commented in its *Report* as follows:

We believe it essential that we should bring every effort to bear on the maintenance of an efficient capital market on which to place new issues which, subject only to minor price fluctuations, provide the necessary capital funds for the large-scale investment programmes of both the public and private sector. In pursuing this objective, we have in mind the experience of others, especially in so far as they go to show that an increase in the quantity of easily monetizable securities often weakens the effectiveness of monetary controls.

Nor must it be overlooked, in planning for a sound money and capital market, that in the Italian banking system as it is at present there is no

[26] E.E.C., *The Instruments of Monetary Policy*, p. 167.

functional relationship between Treasury Bill issues and the Treasury's cash needs. Excess liquidity simply flows into the Treasury and the balance of its current account with the Bank of Italy is apt to convey a false picture of financial ease.

It should be added that to issue Treasury bills in unlimited quantities and at a rate of interest fixed for long periods, may, at times of abundant liquidity, reduce the incentive for the banks to look for productive employment of their resources, precisely because the banks can invest their liquid funds at will in a security which can always be transformed into money and from which they obtain a constant yield not immediately subject to the influence of changing market conditions.

The present system, therefore, reduces the incentive to adjust the rate of productive lending to the level of liquidity which the monetary authorities think it right to leave on the market; but it also prevents the Treasury from borrowing at interest rates in line with the balance of supply and demand on the money market.[27]

To remedy these shortcomings, the Interministerial Committee on Credit and Savings in late 1962 and early 1963 announced reforms whose principal features were a new system for issuing Treasury bills, modifications in the rules governing obligatory reserve requirements, and new regulations concerning commercial bank deposits and loans.

The tap issue of Treasury bills was replaced by a regular monthly issue. Procedures for this issue were described in the *Report* of the Banca d'Italia for 1962 in these words:

At present, the Treasury bill rate is 3.5 per cent, which corresponds to an issue price of 96.50 for every 100 lire nominal value. This is called the basic price, and bidding above it must be in 10 hundredths of a lira or multiples thereof.

Treasury bills are allocated exclusively to banks and banking associations. These receive, at the basic price, the full amount they need to fill up their compulsory reserves; the rest of the monthly quota is allocated to them for free investment at the so-called free price, that is, the lowest still successful bid. Any unallocated Treasury bills can be bought by the Bank of Italy at the basic price. At any time during the month the banks can deal in Treasury bills with the Bank of Italy, and private investors wishing to buy or sell them can do so at the Bank of Italy or at other banks.

The Bank of Italy buys Treasury bills from banks or the public at a price adjusted to the remaining maturity by the basic rate, and sells them at a price similarly adjusted by the free rate, that is, the last successful bid.[28]

This is hardly a description of a money market abandoned to the free play of supply and demand. Banks are guaranteed their customary 3.5 per cent yield on Treasury bills purchased at time of issue and used to meet obligatory reserve requirements. On "free" Treasury bills, the yield may not exceed 3.5 per cent because the Banca d'Italia will buy any bills not absorbed by the banks at or below that yield.

[27] Banca d'Italia, *Report,* 1961, p. 93.
[28] Banca d'Italia, *Report,* 1962, p. 68.

Between monthly tenders, the central bank provides a market floor to the price of outstanding bills by buying and selling at well-defined rates based on the remaining life of the bills in question.

Nevertheless, the arrangements do provide for some flexibility in the yield on free bills downward from 3.5 per cent. To this extent the central bank achieved a small range within which to employ open market policy should it choose to do so. However, the Banca d'Italia continued to underwrite the monthly Treasury bill issues so that the nominal yield would not exceed 3.50 per cent.[29] It continued this practice until a further reform of the Treasury bill issue system in May 1969.

The reform of Treasury bill issue procedure in May 1969 is the most recent attempt of the monetary authorities in Italy to create a flexible money market. Paradoxically, the rationale for this latest reform advanced by the authorities is directly opposite to that of the 1962 reform. In 1962, they expressed a desire for greater flexibility in the money market so as "to facilitate the transfer of funds from the money market to the capital market," observing that "the measures by which short-term rates can be controlled are more effective in regulating economic activity in general when they are seen to have an impact also on long- and medium-term rates." [30] By contrast, in 1969 following application of restrictive measures by the Banca d'Italia, they commented:

> . . . an attempt was made to concentrate the restrictive effect only on the short-term end of the market. However, the well-known absence of a wide and efficient money market, capable of acting as a shock absorber between short- and long-term rates, caused these effects to be rapidly transmitted to the long-term market.[31]

Thus, in 1962 the authorities express frustration that the mechanisms of the Italian money market fail to transmit the effects of abundant bank liquidity from the short-term to the long-term market. In 1969 they lament the rapidity with which such effects are transmitted. The difficulty common to the two episodes is the authorities' lack of control over the long-term rate. Comparison of these two situations suggests that additional forces are at work in determining the relation between short and long rates of interest to those included in the authorities' conceptualization of the problem.

The basic purpose of the 1969 reform of the money market was to free the Banca d'Italia from the responsibility of being the residual buyer of newly issued Treasury bills at the fixed price required to preserve 3.50 per cent as the maximum yield on these bills. By introducing some variability in the issue price of Treasury bills, the reform

[29] For confirmation of this practice, see Banca d'Italia, *Report,* 1968, p. 78.

[30] Ibid., p. 92.

[31] Banca d'Italia, *Report,* 1969, p. 100.

sought to break the link between the Treasury deficit and the expansion of reserve money in the form of deposit claims against the central bank created by the latter's purchase of Treasury bills at their support price. At the same time, the reform sought to preserve a fixed return to the banks on Treasury bills held to meet obligatory reserve requirements; and it sought also to prevent an increase in the cost to the Treasury of interest payments on grain storage bills discounted with the central bank, and on cash deposits of the banks at the central bank held for reserve purposes. Under the Italian system, both of the latter interest payments are Treasury obligations to be met by the government budget. It is this mixture of controlled and market-determined elements that induces complexity in the new system of issuing Treasury bills.

The Banca d'Italia provides these details on the new system:

The new Treasury bill issue system, introduced with effect from May this year, enables the Bank of Italy to extend its open market operations to the monetary sector. The governing criterion is that the Treasury shall in principle finance its requirements in strict relation to its temporary needs for cash, and at rates conforming to market conditions.

From time to time the Minister of the Treasury lays down, by a decree published not later than the 10th of the month in which the issue is to be effected, the maximum limits for the issue of Treasury bills keeping thus the portion used for obligatory reserves distinct from that for free investments.

On the first of these portions interest will be paid in advance at the annual rate of 3.75 per cent and allotments will be made on pro rata basis if the bank's applications exceed the total fixed for the monthly issue, provision having been made for the banks to put up the balance due in cash reserves.

On the portion earmarked for free investment the rate of interest will be determined each month, as well as the amount of bills to be offered, at the time when the decree concerning the issue is published. Demand is reconciled with supply by a process of tendering as follows: (a) If the demand exceeds the supply, applications are appropriately scaled down with due regard for any premium which the applicant may offer to pay in comparison with the par value; (b) if the supply exceeds the demand, the amount alloted will be less than that proposed by the Treasury unless the Bank of Italy decides at its discretion to intervene.[32]

The new system provides for a variable market price on outstanding Treasury bills.

It has been laid down that the Bank of Italy will sell Treasury bills at a rate of discount not greater: (a) than the average weighted rate for fixed term advances (by the central bank to the credit institutions) in force during the previous week, in the case of Treasury bills with more than four months still to run, or the tender rate if this is lower; (b) than the official

[32] Banca d'Italia, *Report*, 1968, pp. 75, 78.

rate of discount during the last four months of the bill's life, or than the tender rate if this is lower.[33]

These provisions have the effect of permitting the market price of free Treasury bills to vary within controlled limits. The floor price on bills over four months is set by the average weighted rate for fixed-term advances. This rate is scaled upward from the official rate on fixed-term advances by a formula that increases the rate gradually as the volume of borrowing increases. (See our discussion of discount policy above.) The floor price for bills under four months in maturity is directly determined by the discount rate. When abundant liquidity drives the tender rate on bills below these official rates, the central bank sells bills at the tender rate.

Clearly the reform has not altered the central role of the Banca d'Italia in the Treasury bill market. What are the implications of the new procedure for the freedom of the Banca d'Italia to use open market operations as a flexible instrument of monetary and credit policy? The answer to this question depends on what happens when a Treasury bill issue is undersubscribed. If the central bank must then serve as residual buyer, the link between Treasury deficits and monetary expansion has not been broken. The evidence is fairly clear that this is indeed the case and that central bank open market operations continue to be subordinated to the requirements of financing the Treasury deficit by monetary expansion if this is necessary. The Banca d'Italia's statement on this point is slightly misleading: In a comment on the new procedure for Treasury bills they say:

The effect is thus to loosen the rigid link between the cash deficit of the Treasury, the creation of monetary base and long-term rates. More precisely, since the previous practice was to cover the Treasury's deficit by creating monetary base or by issuing long-term securities, pursuing at the same time a policy of keeping prices for such securities stable, the creation of monetary base depended closely on that deficit. The size of the deficit could moreover fluctuate, especially in the short run, to an extent not compatible with orderly management of credit and liquidity.

The new Treasury bills are hence designed to cover the gap between the Treasury's deficit, on the one hand, and financing with monetary base and long-term securities on the other, to such an extent as may be deemed most appropriate for purposes of monetary policy.[34]

There is an implication in this statement that a Treasury deficit that cannot be financed by selling the "free" Treasury bills without an expansion of monetary base will be covered by means of such an expansion or by the sale of long-term government securities. Normally,

[33] Ibid.
[34] Banca d'Italia, *Report*, 1968, pp. 102–3. On this rationale "free bills" have been excluded from the statistical measure of the monetary base since the 1969 reform of the Treasury bill market.

however, the Treasury will already have sold as many bonds as possible before determining the size of its bill offering. In such circumstances, further sale of Treasury bonds will be possible only if the central bank supports the bond market by buying bonds itself or providing additional reserves to the banks. In either case the monetary base expands and the link between the Treasury deficit and some form of central bank credit is restored. That this indeed is the implication is supported by the Banca d'Italia's terse comment on Treasury financing in its 1969 report:

> In 1969 the Treasury's overall requirements were mainly financed by sales to the Bank of Italy of medium- and long-term securities, which were concentrated especially in the second half of the year at the time of the tensions on the capital market. The issues of Treasury bills, too, not having been taken up by the banks, were subscribed almost entirely by the Bank of Italy.[35]

Thus, despite the recent procedural reforms, there is still no free money market in Italy. Business firms and individuals, as distinct from banks and credit institutions, cannot participate in the tender for Treasury bills but must acquire bills from their banks or the central bank at regulated prices. The authorities are unwilling to accept the level and structure of interest rates that would be determined by the market under free market conditions. Under the reformed procedures for issuing Treasury bills, the authorities seek to determine both the quantity of bills and their maximum yield. Market conditions often are such as to make this impossible without central bank intervention to expand the money supply. Thus, within the Italian system of monetary and credit controls the Banca d'Italia still does not and cannot use open market operations in Treasury bills as an instrument of general monetary control.

Open Market Operations in Long-Term Bonds. The primary experience the Banca d'Italia has had to date with open market operations in long-term bonds occurred in the years 1966 through 1969 in conjunction with an announced policy by the Italian central bank to stabilize prices and yields on such bonds through active participation in the market. The pegging policy was inaugurated in mid-1966 in an effort to offset the expansionary effects on the monetary base and money supply of increasing deficits in the state budget. It was thought that stable prices and yields for long-term government and government-guaranteed bonds would increase their attractiveness as investments for the banking system and for the public. By encouraging the banks to switch from short-term liquid assets into medium- and long-term bonds, the pegging policy would offset the expansionary effect of a government deficit on the monetary base. By enticing the public to give up bank deposits, especially time and savings deposits, in ex-

[35] Banca d'Italia, *Report,* 1969, pp. 75–76.

change for long-term bonds, the pegging policy was intended to reduce the growth in money supply accompanying the financing of the Treasury deficit. In short, pegging of prices and yields on long-term bonds was viewed as an anti-inflationary policy. To maintain the peg, the Banca d'Italia undertook to deal actively in the market to correct short-term fluctuations in bond prices.

This pegging policy was continued until mid-1969, when it was abandoned with the explanation that high interest rates abroad in comparison with lower interest rates in Italy were causing net capital exports that were contributing to a balance-of-payments deficit at a rate that could no longer be sustained. The pegging experiment was interpreted as a successful anti-inflationary measure in terms of its domestic effects, with the onus for its abandonment assigned to the rise of interest rates on foreign money and capital markets.

There can be no denying that the interest rate differential between the Italian and foreign capital markets did attract private investors into foreign securities available through the Eurocurrency and Eurobond markets and through the sale of foreign mutual fund shares in Italy. (See the section on measures to influence international flows of money and capital, below.) On this aspect of the pegging policy and reason for its abandonment, the interpretation offered by the Banca d'Italia is certainly reasonable. But in their interpretation of its domestic influence as an effective anti-inflationary measure, officials of the Banca d'Italia are open to challenge.

The short-run effects of a central bank policy to peg yields on long-term bonds may appear to be anti-inflationary while actually concealing an underlying inflationary expansion of monetizable assets leading to loss of control over the money supply. This will certainly be the case if continued government deficits add to the supply of long-term bonds at a rate that exceeds that at which investors in a growing economy are willing to acquire bonds without an increase in their rate of return. Under such circumstances, the central bank will have to add steadily to the money supply to prevent the price of bonds from falling and their yield from rising. The central bank may do this by purchasing bonds itself, by lending directly to commercial banks or the Treasury, by failing to neutralize the effects on bank reserves of a balance of payments surplus, or by some combination of these measures.

So long as the banks are confident that the central bank will maintain its pegging policy, they may prefer to hold liquid secondary reserves in the form of higher-yielding bonds whose prices are pegged, since they can do so without any loss of liquidity. Bonds whose prices are guaranteed in the market by a pegging policy of the central bank are just as liquid as cash or Treasury bills and more desirable because of their higher yield. Should the peg be removed, the banks would experience a sharp decline in liquidity. But the effectiveness of the pegging policy in attracting banks to substitute bonds for shorter-term assets depends on its credibility. Repeated episodes of abrupt withdrawal of market support would certainly impair such credibility and erode or negate even the short-run effectiveness of a pegging policy in making bonds more attractive assets to be held by banks and public.

Accordingly, during a pegging regime, both bank and public holdings of bonds whose prices are pegged must be viewed analytically as part of the monetary base since their liquidity is guaranteed by the central bank's readiness to convert them into cash without loss of market value. Statistics of the monetary base presented by the Banca d'Italia omit the value of outstanding long-term bonds at pegged prices. Thus, during the pegging regime from mid-1966 until mid-1969, both the level and changes in level of the monetary base are understated in these statistics. Accordingly, to assess the effectiveness of the pegging policy as an anti-inflationary technique, it is necessary to consider additional kinds of evidence. (This is done in the evaluation and commentary which concludes this chapter.)

The Banca d'Italia has been constrained in its use of the open market policy instrument in both the money market and the bond market by the goal of maintaining stable prices and yields for government securities whose supply has increased steadily through persistent growth of government deficits. The supply of long-term bonds issued by special credit institutions to obtain funds for capital loans to high-priority investment projects has added to the problem of the central bank in preserving stable prices and yields in these markets. These considerations were outweighed in 1969 and early 1970 by the need to stem capital outflows and deterioration in the current account of the Italian balance of payments. It was the need to reduce the balance-of-payments deficit that led to abandonment of the pegging policy on long-term bonds and to a general rise in interest rates in the Italian money and capital markets in those years. However, the domestic policy objectives of credit controls and moderate interest rates have not been altered and are being pursued by the same techniques as before the removal of the peg in the long-term market. It does not appear likely that the Banca d'Italia will come to place primary reliance on open market policy as a technique of intervention in the near future.

The three classic instruments of central bank policy are the rediscount rate, reserve requirements, and open market purchases and sales of securities. In their simplest forms, these instruments have their primary effect on the amount of base money in the system and on the cost of obtaining more of it from the central bank. With central bank policy as expressed in these three instruments, it is left for market forces to determine the level and structure of interest rates, the size of the money supply, and the volume and allocation of credit, both short- and long-term and both private and public.

The Italian system of monetary and credit controls seeks to restrict the role of market forces as compared with this classic system. In the Italian system, neither rediscount policy, nor reserve policy, nor open market operations can be considered as a policy instrument of prime importance. The forms are there but the substance is lacking because monetary policy is subordinated to credit policy. Thus these instruments of monetary policy have played a relatively passive role in Italy in the past two and one-half decades. Interest rates in the Italian system are disequilibrium rates for the most part and can be preserved only with the support of a substantial system of administrative controls. Principal among these are controls applied to banks and other credit institutions, controls over new issues in the capital market, and foreign exchange controls. The effect of these on credit conditions and credit allocation is complemented by national budget policy and the activities of the special institutions for long-term credit.

Administrative Controls in the
Short-Term Credit Markets

Since the 1930's, Italian banking has been heavily cartelized, with the tacit and even express approval of the monetary authorities. The voluntary cartel's Interbank Agreement of 1954 provided a comprehensive guide for bank deposit and loan rates of interest and for commission charges on bank services to customers.[36] This agreement among bankers has been continued by successive renewals and is under the supervision of the Italian Bankers Association. In 1963 it was given specific sanction by the monetary authorities, who have not, however, taken an active role in enforcing the agreement.[37] In 1969, for the first time in many years, the agreement was not formally renewed.[38] It had been violated more frequently in late years under the pressure of growing interbank competition permitted by the authorities and in response to competition from foreign money markets. A new agreement was negotiated in August 1970 among fourteen larger banks and subsequently extended in 1971 on a more differentiated basis to smaller banks.[39]

Under the terms of the Interbank Agreement, banks have been required to observe a detailed schedule of maximum interest rates payable on customer deposits of different maturities and sizes, and of minimum interest rates on customer loans of different types and sizes.[40] The entire rate schedule is tied to the rediscount rate of the Banca d'Italia. Since most bank loans are negotiated at rates in excess of these minima, the freedom of bankers to charge rates appropriate to market conditions ordinarily is not limited by the agreement.

Restrictions on deposit rates have been more effective. Here it is useful to distinguish between *interbank* deposits and *customer* deposits. Many smaller Italian banks hold excess funds on deposit with

[36] Alhadeff, pp. 29–37.
[37] Banca d'Italia, *Report*, 1962, p. 69.
[38] Banca d'Italia, *Report*, 1969, p. 110.
[39] Banca d'Italia, *Report*, 1970, p. 124.
[40] See Alhadeff, pp. 31–33.

larger banks. The larger banks compete for these funds, which they invest in Treasury bills, customer loans, and foreign money market instruments. To prevent such competition from driving up bank costs and pushing up the entire structure of bank deposit and lending rates, the Interministerial Committee in November 1962 imposed a ceiling on *interbank* deposit interest. From 1962 until 1970, banks could not pay on interbank deposits more than the free Treasury bill rate as established in the monthly tenders. Banks that violated this rule could be required to pay into special time deposits at the Banca d'Italia all or part of the deposits received by them from other banks. Rates paid by the Banca d'Italia on these deposits are lower than the interbank rate, so that the bank that violates the ceiling incurs an interest penalty equal to the difference. The ceiling on interest for interbank deposits was removed early in 1970, when other changes in policy occurred.[41]

In January 1963, the Interministerial Committee issued regulations for *customer* deposits.

The Committee furthermore decided that the control of interest rates was an integral part of the interbank agreement, of the agreement among special credit institutes, and of the authorization for the issue of securities. To eliminate ambiguities, it was stated explicitly that 18- to 60-month time deposits were to be regarded as medium-term savings deposits and the interest rate may not exceed 5 per cent; banks may not accept deposits tied for more than 18 months, nor special credit institutes deposits tied for less than 18 months barring exceptions defined by law or by the Committee itself.[42]

The purpose of this regulation was to reduce the banks' competition for funds with the institutions of the capital market, so as to strengthen the government's policy of low and stable interest rates in the capital market. The effect of the regulation was to impose a ceiling below 5 per cent on the interest that banks may offer for customer deposits. The actual structure of deposit rates contained in the Interbank Agreement was scaled downwards from this ceiling in relation to size and maturity of deposits. Details on the new interbank agreement that came into force in early 1971 have not been published. However, the new agreement cites maximum deposit rates and minimum loan rates that are differentiated by size of customer. It is voluntary and has been recognized by the Banca d'Italia. It does not cover the interest rate on interbank (as distinct from customer) deposits, which is now free from its former relationship to the Treasury bill rate.

Authority for the Interministerial Committee and the Banca d'Italia to regulate interest rates paid and received by banks, the terms of deposit and current account transactions, and commissions payable on various banking services is conferred under the Banking Act of 1936

[41] Banca d'Italia, *Report,* 1969, p. 187.
[42] Banca d'Italia, *Report,* 1962, pp. 69–70.

and subsequent revisions. Thus, the authorities have power to regulate these matters directly rather than through the voluntary Interbank Agreement, should they come to regard this as necessary or desirable. Under the same legislation, the authorities have substantial powers to affect the composition of bank assets and thus to influence the allocation of bank credit. They may regulate "the ratio of the various categories of authorized investments either to the liquidity of the credit institution concerned or to the different economic sectors to which the investments are allocated" as well as "the ratio between the net worth of the firm and its obligations." [43] Since the early 1950's, however, this authority has not been used.

In the annual report to stockholders in the year 1963, Governor Carli of the Banca d'Italia responded to suggestions from academic economists that selective controls of bank credit should be introduced. In a thoughtful discussion, Governor Carli referred to the extensive powers of the authorities to determine the allocation of credit through *capital market* controls. He stressed the goal of allocating investment capital rather than working capital and the smaller role of the banking system in financing company investment. He spoke in broad terms of the economic powers of the modern state and the responsibility "to create throughout the whole productive system a degree of competition which is judged optimal from the point of view of reconciling social justice with income growth." [44] Coming to the specific issue of selective controls over bank credit he concluded:

Even if it were possible to introduce more selectivity into bank credit, it is hard to see how to avoid arbitrariness, given the complexity and variety of the sector of medium-sized and small enterprise which relies upon bank credit and given, above all, the great number of medium-sized and small banks operating in geographically restricted areas. If these latter were asked to implement directives implying choices of high-priority sectors, they would be all but paralyzed in practice, or else they would be forced into a concentration of risks incompatible with efficient safeguards for the class of depositors to whom they cater.

For all these reasons I believe that, in the conduct of modern government, qualitative control of bank credit is a tool to be kept in reserve and to be applied with moderation in special conditions rather than as a regular component of credit policy. In certain cyclical phases one kind of credit may indeed have to be curbed in favor of others and, in exercising its overall powers of control and direction, the central bank has from time to time done so and may do so again. But we only have to look at the most recent developments to see that cyclical situations can change very quickly, and for this reason we must be watchful and flexible in anything we do to direct the flows of credit. Moreover, intervention of this kind is apt to have so many general and specific effects of opposite sign and unmeasurable magnitude, that it would seem safer for the monetary authorities not to assume direct responsibility for the innumerable adjustments required by

[43] Aufricht, p. 447.
[44] Banca d'Italia, *Report,* 1963, p. 133.

cyclical developments, but to leave these adjustments to the market processes, within the general conditions created by control of the volume of liquidity.[45]

This philosophy continues to shape the approach of the Italian authorities to short-term credit markets. Although they have legislative authority to do so, the authorities have not imposed overall quantitative limits on the expansion of bank credit nor have they used administrative review by the central bank to control bank loans and terms to individual borrowers. They do attempt to control the general flow of funds through the banking system, partly by influencing the rate of expansion in the monetary base, and partly by regulating the rates banks may offer on deposits to compete for funds with the institutions serving the capital market.

**Measures to Influence International Flows
of Money and Capital**
The difficulty of reconciling passivity in the use of the classic instruments with an active influence on the domestic money supply is partly resolved by reference to foreign-exchange policy. The Italian monetary authorities have employed foreign-exchange regulations both to alter the domestic liquidity of the banking system and to increase the effectiveness of policies concerning the financing and direction of investment in the capital market. The foreign-exchange system is administered by the Italian Exchange Office (*Ufficio Italiano dei Cambi*) under the supervision of the Ministry of Foreign Trade. The Banca d'Italia acts for the Italian Exchange Office on the operating level.[46]

The exchange control system is relatively complex.[47] Financial institutions are subject to special regulations in dealings for their own account that involve foreign exchange. The extent to which Italian banks may take a net debtor or credit position in their foreign operations is controlled by the Banca d'Italia in the light of the balance-of-payments situation and as an aid to regulation of domestic credit conditions. It is this control which affects the monetary base in the manner of open market operations. An increase in the banks' net debtor position abroad adds to domestic liquidity, and a decrease reduces it. The opposite is true for a net asset position. These adjustments are accomplished by the banks pursuant to administrative orders from the Banca d'Italia.

To increase the attractiveness to Italian banks of foreign loans and money market investments during a period of excessive domestic

[45] Banca d'Italia, *Report,* 1963, p. 134.
[46] Bank for International Settlements, *Eight European Central Banks,* pp. 211–12.
[47] The following brief sketch of Italian exchange controls is based primarily on the report on Italy contained in International Monetary Fund, *20th Annual Report on Exchange Restrictions, 1969,* Washington, D.C., 1969, pp. 242–47.

liquidity combined with a balance-of-payments surplus, the Banca d'Italia has sometimes offered to sell spot foreign exchange and re-purchase forward (that is, swap) at rates low enough to add a margin to the yield available on foreign short-term assets. On other occasions of temporary liquidity shortage, especially in the large banks that both deal in foreign exchange and hold the liquid reserves for smaller banks, the Banca d'Italia has repurchased foreign exchange from the large banks and then redeposited the foreign exchange with the banks. This procedure increases the banks' lire reserves while leaving their foreign-exchange position unchanged.

Other regulations apply to foreign-exchange transactions under-taken by individuals and firms other than banks. All sales and pur-chases of foreign exchange must pass through banks authorized for this purpose. A number of import products still must be licensed, especially when originating in Japan or in countries with communist governments. A few export goods also are subject to licensing. Licenses are issued by the Ministry of Finance at the request of the Ministry of Foreign Trade. Export proceeds must be collected within a specified period of time and sold to an authorized bank within thirty days of collection. There are limits to prepayment for imports. The amount of lire currency that a resident may take abroad is regulated.

Various regulations govern capital transfers. There are no controls over inward and outward movement of *nonresident* capital. Certain restrictions apply to *loans* from nonresidents to residents and from residents to nonresidents. These restrictions are less severe for coun-tries that are members of the OECD and particularly for countries that are members of the EEC. Direct investments abroad are regulated except to countries that are members of the OECD.

Residents may purchase and sell foreign securities issued and pay-able abroad and listed on foreign stock exchanges. These transactions must take place through the Banca d'Italia or an authorized bank. With minor exceptions, such securities must be deposited with an Italian bank or with a bank abroad for account of an Italian bank. Residents may also purchase shares of those foreign mutual funds that have been authorized to market their shares in Italy. Purchase or subscription by a resident to any foreign bond not issued or quoted in Italy is subject to exchange control regulations.[48] This control ap-plies, for example, to purchase by residents of foreign government bonds or Treasury bills, which would otherwise provide a ready chan-nel for interest-sensitive or speculative short-term capital movements.

Nonresident firms may not issue fixed interest securities on the Italian capital market without prior approval of the Ministry of For-eign Trade. If such approval is given, the securities must meet the same issue conditions as their domestic counterparts. For private bor-

[48] European Communities, Monetary Committee, *Policy on the Bond Markets in the Countries of the EEC*, Brussels, October 1970, p. 34.

rowers, this includes payment by the issuer of a 38 per cent tax on bond interest (*imposta di richezza mobile*).[49] In practice, permission to issue has been granted sparingly and then primarily to international organizations.

The general effect of Italian foreign exchange regulations is to give the authorities a substantial degree of control over movements of short- and long-term funds between Italian and foreign money and capital markets. Under the present foreign-exchange system, this control is certainly not complete. There is the usual problem of leads and lags in settlement of current account transactions as well as the movement of funds into and out of nonresident accounts. In recent years there have also been large outflows through illegal channels, particularly by the export of bank notes in excess of prescribed limits.[50] Nevertheless, the control the authorities exercise over the net foreign position of banks provides them with a means of compensating in a measure for excessive movement of short-term funds through other channels. Furthermore, the exchange controls do insulate the Italian capital market from their foreign counterparts to a significant extent, thus supporting the authorities' policy of comprehensive domestic controls on the capital market. Finally, the Italian Exchange Office and the Banca d'Italia have legislative authority to operate much tighter foreign-exchange controls and have shown themselves willing to do so when balance of payments or domestic conditions require this.

CAPITAL MARKET CONTROLS

A persistent theme in our discussion of the instruments and objectives of Italian monetary policy has been the importance of goals for investment allocation for economic development as providing part of the basic rationale for monetary policy. Indeed, allocative goals have converted Italian monetary policy to what may be more aptly termed credit policy. Capital market policy has provided the impetus for many measures undertaken by the authorities in recent years in the realms of monetary and credit policy, procedural reform of the Treasury bill issue and of the money market, modification in bank reserve requirements, interest rate policy, and foreign exchange controls. Accordingly, although capital market policy is far from constituting a part of monetary policy as commonly understood, some familiarity with Italian capital market policy is essential to give us perspective on the actions of the monetary authorities.

The Italian capital market is controlled by the Banca d'Italia acting under policy directives from the Interministerial Committee for Credit and Savings and, so far as international capital movements are concerned, the Italian Exchange Office. Authorization from the Banca

---

[49] European Communities, Monetary Committee, *Policy*, pp. 64–65, 86.
[50] Banca d'Italia, *Report*, 1967, p. 62; and *Report*, 1969, pp. 175–76.

d'Italia is required for the issue of any stocks or bonds to the capital market through any of the banking or credit institutions subject to Banca d'Italia control or for listing on any of the Italian stock exchanges. This comprehensive authority dates back to the Banking Law of 1936.[51] Principal borrowers in the capital market have been the Treasury, the National Electricity Board (*Ente Nazionale di Energia Elettrica*), the large government controlled petroleum company (*Ente Nazionale Idrocarburi*), the holding and management agency for government-controlled industry (*Instituto per la Ricostruzione Industriale*), the variety of special credit institutions that specialize in real estate loans and in medium- and long-term loans to industry and agriculture, and private industrial firms. Principal suppliers of funds to the capital market include the banking system, the Central Post Office Savings Fund, social insurance funds, the Banca d'Italia itself, private companies, and individuals.

The monetary authorities are frank to state that capital market controls are used to facilitate the financing of investment activities assigned a high national priority. The *Report* of the Banca d'Italia for 1963 states:

> At present, selective credit control over the medium- and long-term loans of special credit institutes is exercised by the monetary authorities on the occasion of their authorization of bond issues by the institutes; similarly, all other security issues are subject to administrative authorization and at that moment to selective control.[52]

This control of access to capital market funds would seem to be fairly definitive. However, additional obstacles are provided against borrowing by private firms both by relatively heavy taxation of corporate profits and dividends and by the 38 per cent tax on bond interest (imposta di ricchezza mobile) payable by private issuers of corporate bonds. The central government, local authorities, institutions issuing for the account of the Treasury, special credit institutions, and public enterprises all are exempt from payment of this tax.[53]

Preferred investment activities have included electric power and the petroleum industry, roads and railroads, communications, industrialization of southern Italy, agriculture, schools, housing, and the bonds of intermediaries specializing in loans to small and medium-sized businesses and for export credit, among others. Such activities are given priority for direct access to the capital market by control over capital issues. They are also assisted by investment grants or interest subsidies from the state budget, by favorable terms on medium- and long-term loans from the special credit institutions (themselves given preferred access to the capital market), and by long-term loans from the Cassa Depositi e Prestiti, which invests post

[51] Aufricht, p. 446.
[52] Banca d'Italia, *Report*, 1963, p. 131.
[53] European Communities, Monetary Committee, *Policy*, p. 65.

office savings. Certain nationalized industries and government controlled intermediaries also have been permitted to borrow abroad from banks and in the Eurobond market.

In addition to rationing capital issues, the authorities have made extensive use of interest rate policy to support the capital market and investment activities dependent on that market. The Banca d'Italia has sought to ensure an adequate flow of funds to the capital market so that the substantial and growing demand for capital could be satisfied at a relatively low and stable long-term rate of interest. One aspect of this policy has been the authorities' attempt to create a sharp demarcation line between the activities of the money market and the commercial banks in the field of short-term credit and that of the capital market and its institutions such as the savings banks and special credit institutions. The purpose of this distinction has been to reduce the relative attractiveness of bank deposits and Treasury bills in comparison with longer-term savings deposits and bonds in the competition for household savings.

Throughout most of the decade of the 1960's the authorities have tried to keep short-term interest rates from rising relative to the low and stable level of the long-term rate. This effort has involved numerous policy measures. Despite the discontinuance of the tap issue of Treasury bills in 1962, the maximum yield on these bills had been kept in the range 3.50 to 3.75 per cent until 1969, when some slight upward movement was permitted under the pressure of very high rates abroad. Similarly, the rediscount rate for central bank credit has been held virtually unchanged in the same range. Commercial banks may not accept time deposits with maturities that exceed eighteen months and may not offer depositors interest exceeding a stipulated maximum, recently between 5 and 6 per cent. Until January 1970, the rate that banks could pay for interbank deposits was not permitted to exceed the most recent rate on free Treasury bills established at the monthly tender. Since January 1970, the interbank rate has not been subject to a ceiling. Bank lending rates are free of formal controls, but these are not directly relevant to the level and allocation of household savings. Administrative controls over the net foreign asset position of commercial banks limit any tendency of loans made by Italian banks on foreign money markets to push up the prevailing rate in the Italian money market. All these measures are intended to favor the flow of savings into the capital market either directly or via savings banks, post office savings, and special credit institutions.

Besides keeping short-term rates low, the authorities apply other measures either to encourage the flow of funds to the capital market or to keep interest rates in the capital market from rising. Commercial banks have received permission to hold part of their obligatory reserves against savings deposits in the form of various approved long-term securities, principally mortgage bonds, school building bonds, and public works bonds. Savings banks and agricultural banks can meet their reserve requirements completely by investing in appropriate long-term securities. The Treasury provides interest rate subsidies for many capital investment projects and, to a decreasing extent, outright grants of capital funds. Foreign exchange controls on capital movements have been used to keep foreign borrowers from placing any substantial issues on the bond market. Foreign borrowers have also been deterred by the 38 per cent tax on bond interest payable by private issuers. Lastly, the central bank intervenes directly in determining bond yields.

As regards medium- and long-term funds, the rates of interest which are less subject to fluctuations, are determined by the direct intervention of the monetary authorities, especially in the case of bond issues. The rate of interest and all the other conditions which determine effective bond yields are agreed in each separate case with the Bank of Italy in the light, naturally, of the present and prospective conditions of the capital market and the money market.[54]

These "prospective conditions" are themselves strongly influenced by other actions of the monetary authorities. Moreover, the direct intervention by the central bank is not limited to setting the permissible terms on new issues. When it is necessary to prevent the long-term rate from rising, the Banca d'Italia buys long-term securities in the market for its own account, thus expanding the monetary base. It may also buy Treasury bills, acquire foreign exchange from the commercial banks, or take other measures to increase the liquidity of the banks so they can purchase long-term bonds for their own investment accounts.

Thus, capital market policy has exerted a pervasive influence on the approach of the Italian monetary authorities to many of the areas identified with conventional monetary policy. The lack of flexibility in the use made by the Banca d'Italia of its rediscount rate, the passivity of open market operations, the stability of reserve requirements and their satisfaction in part by Treasury bills and certain long-term securities all are traceable to efforts to increase the flow of funds to the capital market and to prevent the long-term rate of interest from rising. So too are various controls over interest rates, whether in the form of direct regulations or through official approval of the interbank agreement that governs rates paid and charged by banks and specifies commissions to be charged for bank services. Capital market controls and controls over international capital movements also have their place in the Italian program to allocate capital to high-priority investment projects. The Banca d'Italia is responsible for implementing policy in these latter areas as well as in the more customary areas related to money supply and interest rates. The

[54] Banca d'Italia, *Report,* 1962, p. 114.

rationale for much of the activity of the Banca d'Italia in these diverse areas becomes coherent from the perspective of capital market policy.

THE THEORETICAL FRAMEWORK FOR
MONETARY POLICY IN ITALY

Clearly formulated monetary theories appear to have exerted a substantial influence on the approach taken by the authorities to monetary policy in certain countries such as the Netherlands and the United Kingdom. Until recently, this has not been the case in Italy. Whether this has been due to the absence of a strong tradition in monetary theory in the Italian economic literature or to lack of relevance of monetary theory generally to policy goals selected by the authorities is not so clear. While it is true that Italian economic literature is not rich in monetary theory, it is also true that the authorities have sought to implement policies intended to have explicit selective and allocative effects on credit. For such objectives, the received body of monetary theory offers limited assistance, since much of it is macroeconomic in orientation.

Since the mid-1960's, however, the research staff of the Banca d'Italia has been engaged in a substantial effort to formulate and estimate econometric models of the Italian economy to assist the authorities in making policy decisions. These models are still being developed. Moreover, their treatment of financial markets is much further advanced than their treatment of the real sector. These models are neo-Keynesian in general approach and are of the multiple equation, disaggregative variety. A principal thrust of the research to date (most of which has appeared primarily in the form of working papers and research reports) has been to investigate the relationship between monetary policy and the structure of interest rates and flow of credit in the Italian setting. In the context of these studies, chief emphasis has come to be placed on control by the Banca d'Italia of the so-called monetary base as the key monetary aggregate through which the monetary authorities should attempt to exert their influence on the economy.[55]

Since the effort to develop these detailed models is still experimental and incomplete, the authorities in their analysis and interpretation of economic developments necessarily rely also on more general and more aggregative models or theories. In 1965, Franco Modigliani and Giorgio La Malfa tried to give explicit formulation to the implicit macroeconomic theory of the Banca d'Italia and to criticize

[55] See Antonio Fazio, "Monetary Base and the Control of Credit in Italy," in Banca Nazionale del Lavoro, *Quarterly Review*, no. 89, June 1969, pp. 146–69; and Antonio Fazio, *The Monetary Base, Credit, and Bank Deposits*, trans. H. Rodney Mills, Jr., and republished in Federal Reserve System, *Review of Foreign Developments*.

it as a representation of forces and relationships determining aggregate demand, employment, the price level, and the current account balance of the balance of payments for Italy in the first half of the 1960's.[56] These authors view the implicit theory of the Banca d'Italia as consistent with most modern macroeconomic theory of the post-Keynesian type, a theoretical preference the authors themselves share. But they differ in the importance they attach respectively to cost-push and demand-pull inflation. The authors regard *excessive monetary expansion* as having been the source of demand-pull inflation that set off wage increases in excess of increases in productivity, altered income distribution, increased consumption, contributed to inflation, and thus caused a balance-of-payments deficit. They interpret the Banca d'Italia as viewing *excessive wage increases* as the causal factor for income redistribution, a decline in profits, and a rise in unemployment, thus creating the necessity for inflationary monetary expansion to neutralize the redistribution of real income, restore profit levels, maintain employment, and eventually produce a current account deficit in the balance of payments.

We have cited these authors' views for two purposes. One is to support our contention, to be developed in the concluding evaluation, that in recent years the Italian monetary authorities have been struggling with problems to a significant degree of their own making. The other is to be able to concur in the view that the Italian authorities' implicit theory is of the Keynesian macroeconomic variety but that the role of excessive monetary expansion as a causal factor in Italian economic developments tends to be underemphasized by the authorities. The reason for this, as we have already indicated, is the subordination of monetary management to the goals of credit allocation for economic development.

EVALUATION AND COMMENTARY

Since the late 1950's, the primary goal of monetary policy in Italy has been to contribute to economic development by helping to ensure an adequate supply of medium- and long-term financing for the ambitious national program of capital investment. The authorities have conceived their problem in terms of measures to increase the flow of funds into the capital market so that the demand for capital financing in that market could be supplied at a relatively low and stable rate of interest. To achieve this objective, the authorities have resorted to a large variety of measures.

One set of measures has been applied to the control of credit

[56] Franco Modigliani and Giorgio La Malfa, "Inflation, Balance of Payments Deficit and Their Cure through Monetary Policy: The Italian Example," in Banca Nazionale del Lavoro, *Quarterly Review*, March 1966, pp. 3–47.

conditions in the markets for short-term credit. The basic objective of these controls has been to prevent the short-term credit markets from competing for funds with the capital market. This problem has been approached by attempting to keep down the cost of funds to the banking system while permitting bank lending rates to be regulated by the banking cartel in at least partial response to the demand for bank loans.

There have been two main lines of attack to keep down the cost of funds to the banking system. One has involved holding down the cost of central bank credit, and the other, controlling the interest rate in the money market. The policy of keeping down the cost of central bank credit accounts for the characteristic lack of variability in the rediscount rate and in the obligatory minimum reserve ratio. The goal of keeping money market rates low and stable is responsible for the passivity of central bank open market operations, and for the heavy controls placed on the Treasury bill market, including issue procedures, prices in the secondary market, and the central bank's price support policy. Controls over interbank competition for deposits (only recently suspended) also had their rationale in the policy of keeping down the cost of funds in the short-term credit market. Measures in this area have included tying the ceiling rate on interbank deposits to the controlled tender rate on "free" Treasury bills, setting a ceiling on the rate banks may pay for time deposits, and imposing geographic and other restrictions (for example, on methods of customer solicitation) on interbank competition for deposits. Interference with these controlled domestic conditions from abroad is moderated by exchange controls and regulation of the net foreign position of Italian banks.

These measures presume a relationship between the market for short-term credit and the capital market that the authorities can manipulate to alter the relative supply of funds in the two markets without affecting their respective interest rates. However, this view neglects the influence on these two markets of the behavior of firms and households, the former primarily as demanders of funds and the latter primarily as suppliers. Households are free to shift between holding assets as deposits or as capital market securities. To a lesser extent, firms can choose between short-term credit and long-term credit. The preference of both households and firms in making these choices depends not only on the term structure of interest rates but on other economic variables, such as anticipated changes in interest rates and in the price level for goods and services, the effects of taxes and subsidies, and the anticipated yield on alternative assets like real property and foreign securities. The extent to which a change in liquidity in the short-term market influences conditions in the capital market depends very much on these and other economic variables such as present and anticipated levels of income. Thus in 1962, the increased supply of short-term funds owing to reduced reserve requirements and a balance-of-payments surplus did not flow readily into the capital market. The newly imposed 15 per cent withholding tax on dividends and the concurrent nationalization of the electricity industry with its heavy demands on the bond market giving rise to expectations of falling bond prices were the causes. In 1968 and 1969, by contrast, the rise in short-term rates in response to the pull of high rates in the Eurodollar and foreign money markets was rapidly communicated to the capital market because it reinforced expectations of rising rates in that market — owing to renewed price inflation, a growing balance-of-payments deficit, and indications of a change in official policy permissive of a rise in bond yields. Thus the authorities' castigation of the money market as inflexible in the first instance and as failing to provide a buffer in the second instance results from a too-partial analysis of the forces determining flows between the two markets.

The authorities have sought, besides control over the short-term credit markets, to increase the flow of funds into the capital market by encouraging the banks to purchase medium- and long-term securities. One technique to this end has been to make specified longer-term securities eligible to satisfy obligatory reserve requirements of banks, the specific provisions differing among banks. Another technique has been for the Banca d'Italia to supply additional liquidity to the banks by increasing central bank advances to them so that they can in turn acquire bonds during periods when new issues are entering the market. Notice that the banking system can purchase bonds equal in value to the increase in central bank credit times the deposit multiplier. Finally, the central bank from mid-1966 to mid-1969 supported the bond market directly by itself purchasing bonds to peg their price in the market.

When monetary policy is used to assist in the allocation of credit flows, there is always the potential danger that the allocative goals will take precedence over the control of inflation. Although the evidence is not decisive on this question, the probability is strong that monetary policy in Italy from mid-1966 to mid-1969 contributed to the gathering strength of inflationary pressures in the Italian economy. The Banca d'Italia has explicitly disavowed this possibility.

To investigate this question, it is helpful to return to the Banca d'Italia's concern with the monetary base as "the strategic variable through which the Bank of Italy influences the availability of credit, as well as the rate of interest." [57]

[The monetary base] comprises legal tender money and financial assets which can be deposited without limitations in compulsory reserves, or are freely convertible into cash at the central bank. The principal assets which can be promptly converted into money are deposits with the Bank of Italy, those with the Post Office, the margin available [at the Bank of Italy]

[57] Banca d'Italia, *Report,* 1968, pp. 181–82.

on [commercial bank] current account advances, the liquid surplus of assets over liabilities in convertible currencies and, until the end of last April [1969], all Treasury bills.[58]

The monetary base includes those obligations of the Treasury that the Banca d'Italia feels obliged to purchase at fixed prices to maintain government credit. They are Treasury bills and indirectly any reduction of the deposits of the private sector with the post office, since these deposits are absorbed into the financing of the Treasury deficit. The Treasury has a direct borrowing privilege at the Banca d'Italia equal to 14 per cent of its current and capital account expenditures. Up to this limit, any shortfall in other forms of financing the Treasury deficit (for example, such forms as sale of Treasury bills or bonds, and increases in post office deposits by the private sector) can occasion an immediate increase in the Treasury's direct borrowing from the central bank. Beyond this limit, the Banca d'Italia has formal discretion to refuse additional credit to the Treasury; in practice, it would probably be subject to extreme pressure to accommodate the Treasury's cash needs.

Accordingly, any Treasury difficulty in financing its deficit by the sale of additional securities to the banking system and the public threatens the Banca d'Italia's control over the monetary base. In such circumstances, the Banca d'Italia has alternatives for assisting the Treasury in financing its deficit. It can strengthen the market for Treasury securities indirectly by increasing its discounts and advances to the banking system. It can act as residual purchaser of Treasury bills and government bonds not purchased by banks or private investors. It can authorize the banks to substitute long-term government bonds for Treasury bills in meeting obligatory reserve requirements. It can authorize private borrowers or special credit institutions to borrow abroad to relieve pressure on the domestic bond market. Each of these measures involves an increase in the monetary base.

By pegging prices and yields on long-term bonds during the period mid-1966 to mid-1969, the Banca d'Italia claimed to have encouraged banks and private investors to invest in these bonds without an increase in the monetary base and thus to have found a noninflationary alternative to those listed above. This conclusion is incorrect. Bonds whose prices are pegged in the market are convertible to cash without loss at the option of the holder. Thus, such bonds become a part of the monetary base. Their omission from the statistics of the monetary base does not alter their being completely liquid. Over the period of pegging, the measured monetary base is understated by an increasing amount so that its measured growth rate also is understated. Naturally banks prefer to hold liquid secondary reserves in the form of pegged bonds whose yields are higher than those of Treasury bills or excess reserve deposits with the central bank.

[58] Ibid.

For private investors, the stabilization of bond yields may increase the attractiveness of long-term bonds in comparison with other assets. In this sense, the improved stability of yields on long-term bonds exerts an influence comparable to a once-and-for-all rise in yields on bonds relative to yields on other assets. For an investor optimizing the distribution of his portfolio among alternative assets, the static effect should be a shift in the portfolio composition toward bonds at the expense of other assets. In a dynamic context marked by growth in asset portfolios, the result should be an increased *share* for bonds in *additions* to asset portfolios compared with the share that would have resulted in the absence of a pegging policy to stabilize bond yields.

Neither the static nor the dynamic effect on investor preferences provides a guarantee against the need for an increase in bond yields to attract investors should a rise in Treasury deficits occasion a sufficiently large increase in the supply of new government bonds offered in the market. In other words, despite the improved attractiveness of government bonds to private investors resulting from the pegging of their yields, the effect in a dynamic growth context is simply to raise somewhat the quantity of government bonds at fixed prices and yields that private investors will be willing to add to a growing portfolio of assets. Should the Treasury deficit fall short of supplying new bonds at this higher equilibrium rate, the central bank could make up the shortfall necessary to stabilize yields by selling bonds from its own portfolio in the open market. By contrast, the central bank would have to purchase bonds in the open market to stabilize their yields should Treasury deficits result in an excessive increase in the supply of bonds to the market.

In an economy experiencing real economic growth accompanied by a rise in productivity, capital accumulation need not depress the yield on real capital, and growth in the money supply is appropriate to stabilize the implicit yield on cash balances and avoid deflation. Thus, some increase in the supply of bonds whose prices and yields are pegged and supported by an increase in the money supply can occur as a result of a government deficit without inflationary consequences. Suppose, however, that an increase in the size of the government deficit supplies bonds at a rate higher than this equilibrium rate. Then, to prevent bond prices from falling and bond yields from rising, the monetary authority will have to expand the money supply at a higher rate, with inflationary consequences. When the rate of growth in both money supply and bonds exceeds that in real assets, investors' considerations of portfolio balance will increase the demand for real assets. This increase in demand for real assets may at first stimulate their production and add to real growth in the economy. But as slack in productive capacity disappears, the price level for goods will begin to rise. In a closed economy, price inflation followed by wage inflation is the end result. In an open economy, a rise in imports relative to exports will result, with attendant reduction of surplus or increase in deficit in the current account of the balance-of-payments.

As investors become aware of price inflation and adjust their expectations to include it, they will wish to continue to purchase bonds only if bond yields rise to include an inflation premium. Under circumstances of pegged domestic bond yields, there will be a tendency both toward increased purchase of real assets such as land and toward the purchase of foreign securities at higher yields if these are available. To the extent that the resulting deterioration of the current and capital accounts in the balance of payments suggests the possibility of devaluation of the foreign exchange value of the domestic currency, a speculative motive will be added to the incentive to purchase foreign securities.

Many aspects of this pattern are evident in the Italian economy in the period 1966–70. Tables 5.2 and 5.3 present relevant statistics. Gross national product in constant prices grows at rates between 5 per cent and 6 per cent per year in the period 1966–70, with the exception of the year 1967, when the rate reaches 6.4 per cent. This is a lower rate of growth than in the early 1960's, save for the recession years of 1964–65. The money supply grows at rates almost double that of the gross national product at constant prices in this period, continuing a pattern also observable in the early 1960's.[59] The Treasury cash deficit, despite some variability from year to year, tends to increase significantly throughout the period 1965–70 and is on a much higher level in the second half of the decade than during the first half. As a result the rate of increase in the public debt tends to rise relative to that in the gross national product in constant prices and to that in the money supply. In free markets, for such an increase in public debt to be financed without requiring an increased rate of growth in the money supply should occasion a fall in security prices and a rise in effective interest on the debt.

By pegging bond prices, the Banca d'Italia increased the demand for bonds by banks and private investors in the period 1966–69. But they did so only by making the bonds as liquid as cash. Thus, during the pegging period, the growth in both the money supply and the monetary base is, in effect, understated. By the late 1960's, this more rapid growth in liquid assets over real gross national product begins to reveal its inflationary potential through a rise in the price level as measured by the implicit price deflator for gross national product and through deterioration in the balance of goods and services and current accounts of the balance of payments. There is also a dramatic increase in capital outflows in the period 1967–69, which was further stimulated by rising yields in foreign and international money and capital markets. It is noteworthy that this rising capital outflow took place despite tight official controls on the foreign capital investments

[59] The money supply is defined here to include currency and coin, current accounts, passbook accounts and certificates of the postal administration, and current, time, and savings deposits of credit institutions.

TABLE 5.2   Italy: Money Supply, Monetary Base,
Real GNP, and Price Indexes
(percentage change)

Year	Money supply [a] (% change)	Monetary base [b] excluding compulsory reserves in long-term bonds (% change)	Monetary base [b] including compulsory reserves in long-term bonds (% change)	Real GNP [c]	Implicit price deflator [c]	Consumer price [d] (% change)
1960	....	3.20	2.96	6.3	2.0	....
1961	....	11.25	10.53	7.8	2.9	2.07
1962	17.28	17.09	15.98	6.2	6.1	4.66
1963	15.10	7.39	8.24	5.5	8.7	7.46
1964	7.91	9.02	9.66	2.8	6.6	5.88
1965	16.52	11.32	11.69	3.5	4.0	4.56
1966	11.52	9.44	11.03	5.5	2.3	2.31
1967	12.33	8.63	11.15	6.4	2.7	3.66
1968	11.25	8.10	10.02	5.7	1.5	1.34
1969	11.81	7.52	8.79	5.9	4.2	2.66
1970	13.72	12.11	13.12	5.1	6.3	4.91
Compound annual rate of growth						
	13.00	9.53	10.25	5.45	4.48	3.83

[a] Currency and coins, postal administration current accounts, savings accounts and certificates, banks current and savings accounts.

[b] As defined by the Banca d'Italia, the monetary base "comprises legal tender money and financial assets which can be deposited without limitation in compulsory reserves, or are freely convertible into cash at the central bank. The principal assets which can be promptly converted into money are deposits with the Bank of Italy, those with the post office, the margin available [at the Bank of Italy] on [commercial bank] current account advances, the liquid surplus of assets over liabilities in convertible currencies and, up till the end of last April [1969], all Treasury bills." Banca d'Italia, *Report* 1968, pp. 181–82. Note that long-term bonds held as compulsory reserves are included but other bonds made fully liquid by the Banca d'Italia's pegging policy from mid-1966 to mid-1969 are excluded from the measured monetary base. Sources for data on monetary base from which percentage changes have been calculated are as follows: Level as of December 31, 1966, provided by Banca d'Italia in correspondence. Changes for other years from table on sources and uses of the monetary base in Banca d'Italia, *Assemblea Generale Ordinaria dei Partecipanti*, 1968, from Appendix pp. 72–73, and from *Report* (Abridged English Version), 1969, pp. 98–99, and 1970, pp. 94–95.

[c] Figures calculated from Banca d'Italia reports: 1960–66 figures from *Report* 1966, p. 18; 1967–68 figures from *Report* 1968, p. 20; 1969–70 figures from *Report* 1970, p. 47.

[d] Figures calculated from Instituto Centrale di Statistica, *Annuario Statistico Italiano:* 1961–63 figures from 1964, p. 327; 1964 figure from 1966, p. 344; 1964–69 figures from 1970, p. 309; 1970 figure from 1971, p. 300.

TABLE 5.3   Italy: Balance of Payments and Public Debt

Year	Goods and services a (million dollars)	Current account b (million dollars)	Capital movements c (million dollars)	Monetary movements d (million dollars)	Exports of Italian bank notes e (million dollars)	Treasury cash deficit f (billion lire)	Treasury public debt g (% change)
1960	971	317.0	....	− 442.5	....	332	....
1961	236.4	508.5	409.9	− 577.4	− 329	333	
1962	− 0.1	293.8	577.3	− 49.9	− 776		
1963	− 986.0	− 701.0	− 485.4	1251.8	− 1470	865	
1964	308.5	619.6	110.3	− 773.9	− 578	847	8.09
1965	1888.4	2234.0	− 458.0	− 1594.2	− 313	1529	7.33
1966	1727.5	2117.2	− 1276.5	− 695.6	− 559	1839	14.82
1967	1236.0	1599.1	− 1023.4	− 323.6	− 801	1243	8.72
1968	2304.7	2626.9	− 1690.7	− 627.3	− 1127	2021	13.05
1969	1927.6	2368.5	− 3623.9	1391.2	− 2256	1692	9.66
1970	624.2	813.6	− 223.7	− 355.8	− 951.2	3231	16.83

a A minus sign indicates a deficit. Figures from Banca d'Italia, Report: 1960 figure from 1961, p. 21; 1961–62 figures from 1962, p. 29; 1963 figure from 1964, p. 42; 1964–65 figures from 1965, p. 43; 1966 figure from 1967, p. 53; 1967–68 figures from 1968, p. 46; 1969–70 figures from 1970, p. 69.

b A minus sign indicates a deficit. Figures from Banca d'Italia, Report: 1960 figure from 1961, p. 21; 1961–62 figures from 1962, p. 29; 1963 figure from 1964, p. 42; 1964–65 figures from 1965, p. 43; 1966 figure from 1967, p. 53; 1967 figure from 1968, p. 49; 1968–69 figures from 1963, p. 53; 1970 figure from 1970, p. 69.

c A minus sign indicates a deficit. Figures from Banca d'Italia, Report: 1961–62 figures from 1962, pp. 38–39; 1963 figure from 1964, p. 40; 1964–65 figures from 1965, p. 60; 1966 figure from 1968, p. 58; 1968 figure from 1969, p. 63; 1969–70 figures from 1970, p. 69.

d A minus sign indicates a surplus. Figures from Banca d'Italia, Report: 1960–61 figures from 1961, p. 21; 1962 figure from 1962, p. 53; 1963 figure from 1964, p. 45; 1964–65 figures from 1965, p. 48; 1966 figure from 1967, p. 53; 1967 figure from 1968, p. 49; 1968 figure from 1969, p. 63; 1969–70 figures from 1970, p. 69.

e A minus sign indicates a deficit. Figures from Banca d'Italia, Report: 1961 figure from 1962, p. 29; 1962–68 figures from 1968, p. 56; 1969 figure from 1969, p. 62; 1970 figure from 1970, p. 68.

f Figures from Banca d'Italia, Report: 1960–61 figures from 1961, p. 36; 1963 figure from 1964, p. 76; 1964 figure from 1965, p. 73; 1965 figure from 1966, p. 70; 1966 figure from 1967, p. 78; 1967 figure from 1968, p. 73; 1968 figure from 1969, p. 75; 1969–70 figures from 1970, p. 88.

g All figures calculated from Banca d'Italia, Report 1970, p. 90.

of Italian banks and business firms. It reflected, therefore, withdrawal of funds by nonresidents as well as growing purchases of foreign securities by resident private investors attracted to the Eurocurrency and Eurobond markets and to offers of shares in foreign mutual funds marketed in Italy with the aid of Italian banks and fund representatives. A substantial and increasing capital export occurred clandestinely by means of export of Italian bank notes for deposit in foreign banks, principally Swiss. A desire to escape domestic taxes on interest and dividend income by investing abroad anonymously contributed to the bank note outflow.

The combination of rising domestic inflation with the large balance-of-payments deficit of 1969 led the Banca d'Italia to terminate its pegging policy and permit interest rates to rise in mid-1969. This action together with a further large increase in the Treasury cash deficit in 1970 caused sharp increases in both the measured monetary base and the money supply in 1970 as public and banks reduced their purchases of long-term government securities and the Banca d'Italia increased its purchases. The rise in the rate of increase in the monetary base relative to that in the money supply reflects the shift of bank liquid-asset accumulation away from (formerly) pegged bonds, omitted by convention from the measured monetary base, toward the category of cash and Treasury bills included in the measured monetary base. As can be seen in Table 5.3 the capital outflow was dramatically reduced and the overall balance of payments swung back into surplus despite the relatively poor performance of the current account.

The Banca d'Italia has interpreted its pegging policy during the period 1966–69 as a successful anti-inflationary use of open market technique in the long-term bond market. We have argued above that this interpretation is not correct. The crucial defect in the policy was the unwillingness of the Banca d'Italia to permit long-term bond yields to rise in order to find willing holders outside the banking system for the increasing volume of government debt.

In its 1969 *Report*, the Banca d'Italia defended its support policy as well as its abandonment in 1969 in the following terms:

It certainly cannot be said that, during the period under review [1966–1969], the policy pursued by the Bank of Italy had the result of making it lose control of the process of creation of the monetary base. The latter increased to the same extent as the national income in current terms, during a period in which the price rise showed no sign of acceleration. The base created produced a growing expansionary effect because the banking system operated with a lower ratio between liquid funds and deposits, and this was in fact why the Bank of Italy, in the middle of 1969, exercised tighter control over the system's liquidity. The money volume increased at rates below those of the long-term average trend, and this development may be attributed to the stabilization policy pursued with a view to transferring the public's preferences towards bonds. This assertion does not contradict the preceding one, to the effect that the financial circuit via which firms financing took place led to the formation of large monetary and quasi-monetary balances consisting mainly of bank deposits; it merely means that the process of formation of these balances was not accelerated by the central bank's policy regarding the purchase and sale of bonds.[60]

This is an amazingly disingenuous statement. The central bank seeks to disavow responsibility for "the growing expansionary effect" of the increase in the monetary base, assigning this responsibility instead to the banking system's decision to operate with a lower ratio between liquid funds and deposits. But this lower ratio is more apparent than real, since the banking system's long-term bonds whose prices were pegged by central bank policy were as liquid as Treasury bills or cash. Thus, the banks were merely adapting their portfolios of secondary reserves to the pegging policy of the Banca d'Italia. Had the banks held short-term liquid assets of the type included in the measured monetary base instead of the long-term bonds, the money supply increase would have remained the same but the rate of increase in the measured monetary base would have been higher. The primary responsibility for the increase in money supply in either case remains with the central bank and the Treasury.

The quoted statement seeks to reassure by noting that the money supply is not increasing more rapidly than national income at *current* prices, a measure that incorporates inflationary price developments. Finally, it says the price rise shows no signs of accelerating. This assurance is not very satisfactory, since it assumes that a specific rate of inflation once established becomes acceptable and that only increases above that rate are disturbing. Moreover, the claim is contradicted by the rise in rate of increase in prices for the years 1969 and 1970. In view of these considerations, it does not appear unreasonable to assess the pegging policy of the Banca d'Italia in the bond market in the years 1966–69 as inflationary.

The authorities have used various rationing devices in their attempts to channel credit flows into the domestic capital market while maintaining low and stable interest rates. Investments assigned a high priority have benefited from preferred access to capital-market borrowing, either directly through the control of capital issues by the Banca d'Italia or indirectly through grants and interest subsidies from the state budget, and eligibility for loans from the specialized credit institutions and from the post office savings fund. The Treasury, nationalized industry, and the specialized credit institutions are given preferential access to the capital market. Since these public borrowers borrow in the bond market rather than the stock market, investor enthusiasm for the stock market relative to the bond market is deliberately dampened by a 15 per cent withholding tax on stock

[60] Banca d'Italia, *Report*, 1969, p. 191.

dividends. In the bond market private borrowers must pay the 38 per cent tax on interest paid (imposta di richezza mobile), from which public borrowers are exempt.

The authorities face a dilemma in that domestic real investment remains insufficient to meet growth objectives even when encouraged by credit market policy and by favorable treatment in the capital market. Moreover, savings that might be invested domestically continue to flow abroad, creating a substantial net deficit in the capital account of the balance of payments.[61] A difficulty central to both problems appears to be apprehension by Italian investors concerning possible domestic social and political instability, combined at times with speculation on devaluation of the lira. On occasion the capital outflow has been accentuated when yields in foreign capital markets rose relative to those in Italy.

Recent social and political unrest in Italy has reflected growing dissatisfaction of workers with the quality of life. Wage increases secured by labor in recent years have shown a persistent tendency to exceed productivity gains, thus pushing up costs of production, reducing profit margins, and posing an uncomfortable choice for the authorities between inflation and unemployment. The reduction in profit margins together with concern over social unrest has impaired incentives for real investment. In these circumstances an increase in domestic interest rates to reduce capital export may also curtail domestic investment unless the rise in interest costs is offset by increased state subsidies. These in turn would tend to increase the deficit in the government budget, requiring expanded central bank support for the government securities market accompanied by inflationary expansion of the monetary base and money supply. The alternative of a reallocation of budget outlays to subsidize investment through a cut in government-provided services or transfer payments does not appear politically feasible.

The Italian monetary authorities face an exceedingly difficult task in their efforts to contribute to economic growth by helping to channel funds toward domestic investment at low and stable interest rates while avoiding inflationary expansion of the domestic money supply and seeking to reduce the capital account deficit in the balance of payments. One way out of this dilemma is for the budget of the central government to assume a stronger role in income allocation and aggregate demand management. For this to occur presumes greater political consensus and more social stability than appears likely to prevail in Italy in the near future.

[61] A measure of the importance of savings diverted abroad is provided by the surplus in the current account of the Italian balance of payments. For the period 1964–70, this current account balance represented, on the average, 17 per cent of total net saving in the Italian economy. Banca d'Italia, *Report*, 1970, p. 53, Table 9.

6 The Netherlands

Certain features of the Netherlands economy and certain aspects of its approach to monetary policy make it unique among the countries studied in this work. Of singular importance for monetary policy is the dependence of the Netherlands economy on foreign trade. The volume of foreign trade is 50 per cent as large as the gross national product. Moreover, the marginal propensity to import reaches approximately one-third of any increase in gross national product. This pattern produces large foreign exchange drains during cyclical expansions and inflows during contractions through its influence on the current account of the balance of payments. To counterbalance the effects of these swings on domestic money supply and liquidity, the central bank frequently has had to pursue a policy of tightening domestic sources of liquidity during cyclical business contractions and of expanding domestic sources of liquidity during cyclical expansions: just the opposite counter-cyclical policies to those customarily followed by central banks. In the circumstances of the Netherlands, these inverted policies make sense, at least within reasonable limits.

Whether the limits are reasonable or not depends on a variety of economic circumstances that require analysis. Here we encounter a second phenomenon comparatively peculiar to the Netherlands — the degree of explicitness with which the monetary authorities have articulated and communicated a theoretical framework that serves as a guide to their decisions and pronouncements in the realm of monetary policy. This theoretical view defines *monetary equilibrium* in a manner that permits the spokesmen of the *Nederlandsche Bank* to analyze causes of disequilibrium and assign responsibility to such primary influences as the behavior of the central government, local authorities, the private nonbank sector, monetary developments abroad, and the like. Not only has the theory been made fairly explicit, but its application in policies and statements of the Nederlandsche Bank is clearly evident. Such a clearly visible union of theory and practice is rare in the realm of central banking.

Whether the theory is a complete and infallible guide to policy is another question. One highly salutary consequence is undeniable: the monetary authorities in the Netherlands are under no illusion concerning their hegemony in the realm of monetary policy. They are highly sensitive to the role of government finance in monetary policy through its effects on the money supply and liquidity. Moreover, their theoretical framework gives them a realistic view of the limitations of monetary policy to achieve objectives of general economic policy and of its limitations in counterbalancing such phenomena as excessive increases in nominal wages or shifts in the pattern of demand in international trade.

We shall begin with a description of the organization of financial institutions and markets. This will be followed by a discussion of the instruments of monetary policy used by the central bank with attention to their modification as circumstances have changed in recent years. This section will include a discussion of the Netherland's system of exchange control which is relatively strict with respect to capital movements but liberal for current account transactions. Next we shall examine the theory of monetary equilibrium and related theoretical views of the monetary authorities as found in published writings and note certain of their principal implications for policy. Finally we shall close our discussion with an appraisal and commentary on the effectiveness of monetary policy as practiced in the Netherlands.

THE INSTITUTIONAL STRUCTURE

Certain aspects of the organization of financial institutions and markets in the Netherlands have important consequences for the mode of operation of monetary policy. These include the high degree of concentration in the commercial banking system; the limited number of banks and other "registered credit institutions"; a fairly sharp though diminishing distinction between, on the one hand, financial institutions that deal in short-term assets and liabilities and use the money market, and on the other, those that issue long-term obligations and invest in the capital market; a money market that in practice is relatively narrow though in principle it is open to a wide variety of lenders and borrowers; and a domestic capital market heavily controlled both to protect domestic issuers from foreign competition and to prevent changes in the domestic stock of liquidity through capital market transactions between Dutch residents and foreigners. These features of institutional organization facilitate monetary policy in the Netherlands; they allow the monetary authorities to exercise control through a limited number of key credit institutions about whose operations information is readily obtainable, without stimulating large flows of credit through open market channels (that is, disintermediation) to avoid the effects of central bank controls.

Four types of credit institutions are subject to central bank supervision by the act of 1956 on the supervision of the credit system. These are commercial banks, agricultural credit banks, security credit institutions, and general savings banks. These are the primary financial institutions that combine the functions of accepting deposits and granting credit. The act also applies to central institutions established by the member credit institutions so far as these central institutions themselves carry on the business of a credit institution. All these institutions are required to be listed on a register maintained by the Nederlandsche Bank.

The classification of "registered credit institutions" is not identical to that of "money-creating institutions" employed by the Nederlandsche Bank in its monetary analysis (see the section on theoretical framework, below). Until January 1, 1969, general savings banks were excluded from the category of money-creating institutions, and so were agricultural credit institutions that confined their activities to accepting savings deposits and making long-term investments. However, in recent years savings banks increasingly have sought to encourage the deposit of wages, salaries, and pensions into savings accounts and have provided savings depositors with services comparable to checking accounts. For this reason since January 1, 1969, savings banks have been subject to suitably adapted general credit measures promulgated by the central bank in conducting monetary policy. The Netherlands Postal and Savings Bank, certain giro departments and services, and the Postal Check and Giro Transfer Service are regarded as money-creating institutions for purposes of monetary analysis, but they are not required by the Act on the Supervision of the Credit System to register with the central bank. The central government and the Nederlandsche Bank are money-creating institutions but for obvious reasons are not treated as credit institutions under the 1956 act.

Commercial banking in the Netherlands has become increasingly concentrated in the past decade as a result of mergers. There were 114 commercial banks at the end of 1961 (not counting branches), whereas at the end of 1969 there were only 80. In 1964, the four largest banks merged into two banks, with the *Amsterdamsche Bank* and the *Rotterdamsche Bank* forming the *Amsterdamsche-Rotterdamsche Bank*, and the *Netherlandsche Handel-Maatschappij Bank* and the *Twentsche Bank* forming the *Algemene Bank Nederland*. In 1967, the latter was further increased in size when the *Hollandsche Bank* unit merged into it. At the end of December 1965, twenty-nine commercial banks, referred to as the representative commercial banks, accounted for 92.4 per cent of the deposits and 94.0 per cent of the loans of all commercial banks. As of December 1970, the two largest banks had 82 per cent of the deposits and 73 per cent of the loans of all commercial banks. Their comprehensive branch systems and their key role in international banking and in stock brokerage and new issue business further enhances their importance.

As can be seen in Table 6.1, commercial banks control financial resources that are larger than the combined total of the other three types of registered credit institutions. At year-end 1969, commercial banks held 58.5 per cent of total deposits and 55.7 per cent of total loans of registered credit institutions. Only in savings and time deposits does the share of commercial banks drop below half of the total, accounting for 47.7 per cent.

Agricultural credit banks and their savings affiliates constitute the second most important class of registered credit institutions. These began as credit cooperatives to collect savings and make loans in rural areas. In recent years, however, they have broadened their services to provide their customers with more of the services of commercial banking and have steadily built up their demand deposits as a result. Their earning assets include short-term commercial loans but are primarily longer-term credits such as mortgages, loans to local authorities, and bonds of local and public authorities.

General savings banks specialize in savings deposits and mortgage loans. They also make loans to local and public authorities and purchase bonds issued by or guaranteed by these authorities. While the savings banks remain primarily engaged in their traditional business of channeling long-term savings into the capital market, they also have begun to move into such commercial banking activities as stock exchange transactions and providing their customers with guaranteed checks for use in paying bills as a substitute for checking accounts in commercial banks.

The security credit institutions are primarily stockbrokers who offer customers the convenience of deposit accounts and loans against securities. As the figures in Table 6.1 indicate, their deposit and lending activities are insignificant compared with the other three types of registered credit institutions.

The concentrated structure of commercial banking, two widespread branch bank systems being of preeminent importance, assures that interbank competition in the Netherlands will be oligopolistic in nature. The two largest banks are highly sensitive to each other's actions but are also greatly concerned with avoiding any appearance of collusion to restrict competition. For present purposes the importance of this is that interest rates on bank deposits and loans, although free of formal regulation, tend to be governed by well-established conventions, and in this sense are administered prices rather than competitively determined ones. Prime lending rates for the larger banks and thus for all are set at a rigid differential above the rate

TABLE 6.1 Netherlands: Registered Credit Institutions (year-end 1969)

Type of institution	Number	Balance sheet total (millions of guilders)	Loans		Deposits		Savings and time deposits	
			Millions of guilders	Percentage	Millions of guilders	Percentage	Millions of guilders	Percentage
Commercial banks	80	40,549	22,003	55.7	32,536	58.5	18,841	47.7
Agricultural credit banks and affiliated savings banks	2,534	16,576	12,956	32.8	15,125	27.2	12,790	32.4
Security credit institutions	45	166.0	103.8	0.3	63.2	0.2	7	....
General savings banks	205	8,370	4,434	11.2	7,845	14.1	7,838	19.8
Total	2,864	65,661	39,497	100.0	55,570	100.0	39,476	100.0

Source: Nederlandsche Bank, Report for the Year 1969, Table 56, p. 128; Table 60, p. 134; Table 1.2, Annex pp. 4–7.

charged by the Nederlandsche Bank for advances on promissory notes, normally 1.5 to 2 per cent. A system of commission charges for various lending and other services provides a rate structure upwards from the prime lending rate. These commission charges are closely governed by agreements reached through the bankers' association. Since competition via provision of services is potentially damaging to the agreed structure of rates, competitors watch closely for violations of the agreement. Offenders are called to account either directly by the bank that discovers the violation or via the bankers' association.

Competition by cutting lending rates is virtually unknown. For large customers with bargaining strength, there may be rate competition for deposits. Presumably the larger business firms with funds to lend can look to the domestic or even foreign money markets if domestic deposit rates are not attractive. For smaller depositors, competition is primarily via convenience of branch bank office location and through customer services.

The two largest banks own finance company subsidiaries. Since the banks are required to include finance company assets and liabilities on a gross basis in their balance sheets, the device of subsidiaries has not provided an escape from direct controls on bank credit in the Netherlands as it did for some years in Britain.

In contrast to the situation in Italy, France, and Germany, the Dutch money market is open to a wide variety of participants, including industrial firms and individuals as well as credit institutions and institutional investors. Nevertheless, the money market remains primarily an interbank market involving commercial banks, savings banks, bill brokers (discount houses), institutional investors, and the Treasury. Very large industrial firms such as Philips also participate in this market, as local authorities do, the latter primarily as borrowers.

The reliance of the Dutch economy on foreign trade opens the economy to foreign influence through the current account of the balance of payments. The money market is strongly affected by swings in the foreign exchange reserves of the Netherlands economy and the form in which they are held. From 1964 until June 1971, the central bank did not intervene in the money market by means of open market operations, preferring instead to rely on measures to influence the export or repatriation of foreign exchange. These measures are discussed in the following section on instruments of central bank policy.

The Nederlandsche Bank was founded in 1814 and nationalized in 1948. Its present organization and authority derive from the Netherlands Bank Act of 1948 and the 1954 Act on the Supervision of the Credit System.[1] The Bank is governed by a governing board consisting

---

[1] On December 8, 1970, a bill was introduced in Parliament to amend the Act on the Supervision of the Credit System so as to strengthen central bank authority and to extend it to so-called near banks, such as investment banks, insurance companies, and other institutions of the capital market. This bill had not been enacted as of September 1, 1972.

of a president, a secretary-director, and from three to five directors appointed by the Crown. There is also provision for a Bank Council, which consists of seventeen members including the Royal Commissioner, four members from the Bank's Board of Commissaries, representative of the Bank's stockholders (that is, the state as sole stockholder since nationalization), and twelve members appointed by the Crown to represent diverse economic interests in society. The governing board determines Bank policy. The Minister of Finance may issue directives to the governing board when he "deems it necessary for the purpose of coordinating the Government's monetary and fiscal policy and the policy of the Bank." [2] The governing board may appeal from such directives to the Crown, in effect to a cabinet-level review and decision by the central government.

Under various legislative authorizations, the Nederlandsche Bank is charged with conducting monetary policy, supervising the credit system, control of foreign exchange, and regulation of new public issues of stocks and bonds in the capital market. The Bank's authority for monetary and credit controls derives respectively from the Bank Act of 1948 and the Act on the Supervision of the Credit System of 1956. The Bank Act of 1948 confers on the Bank its most general authority for monetary policy:

> The Bank has as its task to regulate the value of the Netherlands currency in such manner as shall be most conducive to the country's welfare, and in that connection to stabilize the said value as far as possible.
> It supplies the money circulation in the Netherlands, so far as this consists of bank notes, facilitates money transfer business in the Netherlands and promotes payment transactions with foreign countries.
> It exercises supervision over the credit system on the basis of the provisions of the Act on the Supervision of the Credit System.[3]

The Bank's authority to lend and rediscount and to engage in open market purchase and sale of securities derives from the Bank Act. Its powers to set minimum cash or liquid asset reserve requirements in relation to the deposits of credit institutions, and to prohibit or set limits for credit institutions with respect to total credits or investments or specific categories of assets or forms of credit comes from the 1956 Act on the Supervision of the Credit System. The latter requires the Bank to seek voluntary agreements with the credit institutions in invoking such controls but provides a procedure for securing obligatory controls should a satisfactory voluntary agreement not be reached. Such controls have been exercised under the terms of voluntary "gentlemen's agreements" between the Bank and the credit institutions.

[2] "The Netherlands Bank Act 1948," Art. 26(1), in *Central Banking Legislation*, vol. 2: *Europe*, ed. Hans Aufricht, International Monetary Fund, Washington, D.C., 1967, p. 471.
[3] Aufricht, p. 466.

THE INSTRUMENTS OF MONETARY POLICY

Under legislative authority and voluntary agreements with credit institutions, the Nederlandsche Bank currently disposes of the following instruments of monetary and credit policy: rediscounting; open market purchase and sale of securities; minimum cash or liquid-asset reserve requirements; ceilings on categories of credit and credit expansion; authority to establish constraining relationships between assets and deposits of specific types; authority to regulate borrowing from or lending to nonresidents by residents whether the latter are credit institutions, firms, or individuals; and certain powers to regulate access to the capital market. Administrative controls over deposit and loan rates of interest are not among the powers of the Nederlandsche Bank.

In recent years, the Nederlandsche Bank has increased its use of credit ceilings and other direct controls while decreasing its reliance on rediscounting, open market operations, and minimum reserve requirements. After 1964, the Bank did not engage in open market operations until June 1971. Minimum cash reserve requirements have been set at zero since September of 1963. The rediscount rate is regarded as primarily symbolic for purposes of domestic policy but as having some influence on short-term capital movements between money markets in the Netherlands and abroad. (We shall subsequently develop the reasons for the decline in importance of these classic instruments of central bank policy.) There appear to be two primary motives for this trend. The first is a desire to control money and credit while reducing reliance on interest rate changes that may induce offsetting reactions through flows of foreign exchange between the Netherlands and foreign money and capital markets. Among the more immediately responsive of such flows are adjustments in the liquid foreign asset positions of Netherlands commercial banks. The second motive is to give the Nederlandsche Bank a firmer grip on domestic sources of liquidity creation. The rationale for this motive is found in the theoretical views of Netherlands monetary authorities concerning "monetary equilibrium."

Discount Policy

Prior to the Second World War, rediscounting and advances on promissory notes secured by appropriate collateral were the primary instruments of central bank policy in the Netherlands. Following the war, however, conditions were at first not conducive to successful use of discount policy. The banks were very liquid, restoration of the economy was the primary task, and selective controls directed to the support of obvious priorities were relatively efficient and effective. During the Korean War, an excessive rise in bank credit threatened monetary stability and led to special liquid asset reserve requirements for credit institutions so that they would have to turn to rediscounting at the central bank for additional resources to support the credit expansion. Since the early 1950's, the Nederlandsche Bank has continued to operate its discount window but has not regarded discount policy as an important policy instrument under the circumstances that have prevailed.

The basic purpose of discounts and advances made to credit institutions is to provide temporary assistance in adjusting liquidity positions. Discounting is a privilege rather than a right. Banks are not expected or permitted to remain permanently indebted to the central bank. There are no formal limits to borrowing for individual banks but central bankers watch such borrowing carefully and will admonish a bank if they regard its borrowing as excessive.

Various credit instruments are discountable. These include Treasury bills and notes, certain export trade bills, and short-term securities issued by local authorities. The latter have been declared discountable, either directly or indirectly, to improve their marketability. However, acceptability for discount of the obligations of *specific* local authorities depends on their observance of certain rules established by the central bank. The Bank regards such obligations as part of the stock of liquid assets in the economy whose volume must be controlled to avoid monetary disequilibrium. To bring pressure to bear on the local authorities to limit their issue of short-term debt, the Bank limits the volume of such obligations of specific local authorities that may be presented for discount. In recent years this limit has been stated as follows:

> ... Promissory notes shall be declared discountable and eligible as collateral up to 15 per cent of the ordinary receipts of a municipality provided its budget is in balance, and provided its net floating debt plus the next twelve months' estimated capital budget expenditure, for which long-term financing has not yet been ensured, does not exceed 25 per cent of the ordinary receipts.[4]

This represents use of the discount privilege to accomplish the specific objective of limiting short-term borrowing by the local authorities rather than as a general instrument of monetary policy. That this method may not have been very effective may be inferred from the extension of formal credit ceilings to loans by credit institutions to local authorities in December 1966.

The Bank posts separate rates for discount of bills of exchange, discount of promissory notes, and interest on advances in current account and loans, the latter differentiated by private sector and "other." When banks borrow they often prefer advances on current account. The mechanics of secured advances on current account are more flexible than those for discounting, with the result that the bank can borrow for as little as one day if it chooses.

[4] Nederlandsche Bank, *Annual Report for the Year 1968*, p. 155.

Under prevailing circumstances, discount policy cannot be regarded as a main instrument of central bank policy in the Netherlands. These circumstances include the persistent liquidity of the economy resulting from balance-of-payments surpluses, the ability of commercial banks to repatriate foreign liquid assets when pressure is brought on their domestic liquidity, and the traditional low interest rate policy pursued by the monetary authorities. Within the normal range of interest rate variations in the Netherlands, it is doubtful that interest rates serve as significant deterrents to domestic borrowers. In 1958, Dr. M. W. Holtrop, then president of the Nederlandsche Bank, put the matter thus in a discussion with the Radcliffe Committee:

> I believe that a rise in Bank Rate, if it is sufficiently large, will have by itself a certain effect on demand for credit, but not too much. If it is the Bank's policy that the banks should be very careful about their lending policies, apart from raising the Bank Rate we will also talk with the banks and try to influence their operations. One might even say to the banks: "This is a credit ceiling and you must not go beyond." If I used the Bank Rate as a means of influencing monetary policy I should also look to other means. If, however, I was using the Bank Rate only to affect the movement of short-term funds, I should only move the Bank Rate and nothing else, in order to make it a little more or less attractive to invest short-term funds on the Dutch market instead of on other markets.[5]

Thus, the official view appears to be that the discount rate can be used to influence short-term capital movements between the Netherlands and other countries but is not an effective instrument of domestic monetary policy except as induced movements in these short-term funds alter the stock of liquidity in the economy.

Minimum Reserve Requirements

Minimum cash reserve requirements were first introduced in the Netherlands in 1954. Their purpose was to aid in absorbing surplus liquidity that had arisen through a large influx of foreign exchange. Application of minimum cash reserve requirements was and is based on a gentlemen's agreement concluded between the central bank, the commercial banks, and the two central associations of the agricultural credit banks. Under this agreement, which is periodically renewed, the central bank can impose a minimum cash reserve not to exceed 15 per cent, to be met in the form of non-interest-bearing deposits with the Nederlandsche Bank. The requirement is calculated as the monthly average ratio between a bank's reserve deposit at the central bank and its own reserve eligible obligations: customers' sight and time deposits, deposits of credit institutions not participating in the agreement, and other short-term obligations similar to deposits. The minimum reserve requirement does not apply to general savings banks

[5] The Committee on the Working of the Monetary System (Radcliffe Committee), *Minutes of Evidence*, p. 815, para. 11873.

and to security credit institutions nor to very small commercial banks. It does apply to the postal check and giro transfer services.

In the period 1954–62, the Nederlandsche Bank varied the minimum cash reserve requirement between 4 per cent and 10 per cent. In September 1963, the requirement was reduced to zero, where it remained until activated at 2 per cent in September 1972. The ability of the Nederlandsche Bank to conduct monetary policy for a decade without the aid of this instrument has depended in part on spontaneous and induced fluctuations in foreign exchange reserves and their effects on bank liquidity. In part, reliance on minimum reserve requirements has also been reduced by the technique of credit ceilings, first used in 1961 and heavily relied on since then.

Credit institutions that fail to keep within ceilings established to guide credit expansion are assessed penalties in the form of prescribed non-interest-bearing deposits at the Nederlandsche Bank. These deposits are an aspect of credit ceilings and are not to be confused with deposits required as minimum reserves.

Open Market Operations

The Nederlandsche Bank made no use of open market operations from 1964 until June 1971. Prior to 1952, the central bank was unable to use open market operations as an instrument of monetary policy because the Treasury sold bills on tap at fixed interest whether or not it had a deficit to finance thus, in effect, having a passive open market policy of its own. From 1952, following suspension of the Treasury practice, until 1964 the Nederlandsche Bank did use open market policy, but rarely as an active instrument. Rather it would make open market sales when excess liquidity flooded the market and purchases when the credit institutions sought additional cash at prevailing interest rates.

The Netherlands money market is open to a wide variety of participants including credit institutions, the Treasury, local authorities, business firms, and individuals. Brokers (discount houses) service the market and have access to rediscounting at the central bank. However, they do not occupy a privileged position in this regard, as is the case in Great Britain, nor do they have any special understanding about covering tenders of Treasury bills.

Although the money market deals in a variety of credit instruments as suggested by the variety of participants, only central and local government obligations are significantly used in open market purchases and sales by the central bank. As with the other two traditional policy instruments of rediscounting and reserve requirements, open market operations have had little significance in the Netherlands in recent years, and indeed no significance during their suspension from 1964 until 1971. In June of 1971, the central bank tightened exchange regulations, thereby prohibiting nonresidents from using their balances of convertible guilders for the purchase of Netherlands Treasury paper or bank acceptances denominated in guilders. With the inflow of nonresident funds to the Dutch money market reduced in this fashion, the central bank could engage in open market sales to absorb excess liquidity for the first time since 1964.

Measures to Influence International Flows of Money and Capital

Changes in foreign exchange reserves through current account surpluses and deficits and in the form of short-term capital movements strongly influence the money supply and stock of liquid assets in the Netherlands economy. Owing to the dependence of the Netherlands economy on foreign trade, which measures 50 per cent as large as the net national income, and the high marginal propensity to import (one-third) in response to an increase in national income, any inflationary increase in national income tends to be accompanied by losses of foreign exchange through the current account of the balance of payments. Unless offset by capital imports, such drains occasion a prompt and significant decline in domestic liquidity that checks the inflationary development. This combination of circumstances has not infrequently led the Nederlandsche Bank to use its traditional policy instruments in a seemingly perverse fashion but with the objective of moderating counter-cyclical swings in domestic liquidity.

It is fundamental to the concept of monetary equilibrium held by the monetary authorities of the Netherlands that the balance of payments should not be permitted to disturb domestic monetary equilibrium unless in response to prior disequilibrating domestic developments such as inflation or excessive wage increases. They believe that disturbances initiated abroad should be absorbed by outflows from a buffer stock of foreign exchange so far as this will tend to equilibrate the international trade balance. An exception is a change in basic world trade patterns resulting from changes in technology, new products, tastes, and the like. Then a change in exchange parities may be necessary to restore equilibrium. Similarly, experience has taught that deficits in the balance of payments of reserve currency countries also may not be self-equilibrating through the price-specie flow mechanism under the present international monetary system. To restore equilibrium in these cases may require cooperation from foreign governments and monetary authorities and may involve complex international negotiations.

This combination of practical and theoretical considerations provides the rationale for a comprehensive set of controls over capital movements between the Netherlands and foreign countries as well as for efforts by the Netherlands central bank to influence short-term capital movements by its swaps policy, that is, its intervention policy in the forward market for foreign exchange.

Basically, all capital movements between Dutch firms, individuals, and credit institutions on the one hand and foreign money and capital markets on the other are subject to controls. Occasional gaps left in the system of controls have been closed when flows through them became important. Accordingly, the determination of Dutch authorities to exercise such controls when regarded as necessary does not appear open to question.

Under present regulations resident nonbank firms and individuals may not borrow from nonresident banks. Loans to such borrowers from other sources (except trade credit) are subject to approval. The net foreign liabilities position of individual Dutch banks is limited to 5 million guilders. Until the summer of 1969, no limits had been placed on foreign *lending* by Dutch banks. During that summer, high rates in the Eurodollar market caused Dutch banks to increase substantially their Eurodollar placements. The volume involved was sufficient to tighten markedly the Dutch money market and to drain official reserves of foreign exchange. In response, the Nederlandsche Bank negotiated an agreement with the commercial banks that set a limit to their net foreign asset positions in relation to such positions during a selected base period. This agreement remains in effect although the particular restrictions are altered or removed in the light of changing circumstances.

Transactions between residents and nonresidents in existing securities are subject to various controls, which have increased in response to unsettled international monetary conditions that existed during 1971 and early 1972. Until 1971, nonresidents were free to purchase at published market rates securities publicly issued in the Netherlands. They were not permitted, however, to purchase privately placed issues; such issues in recent years have accounted for about four-fifths of new security issues in the Netherlands. On June 1, 1971, to check the inflow of speculative short-term capital, nonresidents were barred from using their balances of convertible guilders to purchase Netherlands Treasury paper or bank acceptances denominated in guilders. For some years, Dutch residents other than banks (whose net foreign positions are regulated) have not been permitted to buy foreign treasury bills or other foreign short-term debt instruments. On September 6, 1971, the Ministry of Finance further tightened controls over international capital flows by establishing a so-called closed circuit for bonds. Under that regulation, nonresident purchases of bonds denominated in guilders are permitted only against payment in guilders obtained from the prior sale of such bonds by nonresidents to residents. The regulation prevents a net inflow of capital by means of transactions in bonds. Transactions in listed stocks are unrestricted as net purchases of bonds by residents are. Presumably if such transactions came to be regarded as troublesome, controls over them would be imposed.

Nonresidents may not issue stocks or bonds on the Netherlands capital market without individual permission. Since 1945, such permission has almost never been given. When permission has been given, the issuer has been an international organization and the timing has coincided with a balance-of-payments surplus that the authorities desired to reexport to restore domestic monetary equilibrium. Resident companies may not issue stocks or bonds on foreign capital markets without a license. Such licenses are rarely if ever given and would certainly be denied to support domestic monetary policy. Inward direct investment is freely permitted. Outward direct investment is subject to approval by the authorities.

On March 9, 1972, the authorities further tightened controls over the inflow of short-term capital. While the new regulation remains in effect, nonresidents may not place guilders on time deposit in the Netherlands and expiring time deposits may not be renewed. Moreover, residents may not pay interest on guilder demand deposits of nonresidents. Opportunities for nonresidents to place speculative capital inflows at fixed interest in the Netherlands (for example, bank deposits, Treasury paper, bank acceptances, bonds) have all been denied by these measures.

Clearly, the Dutch authorities operate a nearly comprehensive system of controls over short- and long-term capital movements between Dutch and foreign money and capital markets. Despite these controls, financial transactions related to financing and settlement of current account trade in goods and services, swings in the level of nonresident guilder accounts, and capital transfers that filter by the controls in the guise of current account transactions in the past have made conditions in the Dutch money market responsive in a degree to conditions in the Eurodollar market and principal foreign money markets. By means of controls, the authorities have been able to establish a differential of 1 to 2 per cent between domestic and foreign money market or Eurodollar rates.[6] Larger differentials tend to be reduced to this level by compensating short-term capital movements despite the system of controls.

By intervening in the forward market for foreign exchange, the Nederlandsche Bank has sometimes been able to influence domestic commercial banks to increase or decrease their holdings of foreign short-term liquid assets. By modifying the terms at which it will exchange foreign currencies for guilders in the forward market, the Nederlandsche Bank can alter the profitability of covered short-term investments abroad. Since the banks are limited both by regulation and by conservative policies of management in their ability to hold net foreign assets, the terms on which the Nederlandsche Bank will provide cover through such "swap operations" can influence the profitability of the transaction.

It is perhaps more customary for the Bank not to participate in such swaps than to do so, depending on specific circumstances. Use of swaps as a policy instrument has declined as more direct limits have

[6] Nederlandsche Bank, *Annual Report for the Year 1969*, p. 112.

been imposed on the commercial banks' net foreign positions. In any event, such swaps may usefully be thought of as a technique of monetary policy not too different in their domestic liquidity effects from open market operations but using short-term capital movements in lieu of open market transactions to release and absorb liquidity. In the context of the Dutch economy and financial institutions, neither technique is likely to deter banks and other credit institutions from lending to good customers so long as they have adequate holdings of liquid assets to support a credit expansion.

Measures to Restrict Credit

During the entire period since 1945, the Nederlandsche Bank has had authority to impose quantitative restrictions on the level of bank credit and its expansion and to regulate or prohibit certain forms of credit. This authority was originally granted under emergency legislation following the Second World War; it was revised and renewed under the 1952 Act to Control the Credit System, and most recently granted under the 1956 act by that name. Controls were employed selectively for the most part, in the immediate postwar period. From 1952 to 1960, no such controls were in use, although the Bank retained the authority to invoke them. Since 1961, quantitative credit controls have been in constant use, with varying degrees of intensity and comprehensiveness, save for one year's respite that ended in September 1963.

Quantitative credit controls are currently exercised under the terms of "gentlemen's agreements" concluded between the Nederlandsche Bank and the commercial banks, central institutions of the agricultural credit banks, and those of the general savings banks. The agreements with the commercial and agricultural credit banks date from May 1960. General savings banks were previously exempt from credit ceilings on the theory that they were exclusively capital market intermediaries and therefore could not add to domestic liquidity and thus disturb monetary equilibrium. Their entry into commercial banking activities has modified this presumption. They are now subject to credit regulation under an agreement concluded in March 1969. Finally, an agreement of September 1970 between the central bank and the Post Office's director general brought lending by the postal check and giro services to the domestic private sector and to local authorities within the scope of credit ceiling regulations.[7] Extension of credit ceilings to these lenders was motivated by considerations of monetary control as well as equity.

From 1961 until 1965, credit ceilings were applied only to short-term bank loans to business firms and individuals. During this period some banks began to evade the ceilings by lending at longer term. To bring this under control, the central bank sought and received in 1965

---

[7] Nederlandsche Bank, *Annual Report for the Year 1970,* p. 141.

an agreement concerning *longer-term credits*. Effective in May 1965, the banks agreed to restrict the growth in their longer-term assets to the growth in their longer-term liabilities. This development required a more precise definition of both long-term assets and long-term liabilities:

> Long-term assets are deemed in this context to comprise loans privately granted to the Government, domestic securities and foreign guilder bonds quoted at Amsterdam, lendings to local authorities with an original life of more than one year, lendings to the private sector with an original life of at least two years, participations, syndicate holdings, and real properties.
> Long-term liabilities are deemed to include capital, reserves, time deposits with an original life of at least two years (in certain cases one year), and real savings balances.[8]

In the case of savings deposits, the extent to which they are regarded as real savings is determined with reference to their annual rate of turnover.

In December 1966 under its agreement with the banks, the Nederlandsche Bank extended credit ceilings to cover short-term bank loans to local authorities in view of the fact that such credit had expanded in a manner regarded excessive in the preceding year. Credit ceilings on bank loans to local authorities have remained continuously in force since that time with varying degrees of intensity.

Ceilings for short- and long-term bank credit to the private sector were removed in June 1967 but restored in January 1969. At the same time, general savings banks were brought under the agreement for the first time and requested to limit the growth in their long-term assets to that in their long-term savings deposits. They were also requested to hold their short-term lending to the private sector to its customary modest level. Moreover, in 1969, the Nederlandsche Bank made a specific request to the commercial and agricultural credit banks concerning their personal loans, asking them to hold the expansion of these to the increase laid down for loan societies in the Personal Loan Order of 1969. Thus the variety and complexity of direct credit controls that rely on administrative rather than price rationing has steadily expanded in the Netherlands in the past decade.

Ceilings are defined in terms of a permissible percentage increase over the volume of credit in a specific base period. When collective bank credit expands over the prescribed percentage, those individual banks that have exceeded their own ceilings are assessed the penalty of a non-interest-bearing deposit with the central bank. The required deposit is calculated as a prescribed percentage of the amount by which a bank has exceeded its ceiling. The Nederlandsche Bank has varied the percentages used in calculating the penalty deposits from time to time depending on its view of general credit conditions. Also,

[8] Nederlandsche Bank, *Annual Report for the Year 1965*, p. 129.

various temporary exceptions and abatements of the penalty have been offered by the Nederlandsche Bank on occasions when it wished to respond to temporary changes in money market conditions. To gain flexibility, it has at times granted brief suspensions of the penalty clause and on other occasions informed the banks they could finance their penalty deposits by borrowing at the central bank.

Unquestionably the Nederlandsche Bank has come to rely more and more on credit ceilings until these have now become its most important flexible policy instrument. Balance-of-payments considerations undoubtedly provide the basic rationale for this development. These considerations are compounded out of two factors: (1) the influence of balance-of-payments surpluses and deficits on domestic monetary equilibrium as a theoretical guide to monetary policy in the Netherlands, and (2) continuous efforts by the Netherlands monetary authorities to insulate the domestic money and capital markets sufficiently from their foreign and international counterparts to preserve some autonomy in monetary management. The interactions among policy instruments and objectives is complex.

Capital Market Controls

A logical and practical complement to credit controls is furnished by capital market controls. In the realm of domestic capital issues, we must distinguish between publicly floated issues and private placements and between private sector demand and public sector (central government and local authority) demand.

Under a gentlemen's agreement concluded in 1954, the banks are required to notify the Nederlandsche Bank of plans for public issue of bonds in the capital market. The central bank may then make recommendations concerning timing and even terms of the proposed offer. In the Netherlands, volume of privately placed issues and loans against borrowers' notes is three to four times as important as that of issues floated publicly.[9] Over these private placements the central bank has only such influence as the weight its prestige may give it in informal negotiation with the banks. No doubt more binding authority could be obtained by the central bank should cooperation ever become a problem.

The central government and local authorities confer informally with the banks to arrange their schedules of offerings on the capital market so as not to interfere with private issues nor to overburden the market's capacity in a given period of time. Moreover, the Minister of Finance with subsequent approval of Parliament can limit or prohibit municipal issues of more than one year in maturity during a period of excessive strain in the capital market. By another provision of the

[9] European Communities, Monetary Committee, *Policy on the Bond Markets in the Countries of the EEC,* Brussels, 1970, p. 29.

same enabling legislation (the Public Bodies Capital Expenditure Act of 1963), the government has the power to order that the local authorities' demand for capital shall be centralized when overstrain occurs in the capital market. Such centralized municipal borrowing in the capital market has been required continuously since 1965, mainly through the Bank for Netherlands Municipalities.

From this brief survey of measures to regulate lending in credit markets and borrowing in the capital market, there emerges a fairly comprehensive, albeit not fully complete, system of administrative controls over major financial flows. In its present form this system has been developed chiefly during the decade of the 1960's. The system appears to have been used more to support general stabilization policy than to achieve selective goals. We shall consider its rationale and implications more fully in our evaluation and commentary. However, before attempting an evaluation, we must become acquainted with certain theoretical views that influence the Netherlands authorities in their approach to monetary policy.

THE THEORETICAL FRAMEWORK FOR
MONETARY POLICY IN THE NETHERLANDS

The monetary authorities in the Netherlands have articulated and communicated their theoretical views to an unusual degree; and such views find expression in practice with apparent consistency. Dutch authors as well as practical bankers attribute these theories primarily to such men as J. G. Koopmans, W. M. Holtrop, and G. A. Kessler. Koopmans was a Dutch academic economist. Holtrop, now retired, was for many years president of the Nederlandsche Bank and a distinguished figure in international central banking circles. He was one of a select number of foreign central bankers invited to meet with the Radcliffe Committee in England in the development of their famous report on monetary policy in the United Kingdom. Kessler is currently a managing director of the Nederlandsche Bank, and he combines both academic and practical banking credentials.

Much of the basic theoretical literature written by these men is available only in Dutch and therefore of limited accessibility. Fortunately, statements of the theory are available in English although somewhat less systematic in nature. These include various published speeches of Holtrop, his initial statement and subsequent responses to detailed questions by members of the Radcliffe Committee and its staff, sections of various annual reports published in English by the Nederlandsche Bank, and an English language summary of Kessler's doctoral dissertation. These English language sources are the primary ones drawn upon in preparing the following summary of the theory. In addition, there is available in French a systematic review and critique of the monetary theory of the Nederlandsche Bank prepared by a

Dutch economist, Professor Frits J. de Jong and published in the monthly *Bulletin* of the Belgian central bank.[10] In the summary that follows specific reference to these sources will be made only for direct quotations or to establish a source for a particularly important point.

The concept of "monetary equilibrium" is central to the theoretical framework employed by the Nederlandsche Bank. Monetary equilibrium holds when the demand for liquidity equals the supply of liquidity at an unchanged price level for goods and services. In this situation there are on balance neither inflationary nor deflationary pressures. The stock of liquidity in the economy consists of the money supply in the form of cash and demand claims against banks and other credit institutions that issue demand obligations, plus certain other "secondary liquid assets" that can be converted into money at the holders' option with little delay, trouble, and expense. These secondary liquid assets include certain claims on public authorities and money-creating institutions, so far as they are held by holders other than money-creating institutions. The 1969 *Annual Report* of the Nederlandsche Bank mentions the following among such assets considered as liquid:

> Secondary liquid assets representing a liability of the Government comprise Treasury bills, Treasury notes, tax certificates, reconstruction bonds, short-term loans and freely available balances at the Treasury.
> Secondary liquid assets representing a liability of local authorities comprise money at call and short-term loans, and credits in current account granted to provinces, municipalities and polder boards; also short-term claims of various descriptions on the Bank for Netherlands Municipalities and the Netherlands Polder Boards Bank.[11]

Savings deposits of commercial banks or other credit institutions formerly were excluded from secondary liquid assets. In recent years, however, savings accounts have been used increasingly in lieu of checking accounts to make payments. Accordingly only those savings accounts whose annual rate of turnover is 50 per cent or less are now excluded from liquid assets. Those with an annual turnover rate of 2.00 or above are fully included in liquid assets. Those whose turnover rate lies between 50 per cent and 2.00 are included in part on a sliding scale. The category of secondary liquid assets also includes the private sector's foreign currency deposits and money market investments. These can be repatriated at the option of the holder and thus are counted in domestic liquid assets.

Clearly, the definition of liquid assets that are very close substitutes for money depends on financial practice and tradition, the policy of

[10] F. J. de Jong, "L'Analyse Monetaire Elaborée par la Nederlandsche Bank," in Banque Nationale de Belgique, *Bulletin d'Information et de Documentation*, April 1965, pp. 425–48; May 1965, pp. 569–85. This article may be consulted for greater detail and for references to published writings of other Dutch authors mentioned in the text.

[11] Nederlandsche Bank, *Annual Report for the Year 1969*, Statistical Annex, footnote to Table 3.1, pp. 16–17.

the central bank as influenced by its view of the consequences of its actions in refusing to provide money in exchange for liquid assets, and in some degree, on attitudes of firms and individuals in the private sector, for example, whether savings deposits represent long-term commitments or simply a temporary resting place for funds soon to be used elsewhere. Practice, tradition, and central bank policy differ among different countries. In the Netherlands, the central bank's classification of these assets as liquid implies its willingness to guarantee their convertibility into money on short delay and at very little sacrifice to the holder. Behind this guarantee are central bankers' views concerning the need to prevent bank failures and to protect the ability of the central and local governments to honor their financial obligations. Spokesmen for the Nederlandsche Bank acknowledge that other central banks may view matters differently, but they are skeptical concerning the willingness of these other central banks to stick to their principles when a credit squeeze becomes tight enough to cause a liquidity panic. This is a pragmatic judgment whose details the Nederlandsche Bank has shown itself willing to modify with changing circumstances, as in the treatment of savings deposits. Formerly these were entirely excluded; now they are included in part. At this stage of our discussion, it is more useful to accept the definition of liquid assets adopted by the Nederlandsche Bank and to examine consequences of its use than it is to debate it in principle.

The supply of liquid assets depends on the borrowing behavior of the central government and local authorities, the lending behavior of money-creating institutions responding to demands for their credit by the private sector, the surplus or deficit position of the balance of payments (including both current and capital accounts), and the policy actions of the central bank. The demand for liquidity is divided into two parts: a necessary, or transactions, liquidity and a desired, or precautionary, liquidity. Jointly and separately these are thought of as being strictly proportional to the level of real gross national product; or rather, their incremental relationships are regarded as strictly proportional. What this proportionality defines, however, is the long-run trend relationship. Variations around this relationship, often expressed as the ratio of liquidity to gross national product, are recognized as temporary distortions due to short-run factors of various kinds.

Disturbances to the normal, or long-run, liquidity ratio reflect monetary disequilibrium. These disturbances occur in part for monetary reasons and in part owing to other economic or political forces. Among the monetary causes are hoarding or dishoarding of liquidity by the private sector or sometimes the central government; liquidity creation when central and local governments engage in deficit finance by issuing any of the short-term obligations listed above; lending operations by money-creating institutions that expand monetary deposit claims against these institutions); and a net inflow of foreign exchange from abroad if monetary developments abroad were the responsible factor. Nonmonetary disturbances of equilibrium include increases in money wages that cannot be absorbed without raising prices, and changes in tastes or in technology that change the basic pattern of world trade. In general, the central bank should have the task of offsetting monetary causes of monetary disequilibrium unless these initiate processes, which in the end will restore equilibrium without permanent inflation or deflation, having occurred. Under most circumstances of disequilibrium produced by nonmonetary causes, the economy cannot successfully be restored to long-run equilibrium by monetary measures; other and more appropriate nonmonetary measures should be used, such as taxation, reduction of money wages, subsidies, and changes in exchange parity.

The monetary theory of the Nederlandsche Bank in general reflects modern macroeconomic theory. Both stress interaction between financial and real variables in determining interest rates; both employ the concepts of aggregate demand, employment, price level, and balance-of-payments surplus or deficit. A principal difference in emphasis is the substitution in the theory of the Nederlandsche Bank of the stock of liquidity for the stock of money. In their emphasis on the stock of liquidity rather than the stock of money, Dutch theoreticians differ from both standard Keynesian views and standard quantity theory views, which stress the money stock as the key variable for monetary policy. Moreover, the Dutch central bank's view is also very different from the view of the Radcliffe *Report* and that of the monetary authorities in Great Britain. Both of these choose the stock of liquidity over the stock of money as the crucial financial magnitude, but regard it as ill defined and somewhat subjectively determined. Thus, for policy purposes, they concentrate on interest rates as the key financial variables. The Netherlands central bankers by contrast give a precise working definition to the stock of liquid assets and regard this rather than interest rates as the key variable for monetary policy.

Other aspects of the theoretical framework employed by the Dutch monetary authorities are standard in modern macroeconomic and international trade theory. These include marginal propensities to save, invest, and import; wage, price, and employment relationships; the influence of interest rates and expectations on liquidity preference and on investment; compensatory variations in government expenditures to stabilize aggregate demand; and the influence of international price differentials on the current account balance of trade.

From their theoretical views of the economy and of monetary equilibrium, the Dutch monetary authorities have drawn important implications for monetary policy. The clarity and consistency with which theoretical views find expression in practice, as well as certain specific practical implications drawn from the theory, are distinctive when compared with central banking practice in other countries.

Perhaps the most important practical consequence of Dutch monetary theory is the central bankers' emphatic insistence on the role of central government finance in monetary policy. According to Kessler:

Monetary policy may be generally described as the managing of the price and availability of money. It embraces both central bank policy and government policy, the latter *in so far* as it influences the liquidity in- or outside the banking system. It is characteristic of monetary policy that its primary impact lies in the financial sphere. Fiscal policy (proper) on the other hand, consisting of the managing of the level and the nature of government expenditure and of tax policy, has its primary impact in the income sphere.[12]

Or as stated by Holtrop in his discussion with the Radcliffe Committee in England:

. . . Monetary policy and central bank policy are by no means identical. Central bank policy is only that part of monetary policy that comes within the domain of the operations of the central bank. There are, however, instruments of monetary policy that are only under the control of the Government.[13]

And further, regarding central bank policy:

If supported by Government monetary policy it can be very effective; if counteracted by Government policies it can be nearly powerless.[14]

In short, whenever a surplus or deficit in the government's budget alters the amount of liquid assets outstanding in the economy through a change in the amount of short-term government debt, the government is engaged in monetary policy. It is the manner in which government financing is carried out that is crucial. In the view of the Netherlands authorities, sale or redemption of long-term government bonds is a capital market transaction rather than a money market one and cannot disturb monetary equilibrium. This is so because the demand for obligations in the capital market generally comes from genuine long-term savings out of current income and thus implies a decline in aggregate demand to offset the real investment funded through the capital market. On the other hand, a government deficit is regarded as constituting expansionary monetary policy when financed by short-term government debt; this view holds even when this debt is purchased by the public and thus does not expand the money supply in the strict sense as it would have done if purchased by the banking system.

These views depend on regarding money and liquid assets (as defined by the Nederlandsche Bank) as almost perfect substitutes for each other. From this perspective both the current and potential

[12] G. A. Kessler, *Monetair evenwicht en betalingsbalansevenwicht* (Leyden: 1958), English language "Summary and Conclusions," p. 461.
[13] The Committee on the Working of the Monetary System (Radcliffe Committee), *Principal Memoranda of Evidence,* vol. 1, p. 265, para. 81.
[14] Ibid., para. 85.

longer-run inflationary implications of government finance are subject to far closer scrutiny and assignment of responsibility than is the case when only the money supply per se is the focus for attention. Moreover, the responsibility of government deficit finance in adding to the supply of liquid assets that overhang the money market with potentially inflationary consequences is more clearly defined.

The condition of general monetary equilibrium may be disturbed by causes originating in the financial sphere, or the real economic sphere, or through the balance of payments. The central bank with the monetary cooperation of the central government has special responsibility for maintaining liquidity equilibrium in the financial sphere and to a lesser degree for offsetting disturbances to liquidity equilibrium through the balance of payments. The central bank can use its powers to offset excessive changes in the stock of money caused by the lending of credit institutions, or to offset inflows or outflows of foreign exchange when these are due to domestic or foreign monetary impulses. It can also seek to compensate for private sector hoarding or dishoarding by measures to change the stock of money. However, to cope with big swings in private sector liquidity preference, the central bank will require assistance from appropriate surpluses or deficits in the government budget. Moreover, concerning its role as lender of last resort, "a moment may come that the Bank has to allow some further inflationary financing rather than to let come the sudden break-down which might result from a too abrupt refusal." [15]

Following such views, central bankers in the Netherlands assign to monetary policy a more modest and restricted role than is frequently claimed for it in other countries. To quote again from Holtrop's views as stated to the Radcliffe Committee:

> To sum up I would say that it is not correct that monetary policy is only one of the instrumental possibilities of general economic policy. I think that monetary policy is a thing of its own which strives for a purpose which should be the purpose of good government under all circumstances, namely, the maintenance of monetary equilibrium, in whatever sense this may be defined, as for instance, price stability, maintenance of the value of money or the prevention of monetary causes for disequilibrium in the economy. Other purposes of economic policy should be pursued by the use of other instruments than monetary ones. [16]

Central bankers at the Nederlandsche Bank, from their strong sense of the limitations of monetary policy and even more of central bank policy, combined with their confidently held theoretical views on monetary and general economic equilibrium, have been outspoken in their assignment of responsibility to various causes of inflationary or deflationary disequilibrium. For some years, the *Annual Report* of the

[15] Ibid., p. 266, para. 89.
[16] Radcliffe Committee, *Minutes of Evidence,* p. 813, para. 11854.

Nederlandsche Bank has published statistical tables and commentary on the contribution of various sectors and institutions to liquidity creation, hoarding (liquidity accumulation), and dishoarding (liquidity activation). Among the sectors distinguished are the central government, local authorities, the personal and business sector, and the foreign sector (balance of payments). The institutions include the money-creating institutions (commercial banks, security credit institutions, agricultural credit institutions, and giro institutions), and the institutional investors (life insurance companies, pension funds, social insurance funds, and savings banks).

Basically the approach is to determine the change in short-term borrowing by the various sectors and the overall surplus or deficit in the balance of payments, and to consider this as liquidity creation. To this there is an adjustment for changes in long-term lending by money-creating institutions that increase their monetary liabilities. Changes in hoarding or dishoarding by sector are calculated by comparing the percentage rise in their liquid asset holdings with the percentage rise in national income. An excess of sector percentage over national-income percentage is viewed as hoarding (liquidity inactivation) and a deficiency as dishoarding (liquidity activation). The total national rise in liquidity is also compared in percentage terms with the increase in national income at both constant and current prices to establish liquidity absorption due to rise in real production of goods and services and due to the increase in prices. This statistical exercise then serves to assign responsibility to the various sectors and institutions for their respective contributions to inflationary or deflationary impulses affecting monetary equilibrium.

In the view of Netherlands' central bankers, monetary policy can successfully offset some but not all inflationary and deflationary impulses transmitted through the balance of payments. Domestic inflationary forces tend to produce a balance-of-payments deficit that reduces the domestic money supply through an outflow of foreign exchange and thus is self-equilibrating. Limited monetary expansion abroad produces the opposite phenomenon and also tends to be self-equilibrating. Domestic monetary policy can be used successfully to moderate the rate of change in domestic money supply and liquidity in these cases.

Experience has taught Dutch monetary officials that domestic monetary policy is not an adequate instrument to maintain or restore domestic monetary equilibrium when monetary expansion abroad persists or basic changes occur in the pattern of world trade. Dutch central bankers regard monetary expansion by a reserve currency country (such as the United States or the United Kingdom) as stimulating inflationary pressures that are especially impervious to domestic monetary measures. The only solution in such cases is international monetary cooperation or a unilateral change in exchange parity. A change in exchange parity may also be required to restore equilibrium following a shift in world trade patterns that has arisen from nonmonetary causes.

Two other implications of the monetary theories of Dutch central bankers deserve mention. The first concerns the significance of capital market transactions and the long-term rate of interest; the second, the role of financial intermediaries and their importance for monetary policy.

Holtrop, in his discussions with the Radcliffe Committee, took the position that demand for capital market securities reflected long-term savings that would neutralize the increase in aggregate demand brought about by the investment undertaken with capital market funds. He thought interest rates in the capital market were virtually independent of short-term interest rates at that time (1958) and that capital market developments were irrelevant to monetary equilibrium. Indeed, he considered use of monetary policy to influence the long-term rate of interest "dangerous," as revealed in his answer to the question from Professor Sayers, Why did you use the word *dangerous*?

Because I thought of the other purposes which are known to have occurred in central bank policy, where maintaining the long-term rate was at a certain moment conceived to be the proper purpose of government policy. When the central bank under such conditions has been willing to try to maintain the rate, it was mostly in the direction of preventing it from going up. Central banks have been buying government bonds in the market, thus going in for inflationary financing and creation of an excess supply of money just for the purpose of maintaining the long-term rate of interest. In my opinion, that is totally contrary to the proper purposes of central banking, because there the central bank would knowingly have disturbed monetary equilibrium instead of maintaining it.[17]

At the time of Holtrop's statement, financial practice and institutional behavior in the Netherlands certainly encouraged a market segmentation theory of the term structure of interest rates. Commercial banks did not make long-term loans; savings banks did not offer commercial banking services and checking deposits. Institutional investors channeled their funds exclusively to the capital market. But the past decade has witnessed some blurring of these lines and probably some increased interdependence between short- and long-term interest rates. The Nederlandsche Bank has responded to these developments partly by including certain savings deposits in its definition of liquidity and — more important for the present discussion — partly by regulating lending to the capital market by money-creating institutions. Since January 1969, these institutions have been required to limit increases in capital market loans to increases in their long-term liabilities. This regulation reinforces traditional market segmentation.

[17] Ibid., para. 11846.

A corollary to the Nederlandsche Bank's views concerning the capital market and long-term interest rates is their lack of interest concerning the growth and behavior of financial intermediaries. Since the theoretical work of Gurley and Shaw in the United States and the publication of the Radcliffe *Report* in England, many monetary economists have accepted the view that claims against financial intermediaries are near monies that contribute to the stock of liquidity in the economy, serve as substitutes for money held for precautionary purposes, and thereby reduce the demand for money and add to its velocity and to expansionary pressures in the economy.

On Holtrop's definition, financial intermediaries are essentially those institutional investors whose activities are confined to transmitting genuine long-term savings to the capital market. Thus claims against them are not liquid near monies, and their activities cannot disturb monetary equilibrium. In Dutch practice, any credit institution whose obligations *are* convertible by it with little delay into money on request is classified as a money-creating institution and is subject to regulation, like a commercial bank. Perplexed questioning by the Radcliffe Committee on the lack of concern by Dutch monetary authorities over the activities of financial intermediaries finally resulted in this exchange between Sayers and Holtrop:

> I am trying to find out why you bother about what the banks are doing, and yet do not bother about what the financial intermediaries are doing in the same way; and why in explaining why you bother about Bank Rate you explain it by reference to its effect on the banks and nobody else. Are you really not concerned with its effect on the capital market generally?

> I think that that effect is very indirect, and not the essential effect. I find it difficult to follow exactly what you mean without an example of the intermediaries you are thinking of. In Holland we have a sharp distinction between registered credit institutions which are subject to the control of the central bank, and others. I know that you have financial institutions which can take deposits and are not considered banks. We think that that is a potentially dangerous situation, because it leaves people who create liquidity outside the control of the central bank. In my opinion these institutions are to be considered banks. According to the Netherlands law everybody who in the course of his ordinary business takes deposits and at the same time grants credits is a bank. The savings banks are credit institutions, but I do not consider them money-creating institutions. I am safe in considering deposits with the savings banks as having no virulent liquidity. This is a matter of actual conditions, of course. On the other hand, the banking system in Holland has very little savings deposits. In practice deposits with the banking system in Holland are corporate and business deposits, and are therefore liquid.[18]

Clearly, therefore, the Dutch central bank is concerned with the activities of those financial intermediaries that issue demand deposit

---

[18] Ibid., p. 810, para. 11822.

obligations or obligations convertible by them at the depositor's request with little cost and delay into monetary claims. Indeed, they are sufficiently concerned to subject these institutions to the same regulations as commercial banks. Their apparent lack of concern may be traced to semantic differences that in turn reflect national differences in financial organization and practice.

In summary, to understand many of the decisions, practices, and public statements on monetary policy by the Netherlands monetary authorities, it is particularly important to be familiar with their analytical framework. Central to this is the concept of monetary equilibrium. This is not a phrase evocative of some vague but desirable condition, as foreign observers frequently regard it, but a concept that has been given specific empirical and practical content in the statistics and policy decisions of the Netherlands central bank. No doubt the theoretical framework's formulation and translation into practice has been strongly influenced by some peculiarly Dutch economic circumstances and institutional patterns. Nevertheless, in its role as guide to monetary policy, the theory has proved to have some strong positive features. Among these may be mentioned for reemphasis its clear vision concerning the role of government finance in monetary policy, its attention to the stock of liquid assets other than money as a constraint on future policy decisions of the central bank, and its realistic view of the limits to the effectiveness of monetary policy as an instrument of general economic policy, this last with attendant assignment of responsibility to various nonmonetary causes of disequilibrium.

EVALUATION AND COMMENTARY

We are now in a position to examine the Netherlands monetary and credit, capital market, and foreign exchange controls as an integrated system. The rationale for this system is the maintenance of monetary equilibrium in the Netherlands economy. To accomplish this, the monetary authority seeks to regulate the growth in money supply and other liquid assets so that their total remains in relatively fixed ratio to the national income measured at constant prices. In pursuit of its goal, the Nederlandsche Bank maintains surveillance over domestic sources of liquidity creation and of changes in the velocity of money owing to hoarding or dishoarding of liquidity. It calls attention to disequilibrating changes in liquidity behavior by sectors of the economy and to nonmonetary sources of disequilibrium such as excessive wage increases. The Nederlandsche Bank also watches the balance of payments for inflationary or deflationary impulses introduced into the economy. When, in the light of its theoretical framework, the Nederlandsche Bank determines that offsetting or compensatory monetary and credit measures are beneficial in restoring equilibrium, it undertakes these measures.

Although the Nederlandsche Bank has the authority to use the classical central bank instruments of discount policy, open market operations, and variations in minimum reserve requirements, none of these currently can be considered a principal policy instrument of the Bank in its efforts to maintain monetary equilibrium. Minimum reserve requirements were not altered between 1963 and September 1972. No open market operations occurred in the interval from 1964 until 1971, and changes in the discount rate are thought to be largely symbolic for domestic purposes but to have some significant effect on short-term capital movements between the Netherlands and foreign money markets.

Quantitative controls over the granting of credit by commercial banks, agricultural credit banks, and general savings banks are the principal instruments of domestic credit policy. These controls are supplemented by measures to influence changes in domestic liquidity by capital flows through the balance of payments. Direct quantitative controls over the foreign position of commercial banks, central bank swaps in the forward market for foreign exchange, administrative controls over short-term borrowing or lending abroad by nonbank firms and individuals, and regulation of access to the domestic capital market by foreign issuers are measures used to influence capital flows through the balance of payments. Depending on circumstances, these measures are used to insulate the domestic money and capital markets from their foreign counterparts or to induce controlled flows to help manage the liquidity of the Netherlands economy.

Nonresidents have been permitted to purchase existing securities in the Netherlands, and residents may purchase existing securities on foreign securities markets. Transactions must take place at official market rates. The volume of capital flows occasioned by such security transactions has not normally been very significant. Nonbank resident firms and individuals are not permitted to purchase foreign Treasury bills and other short-term money market assets. Rates on fixed-interest securities in the Netherlands capital market have not normally attracted foreign purchasers. This fact is not entirely coincidental. Four-fifths of new long-term bonds issued by the private sector are privately placed and are not available for foreign purchase. Rates and timing of the remaining one-fifth of private bond issues marketed publicly are subject to recommendations from the Nederlandsche Bank. During 1971 and early 1972 when speculative inflows of capital into the Netherlands were judged excessive, the authorities imposed controls to prevent any net increase in nonresident investments in bonds and time deposits and prohibited residents from paying interest on nonresident demand deposits denominated in guilders.

The money market in the Netherlands, though wide in principle, is narrow in practice and is primarily an interbank market. Nonbank firms and residents are prohibited from buying and selling foreign money market investments. The net foreign positions of resident banks are subject to quantitative controls. These long-standing controls have recently been supplemented by prohibitions on the acquisition of fixed-interest assets by nonresidents. Under these regulations there does not appear to be much opportunity for transactions between residents and nonresidents in the Dutch market to pose a significant problem for the control of domestic liquidity by the Nederlandsche Bank.

The Nederlandsche Bank's reliance on quantitative credit controls as its principal instrument of credit policy has been motivated in part by the desire for a credit-restraining device that does not raise domestic interest rates and in so doing provide a greater incentive for residents and nonresidents alike to find ingenious new methods for avoiding administrative measures to control international capital flows. The stability of bank lending rates under credit rationing is aided by the oligopolistic structure of the banking industry and its dependence on the central bank discount rate for price leadership. The authorities appear to regard low domestic interest rates as beneficial to the international competitive position of Dutch exports provided that they can be achieved without sacrificing domestic monetary equilibrium. Low interest rates also make restraint on wage increases politically more feasible. But there is also an argument favoring credit ceilings from the perspective of domestic monetary controls.

During a domestic economic expansion, the dishoarding of liquid assets can add to inflationary pressure by aiding in transferring money balances from idle holders to active users and thus raising the velocity of the existing money stock. When banks are free to make additional loans at higher interest rates as loan demand increases, they have a motive to sell liquid assets from their portfolios to acquire additional funds to lend. Even if the central bank does not respond to such sales by open market purchases that increase the money supply, sale of liquid assets adds to the lending capacity of the banking *system.* From a banking system perspective, some depositors give up deposits in exchange for interest-bearing assets while the banks transfer these deposits to borrowing customers by making new loans. By this process the banking system provides a channel of intermediation for activating idle deposits. Credit ceilings shut off this customary channel of financial intermediation and thus retard the rise in velocity of the money stock. In the absence of credit ceilings, not only is bank intermediation more effective but demand for credit will produce more pronounced increases in interest rates with attendant consequences for the control of inflows of money from abroad.

The effectiveness of credit ceilings depends partly on the extent to which alternative channels for intermediation exist and remain free from controls. It is understandable, therefore, that having begun with ceilings for commercial bank and agricultural-credit-bank short-term loans to the private sector, the Nederlandsche Bank has found it desirable gradually to extend the coverage of its credit controls. Those by institutions now include general savings banks and those by loan types now include loans to local authorities and personal loans.

One response of the banks to loan ceilings on short-term credit has been to lend at longer-term. The monetary theory of the Nederlandsche Bank regards longer-term or capital market loans as neutral in their effect on monetary equilibrium provided that they are matched by savings. Thus, the commercial, agricultural, and savings banks have been asked to restrict their long-term lending to the level of their long-term obligations. In 1968, the system of credit controls was reviewed and alternative control measures were discussed, including greater reliance on cash reserve requirements, introduction of variable liquid asset reserve requirements, and modification of the existing provisions for long-term lending (to permit banks to increase either short- or long-term loans in proportion to the rise in their long-term liabilities). The combined regulation was rejected because it would tend to increase competition for long-term liabilities. In other words, it would give further impetus to increased interdependence of the money market and the capital market. Liquidity ratios were rejected because of the familiar problem of designing equitable regulations of this sort for banks with widely differing asset structures. The Nederlandsche Bank's reasons for not making more active use of minimum cash reserve requirements have already been made clear.

Another response of Dutch banks to credit ceilings has been to charge customers high enough rates to cover the interest the banks lost in incurring penalty deposits at the central bank, on which no interest is paid. This conversion from availability rationing to price rationing defeats the purpose of credit ceilings, so that the Nederlandsche Bank has requested the banks to discontinue the practice. Both banks and brokers have assisted customers to bypass bank credit ceilings by helping to arrange direct loans between bank customers, often with bank guarantees of the borrowers' credit. Since the banks' longer-run interests are not in helping to develop nonbank credit channels, such bank-guaranteed direct loans are arranged only for very good customers, and their volume thus far has remained modest. Banks have also sold existing loans on repurchase agreements so they could make new loans within credit ceilings. This practice has not become quantitatively significant either.

A borrower who cannot obtain short-term credit from his bank may turn to the capital market. Few borrowers regard these forms of credit as close substitutes, however, so that once again the alternative is of limited quantitative importance. In any event, the monetary authorities accept this substitution, since they consider capital market loans to be matched by real saving and not affecting monetary equilibrium.

The Nederlandsche Bank has a substantial array of instruments to influence domestic liquidity, changes in the velocity of money, and international capital flows. Its theoretical framework gives it a realistic view of the limitations of monetary and credit policy as a panacea for all economic ills. The concern of this theory with the stock of liquid assets, which include but are not limited to money, emphasizes the role of government finance in monetary policy and has contributed to an awareness of responsibility for monetary policy shared between the government and the central bank.

When monetary and credit controls, foreign exchange controls, and the influence of the central bank on the capital market are considered together, a relatively comprehensive system of controls emerges. These controls have been used in pursuing the primary goal of monetary equilibrium rather than in allocating credit to selective ends. Thus selective goals have not been sought at the expense of general monetary equilibrium, as they have in France and in the United Kingdom. Table 6.2 presents data for growth in money supply and real gross national product and for price developments in the Netherlands during the decade of the 1960's. The record of growth in real gross national product is in the middle range for members of the

TABLE 6.2   Netherlands: Money Supply, Real GNP,
            and Price Indexes (annual percentage changes)

Year	Money supply [a] (% change)	Real GNP [b] (% change)	GNP deflator [c] (% change)	Consumer prices [d] (% change)
1960	....	....	....	....
1961	7.65	3.39	2.50	0.98
1962	7.54	3.78	3.22	1.94
1963	9.17	3.72	5.03	3.80
1964	8.07	8.91	7.97	5.50
1965	10.04	4.67	6.03	4.00
1966	6.86	2.50	6.25	5.76
1967	6.22	6.58	3.62	3.45
1968	11.39	6.68	3.76	3.69
1969	8.07	5.09	5.99	7.45
Compound annual rate of growth				
	8.30	5.02	4.91	4.04

[a] Notes, coins, and demand deposits: De Nederlandsche Bank N.V., *Quarterly Statistics*, 1970, nos. 1 and 2, September 1970, pp. 58–60.
[b] 1960–66 figures calculated from Netherlands Central Bureau of Statistics, *Statistical Yearbook of the Netherlands*, 1965–66, pp. 270–1. 1966–69 figures calculated from *Statistical Yearbook*, 1969–70, p. 242.
[c] 1960–66 figures calculated from *Statistical Yearbook*, 1965–66, pp. 270–1; and 1969–70, p. 242 (GNP at current prices); and from real GNP. 1966–69 figures calculated from *Statistical Yearbook*, 1971–72, p. 310.
[d] 1960–63 figures calculated from *Statistical Yearbook*, 1963–64, p. 335. 1963–69 figures calculated from *Statistical Yearbook*, 1969–70, p. 298.

European Economic Community, and price increases over the decade are somewhat above average.

Among the principal unresolved problems that the Dutch monetary authorities face, those recently most pressing are inflationary impulses transmitted through the current and short-term capital accounts of the balance of payments. The degree of openness of the Dutch economy makes it particularly sensitive to cyclical swings in aggregate demand of major trading partners. Inflationary developments abroad may result in enlarged export demand accompanied by an increase in the domestic money supply. Speculative inflows of nonresident funds through the short-term capital account also posed a problem until the tightening of controls in this area in early 1972. Finally, rising unit wage costs have exerted increasing upward pressure on domestic price levels in the Netherlands in the last several years. The inflationary pressures so generated cause concern to the monetary authorities. They do not regard monetary policy as effective against cost-push inflation, however, so that they conceive their role as advisory to the government and to organized labor in efforts to moderate inflation that excessive wage increases occasion.

7 The United Kingdom

On September 10, 1971, the Bank of England announced important reforms in British techniques of monetary policy that were to become effective on September 16, 1971. This announcement capped discussions between the authorities and representatives of clearing banks and other financial institutions that had been initiated by the Bank of England in May 1971. In principle, the reforms represent a dramatic turnabout in the techniques of monetary policy employed by the United Kingdom authorities. The history of British monetary policy since World War II, prior to these reforms, has been one of steady escalation of administrative interventions by the authorities into financial markets, leading to the progressive replacement of general monetary policy by selective credit controls. The thrust of the 1971 reforms was to accord greater significance to control of the money supply as a policy objective; to increase reliance on price rationing of credit rather than quantitative rationing in communicating central bank policy to the economy; and to stimulate competition in banking and financial markets by removing certain official controls and requiring the major deposit banks to suspend their cartel agreements on lending and deposit interest rates. These features represent a return to more general and more market-oriented techniques of monetary policy in contrast to the network of direct and selective controls that they replace.

The reforms have already changed the techniques of monetary policy and the operations of financial institutions and markets in the United Kingdom and promise to change them still more as time passes. Nevertheless, it is desirable and even necessary to devote much of the present discussion of monetary policy and techniques in the United Kingdom to monetary and financial developments that provide the background to the 1971 reforms. There are several reasons for this. The reforms have arisen from dissatisfaction with the performance of financial institutions and markets and with the effectiveness of monetary policy under the system of selective credit controls that had prevailed. Moreover, although the reforms have changed *practices* of the monetary authorities and are changing those of various financial institutions, they have not basically altered the *structure* of financial institutions and markets, although such structural changes may occur in the long run. Thus, the situation prior to the reforms of 1971 constitutes essential background for understanding the purpose of the reforms, the environment in which they occur and which they are intended in part to change, and the evolving situation of financial institutions and markets in the present and near future.

Finally, the prereform system of selective credit controls still has some advocates in official and financial circles. Under sufficient provocation from rising domestic prices, from a balance-of-payments deficit, and from a substantial deficit in the budget of the central government, the authorities might retreat from the more market-oriented techniques espoused in the reforms to the prior system of selective credit controls.

Our discussion of the British system of monetary and credit controls begins with a survey of British financial institutions and markets. This is followed by a description of the principal instruments and techniques by which the authorities implemented monetary and credit policy in the period from the end of the Second World War until the credit reform of 1971. The next section analyzes the manner in which the system of monetary and credit controls functioned prior to the reform of 1971. Special attention is devoted to those somewhat arcane aspects of the operation of credit controls in the short-term credit markets in which behavior of the participants, especially the clearing banks and discount houses, came to be strongly influenced by various traditional arrangements and noncodified "understandings," as distinct from normal market behavior within a framework of formal regulations. The influence on monetary and credit policy of the government budget, the Exchange Equalization Account, and the authorities' policy toward the gilt-edged market for government securities is discussed. Then the conceptual framework for monetary policy is examined and its influence on policy explored. A final section discusses the credit reform of 1971 and notes some recent developments.

THE BANK OF ENGLAND

The Bank of England is the central bank and key operating agency for monetary policy in the United Kingdom. It was founded under a royal charter in 1694. Among central banks, only the Swedish Riksbank is older, having been established in 1668. Over the centuries since the founding of the Bank of England, this private bank evolved through usage and function to become banker to the government, manager of the public debt, and lender of last resort to other banks — in short, to function as central bank in the British financial system. In 1946, the Bank of England was nationalized. Its present authority and constitution derive from the Bank of England Act of 1946.

The Bank is governed by its Court of Directors, which consists of the governor, deputy governor and sixteen directors, all appointed by the Crown. Four of the directors, known as executive directors, as well as the governor and deputy governor give their full-time services to the Bank. These six are the key policy group within the Bank.[1] The part-time directors are intended to represent the public interest and to provide the Court with channels of communication to various segments of public opinion. They do not play an essential role in policy formation.

The functions of the Bank of England are those commonly associated with central banking. It has exclusive right of note issue in England and Wales. As agent for the Treasury, the Bank of England manages the national debt, the Exchange Equalization Account and the system of exchange controls. The Bank has full responsibility in practice for controlling the monetary system and for supervision of financial institutions with this purpose in view. Even in this area, however, the Bank is in principle subject to Treasury authority as an expression of the authority of the government in power. Section 4(1) of the Bank of England Act of 1946 reads:

> The Treasury may from time to time give such directions to the Bank as, after consultation with the Governor of the Bank, they think necessary in the public interest.[2]

This section has been interpreted to mean "that in the last resort, as between the Treasury and the Bank of England, the Treasury has got to have the last word, after due consultation with the governor of the Bank, in any case of disagreement."[3] The Treasury has never exercised this power to give directions to the Bank.

The authority of the Bank of England to regulate the activities of financial institutions in the public interest is contained in a broadly worded section of the Bank of England Act, which reads as follows:

> 4(3) The Bank if they think it necessary in the public interest, may request information from and make recommendations to bankers, and may, if so authorized by the Treasury, issue directions to any banker for the

---

[1] House of Commons, *First Report from the Select Committee on Nationalised Industries*, Report, Minutes of Evidence and Appendices, Session 1969–70, "Bank of England" (Her Majesty's Stationery Office: May 5, 1970), p. xli.

[2] Ibid., p. 352.

[3] Ibid.

purpose of securing that effect is given to any such request or recommendation:

Provided that.

(a) no such request or recommendation shall be made with respect to the affairs of any particular customer of a banker; and

(b) before authorising the issue of any such directions the Treasury shall give the banker concerned, or such person as appears to them to represent him, an opportunity of making representations with respect thereto.[4]

Here again the formal subordination of the Bank to the Treasury is affirmed. In practice, the Bank is the active directing agency, and regulatory decisions are reached by a process of consultation between the Bank and the Treasury.

The well-known British penchant for rules of custom rather than rules of law is exemplified in the Bank of England's approach to regulation of financial institutions. In practice, this has been based on informal understandings and gentlemen's agreements with representatives of appropriate trade associations for various types of financial institutions. It has not been necessary to invoke the formal powers held in reserve under the Bank of England Act. The British capacity to proceed pragmatically is illustrated by the absence of any clear legal definition of what constitutes a bank as a financial institution to which the regulative authority of the Bank of England applies. There is no clear statutory or other definition in English law or judicial precedent to determine what a bank is. This situation was brought into sharp focus in 1966 in the legal case of United Dominion Trust, which demonstrated how vague and uncertain the criteria in England are for classifying a business as a bank.[5] In a two-to-one vote, a three-judge panel decided that a particular business was a bank for legal purposes because it was generally so regarded by other bankers and not because of any objective criteria or functions performed. But the judges also warned against any use of their decision in the specific case as any precedent whatsoever for future cases.

In practice, different companies are regarded as banks under different legislative acts designed for various purposes. In the past, the Bank of England from time to time issued lists of those companies to be considered as banks for purposes of statistical reporting. On the list issued in June 1971, there were included the London clearing banks, the Scottish banks, the Northern Ireland banks, other deposit banks, the national Giro, all London discount houses, and accepting houses, overseas banks, and other banks. The relative importance of these

[4] Quoted in Ibid., p. 353.
[5] See "Hire Purchase Status Seekers," *The Economist*, June 18, 1966; and "What is a Bank?" *The Banker*, June 1966. On this entire problem, see also J. S. G. Wilson, "Regulation and Control of the United Kingdom Banking and Financial Structure," Banca Nazionale del Lavoro, *Quarterly Review*, no. 89, June 1969, pp. 128–45.

different types of banks in January 1972 in terms of their respective
shares in total sterling and nonsterling deposits can be seen in Table
7.1. After the credit reform of September 1971, the Bank of England
issued a revised list of those companies to be considered as banks
under the obligation to observe the newly established 12.5 per cent
reserve ratio. The discount houses were omitted from this list since
they were subject to a different type of reserve requirement.

TABLE 7.1   United Kingdom: Share of Various Types
            of Banks in Gross Deposit Totals
            (January 19, 1972)

Type of bank	Million pounds	Percentage of total	Other currencies	Percentage of total
Banks in the U.K., summary	22,409	100.00	24,485	100.00
Deposit banks:				
London clearing banks	11,971	53.42	508	2.07
Scottish clearing banks	1,112	4.96	23	0.09
Northern Ireland banks	309	1.37	18	0.07
Others	396	1.76	. . . .	. . . .
Accepting houses	1,621	7.23	1,816	7.41
Overseas banks:				
British and Commonwealth	2,171	9.68	4,372	17.85
American	1,462	6.52	11,486	46.91
Foreign banks and affiliates	597	2.66	2,511	10.25
Others	199	0.88	1,653	6.75
Other banks in U.K.	2,571	11.47	2,099	8.57

Source: Bank of England, *Quarterly Bulletin,* vol. 12, no. 1 (March
1972): 100–10.

Installment credit finance houses likewise have been subject to regulatory requests by the Bank of England concerning the amount of
their lending and are required under the terms of the 1971 credit
reform to maintain minimum obligatory holdings of reserve assets in
ratio to their deposits. This ratio is lower for the finance houses than
for the banks.

FINANCIAL INSTITUTIONS AND MARKETS

The various types of banks, the London discount houses, the finance
houses, and the markets in which all these operate are of primary

interest for our discussion of monetary and credit techniques and policies in the United Kingdom. The London clearing banks occupy the key position in the commercial banking structure. Following merger agreements in 1968, the number of London clearing banks has been reduced to six.[6] Four main branch banking systems dominate the category of London clearing banks. These are Barclays Bank Ltd., National Westminster Bank Ltd., Midland Bank Ltd., and Lloyds Bank Ltd. The London clearing banks held 53 per cent of sterling deposits in the deposit banks in the United Kingdom in January 1972, including the vast bulk of the sight deposits of individuals. They also operate the principal interbank clearing mechanism. Other banks clear interbank balances via this system on terms negotiated with the clearing bank that acts for them. These terms generally are less favorable than for the clearing banks themselves.

For many years, the competition of the London clearing banks with each other and with other financial institutions has been regulated by a variety of conventions and restrictive agreements in a frankly acknowledged cartel arrangement governing interest rates paid for deposits, charged on loans, and commissions charged for various banking services. Also for many years the clearing banks have issued only two types of deposit obligations: the "current account" (sight deposit), on which no interest is paid, and the "deposit account" (time deposit), on which interest has been paid at 2 per cent below the Bank of England's discount rate known as Bank rate. There is an earnings allowance on current account balances that is offset against activity charges, and there has been interbank competition in the form of provision of ancillary banking services and of convenience of branch location. Some breaching of the cartel's restriction on competition for time deposits has developed in recent years via merchant banking subsidiaries and other banking subsidiaries that have competed for larger time deposits at higher rates and longer maturities. Since the credit reform of 1971 (see below), the cartel prohibitions have begun to loosen somewhat further at the behest of the authorities.

Traditionally, the clearing banks have maintained an 8 per cent cash ratio against deposits. Cash assets include vault cash and deposit claims against the Bank of England. The clearing banks have also maintained in addition to the cash ratio a liquid asset ratio of no less than 20 per cent against deposits. Assets eligible for inclusion in the liquid asset category have included call loans to the discount houses, commercial bills, Treasury bills, and export finance paper with a maturity under eighteen months. Some tendency by the clearing banks to permit the combined ratio of cash and liquid assets to deposits to decline in the late 1940's and early 1950's led the Bank

[6] The six London clearing banks are Barclays Bank Ltd., Coutts and Co., Lloyds Bank Ltd., Midland Bank Ltd., National Westminster Bank Ltd., and William and Glyns Bank Ltd.

of England in 1955 to inform the banks that it expected them to maintain the ratio at or above 28 per cent. This provision also has been altered by the credit reform of September 1971. Other assets of the clearing banks consist of advances and overdrafts to commercial and industrial customers and for financing exports, personal loans, loans to local authorities, government ("gilt-edged") securities of longer maturities, and investments in affiliated banks and subsidiary installment finance houses.

The clearing banks' cartel has restrained its members' competition for banking business in a variety of ways. The clearing banks have limited their time deposits to those with a minimum withdrawal notice of seven days, refusing to accept deposits with explicitly longer minimum maturities. This self-restraint has kept them from competing directly with other financial institutions for longer-maturity and higher-interest time deposits from domestic depositors, and from receiving time deposits from nonresident holders who are willing to commit funds for longer than seven days in exchange for a higher rate of interest. (They have, however, competed for these longer-maturity deposits from large depositors via terms offered by their banking subsidiaries.) Clearing banks have refrained from entering the competition for Eurodollar deposits. They have stayed out of installment lending except through their subsidiaries. Only in recent years have they made commercial and industrial loans of medium and longer term. Although not legally barred from providing underwriting and investment trust services, the clearing banks have not done so until quite recently and then on only a modest scale. Traditionally the clearing banks have left the finance of foreign trade and associated business to the accepting houses and overseas banks. By request of the government, however, they have made certain export loans at rates so favorable as to constitute subsidies to the receiving industry. To ease this burden, the Bank of England has come to provide facilities for refinancing these export loans, and there are provisions for including certain of their elements within the liquidity ratio.[7]

The clearing banks adjust their cash position by lending call money to the discount houses or recalling it; they do not deal directly with the Bank of England, with each other, or with other banks. Traditionally the clearing banks also have not dealt directly in markets for short-term funds that have developed parallel to the money market provided by the activities of the discount houses. Thus, the clearing banks have not participated directly in the interbank loan market, nor the market for sterling certificates of deposit, nor have they placed funds in local authority deposits. Since the credit reform of 1971, the clearing banks have begun to operate directly in all these markets as well as in the Eurodollar market. In the past, however, the clearing banks have placed surplus cash by making call loans to the discount

---

[7] *Select Committee on Nationalised Industries,* pp. xxvii–xxviii.

houses, and the latter have made the placements in these other short-term markets. Call loans to the discount houses can be counted toward the clearing banks' liquid asset reserves, whereas direct loans to the parallel markets may not be.

For many years the clearing banks have not competed through interest charges for loans of the types they conventionally make. Collective agreements govern minimum rates charged to nationalized industries, local authorities, building societies, insurance companies, other first-class industrial and commercial borrowers, and hire purchase companies, and also rates charged for export and shipbuilding loans.[8] These rates have been essentially formula rates derived from the Bank rate set by the Bank of England as lender of last resort to the discount houses. For commercial and industrial borrowers not included in the above-mentioned categories and for all private borrowers, the clearing bank agreement has specified an adjustable minimum of Bank rate plus 0.5 per cent (the so-called blue chip rate), with an absolute minimum of 4.5 per cent. The Scottish banks also adhered to these rates, while the Northern Ireland banks used a related but somewhat different and more rigid schedule of agreed rates. The clearing banks also have had an agreed schedule of charges for depositor services and certain other financial services.[9]

A further set of conventions governs the relations of the clearing banks with the discount houses. These relations have been of key importance to the Bank of England's technique for controlling short-term rates of interest.

Deposit-taking and credit-granting institutions other than the clearing and deposit banks include the accepting houses, overseas and foreign banks, hire purchase finance companies, and the discount houses. These are the principal financial institutions that deal in the money and short-term credit markets both as borrowers and as lenders. Local authorities participate in the short-term markets primarily as net borrowers via their deposit obligations and by using their overdraft credits with the clearing banks. Building societies, trustee savings banks, insurance companies, pension funds, and investment and unit trusts are concerned primarily with longer-term savings and investments and with longer-term placements in mortgages, longer-term government gilt-edged stocks (that is, bonds), and capital market bonds and stocks of nationalized and private firms. The Bank of England in implementing monetary and credit policy has been concerned primarily with influencing the activities of the deposit-taking and short-term-credit-granting institutions. Moreover, it is these institutions whose role has expanded most at the expense of the clear-

[8] National Board for Prices and Incomes, Report No. 34, *Bank Charges* (Her Majesty's Stationery Office, Cmnd 3292: May 1967), chap. 5, pp. 36–39.

[9] Ibid.; chap. 6, pp. 40–47.

ing and deposit banks in recent years by taking competitive advantage of the latter's cartel practices to restrain competition.

The accepting houses have traditionally specialized in the financing of foreign trade but have greatly broadened their activities in the past two decades. From a traditional emphasis on bankers' acceptances and loans to the discount houses the accepting houses (known also as merchant banks) have broadened their business to make commercial and industrial loans and loans to local authorities, and they now hold securities of private firms as well as government securities in their investment portfolios. Their activities include factoring, rendering advice on company finance and on portfolio management, establishment of industrial holding companies to acquire equity interests in businesses, participation in consortia with other banks and insurance companies to provide medium-term loans to businesses, and provision of advice and facilities in floating new issues of stocks and bonds. Many of these are activities that the clearing banks have refrained from entering under their self-denying cartel ordinance. On the deposit side, the accepting houses provide their customers with current accounts as well as with time deposit accounts at longer maturities and higher deposit rates than those available on the seven-day notice accounts of the clearing banks. There is no legal barrier to the entry of an established merchant bank or accepting house into the business of providing current or checking accounts along with the other range of financial services offered. Since these banks do not belong to the London Clearing House, their access to its clearing facilities is at higher cost than that for its members. For this reason and because they are not branch banking systems, they do not pose a competitive threat to the clearing banks for current account business. Their primary sources of funds are their time deposits and their borrowings in the interbank market, the market for sterling certificates of deposit, and the market for Eurocurrencies.

Overseas banks (which are British banks traditionally specialized in overseas banking with branches in other countries) and foreign banks with branches in London have also in the past decade increased their domestic business both on the side of deposits and that of loans and investments. Like the accepting houses, these banks depend for funds primarily on the interbank, sterling certificate of deposit, and Eurocurrency markets. The Monopolies Commission investigated the role of the American banks when it was evaluating merger proposals among clearing banks, because the American banks constituted the most rapidly growing major component of the foreign banks in London. The commission found that:

> The American banks' main role in London is, therefore, in the Eurocurrency and interbank markets. In that part of their sterling business in which they compete directly with the clearing banks, rather than with their special subsidiaries and associates, the competition they offer is still largely

for international business, especially the international business of American-owned companies.[10]

The commission also found that the American banks held some 80 per cent of their deposits at interest, compared with only 40 per cent for the clearing banks, and that about 80 per cent of the loans of American banks was to American and other foreign-owned customers, with about 15 per cent to British customers.[11] The circumstances of the American banks relative to the clearing banks may be presumed to be broadly typical of the overseas and foreign banks as a class.

Other deposit-taking financial institutions that compete actively for funds in the short-term money and credit markets are the finance houses. The finance houses issue deposit obligations at competitive market rates of interest with maturity terms adjusted to depositor convenience. The finance houses are primarily engaged in financing installment credit. In the past decade, the clearing banks have increasingly acquired or organized finance houses as subsidiaries through which they could compete outside the cartel agreement for time deposits of longer maturities and higher rates while making installment loans at higher interest charges and longer maturities than was traditional for them.

Table 7.2 shows the relative importance of clearing banks and other categories of banks in gross sterling deposits in 1962 and again in 1972, and also compound annual rates of growth for the various categories over that decade. In interpreting the competitive inroads made on clearing banks by other banks, we should keep in mind the presence of clearing bank subsidiaries in the category "other banks in the U.K." It is important, likewise, to recall that competition between clearing banks and other types of banks on the deposit side has been primarily for time deposits. The clearing banks' branch banking networks and control of the London Clearing House gives them a big advantage in the competition for current or checking accounts. The national giro payments system operated by the Post Office began business in October 1968 and provides an alternative to the clearing banks for payments by check. However, it makes no customer loans, provides no ancillary banking services, and appears to "be of service to those who for one reason or another do not have bank accounts and to those companies and others that have to receive payments on an appreciable scale from, or to make them to, people without bank accounts." [12] Therefore, the national giro does little to remove the competitive advantage for current accounts that the clearing banks have relative to other banks. Its assets are held as cash, call loans to the

[10] The Monopolies Commission, *Barclays Bank Ltd., Lloyds Bank Ltd., and Martins Bank Ltd., a report on the proposed merger* (Her Majesty's Stationery Office: July 15, 1968), no. 319, p. 37.

[11] Ibid., pp. 36–37.

[12] Bank of England, *Quarterly Bulletin*, vol. 9, no. 1 (March 1969): 12.

TABLE 7.2   United Kingdom: Changes in Shares
of Various Types of Banks
in Gross Sterling Deposits (1962–72)

Type of bank	1962 [a] Million pounds	1962 [a] Per-centage of total	1972 [b] Million pounds	1972 [b] Per-centage of total	Compound annual rate of growth (percentage)
Deposit banks:					
London clearing banks	7,903	74.74	11,971	54.38	4.24
Scottish banks	842	7.96	1,112	5.05	2.82
Northern Ireland banks	171	1.61	309	1.40	6.09
Accepting houses	365	3.45	1,621	7.36	16.07
Overseas banks:					
British and Commonwealth	764	7.22	2,171	9.86	11.00
American	141	1.33	1,462	6.64	26.35
Foreign banks and affiliates	201	1.90	597	2.71	11.50
Others	147	1.39	199	0.90	3.07
Other banks in the U.K.[c]	39	0.36	2,571	11.67	52.02

[a] Bank of England, *Statistical Abstract*, no. 1 (1970) pp. 34–64. For deposit banks, the total deposit figure has been used, with no distinction between sterling and nonsterling deposits. No breakdown was available but this is not likely to cause any sizeable error since "... the clearing banks concentrated on domestic branch banking, their assets and liabilities in currencies other than sterling and their lending in the interbank and other specialized financial markets were too small to warrant special identification." Bank of England, *Quarterly Bulletin*, vol. 12, no. 1 (March 1972): 76. Figures are all end-of-year.

[b] *Quarterly Bulletin*, vol. 12, no. 1, pp. 101–10. Figures are all January 19, 1972.

[c] These "other banks" are listed in *Statistical Abstract*, no. 1, p. 67. A substantial share of this category appears to represent finance house subsidiaries of large deposit banks.

discount houses, temporary loans to local authorities, and other forms of government debt.[13]

Table 7.2 reveals a decline in the relative importance of the clearing banks in terms of their share of gross sterling deposits over the decade 1962–72. This is true even if the category of "other banks in the U.K." is attributed entirely to clearing bank subsidiaries, which it should not be. The comparatively more rapid growth in other types of banks has been attributed in part to the heavier burden of monetary controls on

[13] Ibid.

the clearing banks in the form of special deposits and ceilings on loan expansion imposed by the monetary authorities. But the restrictive practices of the clearing bank cartel must also share in the explanation. The relatively small share of the clearing banks in nonsterling deposits in 1972 shown in Table 7.1 indicates that their growth would compare even less favorably with that of other banks should the comparison embrace deposits in currencies other than sterling.

The financial *markets* of primary relevance for an understanding of British techniques of monetary and credit policy are the various short-term money markets and the markets for central government interest-bearing securities — Treasury bills and gilt-edged stocks (that is, bonds). At the core of the money market are the London discount houses that borrow call money from the clearing banks, make the market in Treasury bills, and deal in commercial bills and short-dated government stocks. They also borrow in the interbank and Eurocurrency markets and place funds in sterling certificates of deposit, in local authority deposits, and in nonsterling trade bills. The interbank and sterling certificate-of-deposit markets are used primarily by the non–clearing banks to redistribute excess cash and to borrow funds to be re-lent in their customer loan markets. Excess cash from the clearing banks also enters these markets when the discount houses, having borrowed at call from the clearing banks, make loans to other banks.

The international Eurodollar and Eurocurrency market has its primary institutional focus in London. The net foreign positions of banks domiciled in the United Kingdom are regulated so that they may convert Eurocurrencies to sterling for use in making domestic loans only within prescribed limits. However, until January 12, 1971, British nonbanks were freely permitted to borrow foreign currencies for conversion to sterling without limit, except for purposes for which banks had been asked to be especially restrictive in their domestic lending. Effective on that date such borrowing was limited to terms in excess of five years, a term chosen to prohibit short-term borrowing while permitting borrowing for capital investment.[14] Banks domiciled in the United Kingdom may and do borrow freely in the Eurocurrency market to relend in foreign currencies. The authorities do not specify cash or liquid asset reserves for Eurocurrency deposits, nor have they ever regulated nonsterling loans made with such funds. Some idea of the relative importance of foreign currency deposits for different types of banks may be gained from Table 7.1.

The local authorities obtain funds from the short-term money market by issuing deposit obligations in amounts and for maturities and interest rates that are competitive in the market and attractive to lenders seeking short-term placement of funds. The market for local authority deposits has developed primarily since 1955; in that year

[14] Bank of England, *Quarterly Bulletin,* vol. 11, no. 1 (March 1971): 8.

central government lending to the local authorities through the Public Works Loan Board was curtailed and made dependent on efforts by the local authorities to raise funds in the market. Banks other than clearing banks participate in this market and so do discount houses, financial institutions with orientation primarily to the capital market such as insurance companies and pension funds, commercial and industrial firms, and various foreign lenders.[15]

The remaining market of special importance for British techniques of monetary and credit policy is the market for long-dated gilt-edged stocks of the central government. The Bank of England is the agent of the Treasury for management of the national debt, and its refunding, maturity structure, and interest charges. Throughout the years since 1945, a primary objective of the Bank of England in managing the gilt-edged market has been to preserve the marketability of long-dated stocks. Until 1968, this aim was thought to be best served by maintaining stable prices and yields in the gilt-edged market so as to preserve the confidence of holders of the debt, protect the government's credit, and prevent speculative liquidation crises from occurring. Bank of England doctrine concerning the debt strongly endorsed the view that speculative behavior by investors tended to accentuate price movements in the gilt-edged market and thus act as a destabilizing element. A primary task for the Bank in managing the debt was, therefore, to prevent such destabilizing speculative forces from developing by being prepared to deal in outstanding gilt-edged stocks at prices within a narrow normal range: to sell on a rising market, to buy on a falling market, and to preserve investor confidence in ready marketability of gilt-edged stocks at prices within this narrow normal range.[16] Since 1968, the role of the Bank of England broker in the gilt-edged market has been modified to permit market forces to exert a greater influence on prices and yields. This change is a part of the trend away from selective credit controls toward market-oriented techniques of monetary policy.

TECHNIQUES OF MONETARY AND CREDIT POLICY

Throughout most of the period from the end of the Second World War to the credit reforms of 1971, the techniques of monetary control employed by the Bank of England came increasingly to be those of direct administrative intervention in financial markets. The roots of this system of controls go back at least to the formation of the discount house syndicate in 1934 and various conventions and practices

[15] See N. J. Gibson, *Financial Intermediaries and Monetary Policy*, 2nd ed., Hobart Paper No. 39, Institute of Economic Affairs, 1970.

[16] See "Official Transactions in the Gilt-Edged Market," Bank of England, *Quarterly Bulletin*, June 1966, pp. 141–48, especially pp. 146–48; and "The Operation of Monetary Policy since the Radcliffe Report," Bank of England, *Quarterly Bulletin*, December 1969, pp. 448–60, especially pp. 454–56.

then agreed on informally among the discount houses, the clearing banks, and the Bank of England to rescue the discount houses from extinction in the depressed market conditions of the 1930's. Portions of the system may go still further back to the period of great bank amalgamations in 1900–25 that established the large branch systems of clearing banks and led to the gradual introduction of cartel-like practices in commercial banking in England. The authorities' wartime experience with control over capital issues and with directives to the clearing banks to guide their lending may also have increased their inclination to use direct controls in the postwar period.

At the end of the war, in the mid-1940's, general price controls were in effect, access to capital markets was regulated by a Capital Issues Committee, an elaborate system of exchange controls was in operation, and the clearing banks were accustomed to receiving directives concerning their lending activities. The Bank of England possessed its classic instrument of Bank rate to govern the cost of discounting with it by the discount houses and managed for the Treasury a substantial public debt as a potential vehicle for open market operations. In addition, the entire structure of short-term interest rates through three months maturity was tied to Bank rate by conventions and agreements among the Bank of England, the clearing banks, and the discount houses. As indicated, the arrangements concerning short-term interest rates had emerged during 1934–35 to prevent the failure of a number of discount houses caught in a squeeze between the cost of borrowed money and very low yields on Treasury bills.

Most of the wartime price controls had been lifted by 1953, and the Capital Issues Committee control was suspended in 1959, but exchange regulations of varying degrees of severity have continued throughout the entire period from the mid-1940's to the present. With the relaxation of wartime controls, monetary and credit policy assumed a more active role beginning in 1951. At that time the principal policy instruments the Bank of England used were Bank rate, open market operations involved in management of the public debt via the Treasury bill tender as well as purchases and sales in the gilt-edged market, and reliance on maintenance by the clearing banks of traditional minimum ratios between holdings of cash and liquid assets on the one hand and their deposit liabilities on the other. No formal or traditional minimum cash or liquid asset ratios were in effect for other banks and financial institutions.

To these more or less traditional policy instruments of the central bank, other techniques were added during the decades of the 1950's and 1960's. The authorities asked the banks to limit the rate at which they expanded loans to the private sector, to restrict bank advances to those needed for essential purposes, to withhold credit for speculative purposes, and to limit finance for installment credit (on hire purchase credit the requests were based on statutory authority).

These requests were initially qualitative and limited to the clearing banks, but subsequently they were expressed quantitatively and were gradually broadened to cover other banks, discount houses, and hire purchase finance houses. Quantitative loan ceilings were employed in 1961 and almost continuously from 1965 until the credit reform of 1971. In 1961 also, the Bank of England broadened its request for restrictions on advances to include not only deposit banks but other banks and a wide range of financial institutions. Beginning in 1965, maximum rates of loan expansion were specified not only for all banks but also for finance houses. By the late 1960's, the Bank of England was sending information copies of requests, made to banks and finance houses, to associations of insurance companies, pension funds, building societies, and various commercial finance corporations, asking them to bear the Bank's objectives closely in mind in their lending operations; the Bank did not subject these institutions to formal ceilings, however. From 1962 on, the Bank of England persuaded the London clearing banks and the Scottish banks to undertake loans for financing exports and for shipbuilding on fixed-interest rate terms that with the passage of time became exceptionally favorable for the borrower.[17] These categories of loans and also loans to nationalized industry and to local authorities usually were exempt from the ceilings imposed on bank advances to the private sector.

In April 1960, the device of "Special Deposits" was introduced. This device was based on a voluntary agreement between the Bank of England and the clearing and Scottish banks. It provided for a transfer of a given percentage of the deposits of each of these to a frozen but interest-bearing account at the Bank of England on request of the latter. Calls for Special Deposits were at different percentages for the clearing banks as compared with the Scottish banks. Interest was paid on Special Deposits at the multiple of 1/16 per cent nearest to the average Treasury bill rate at the weekly tender of the preceding week.[18] Customarily, when Special Deposits were called, the Bank of England provided the necessary cash by purchasing the appropriate amount of government securities to be held in its Banking Department as an offsetting asset. Thus, from the perspective of debt management, Special Deposits represented, if indirectly via the Bank of England, a forced freezing of government securities from the security portfolios of banks. From the perspective of monetary and credit policy, a call for Special Deposits reduced the freely saleable liquid assets of the deposit banks and was intended thus to influence their lending policy.

[17] These arrangements were modified with effect from March 16, 1972, so as to formalize terms of access of the clearing banks to refinancing of such loans at the Bank of England and to replace the former fixed-interest rates with regulated rates variable from time to time by the government. (Bank of England, *Report and Accounts for the year ended 29 February 1972*, p. 37.)

[18] See "The Procedure of Special Deposits," Bank of England, *Quarterly Bulletin*, December 1960.

Increasingly over the decade of the 1960's, non-clearing banks and other financial institutions expanded their lending to borrowers whom the clearing banks were unable to accommodate. To increase the effectiveness of credit controls and to make such controls bear more equitably on the clearing banks and other banks and deposit-taking lenders, the authorities in 1967 established a Cash Deposits scheme for the merchant, overseas, and foreign banks to parallel the Special Deposits device applied to clearing and Scottish banks.[19] Moreover, these other banks as well as finance houses came to be included in the Bank's letters setting quantitative lending ceilings. In establishing the Cash Deposits scheme, the authorities took note of the diverse types of businesses and resulting liquidity needs of the merchant, overseas, and foreign banks, and reserved the right to set different Cash Deposits requirements for different institutions. If activated, the scheme would have required these banks to make Cash Deposits at the Bank of England in amounts determined as specified percentages of their principal deposit liabilities in sterling. Foreign currency deposits were exempt. The Bank undertook to pay interest on the Cash Deposits at the equivalent of the market rate on Treasury bills but reserved the right to pay less than this rate. For most of the institutions affected, either rate would have been lower than that on earning assets for which the Cash Deposits would have substituted and thus would have reduced earnings as a penalty measure. In any event, the Cash Deposits scheme was never activated and expired with the credit reform of September 1971. Its place was taken at that time by a required minimum reserve ratio for all banks.

In addition to these instruments of credit policy the Bank of England administered the system of foreign-exchange controls and operated the Exchange Equalisation Account, both of which can be used to influence domestic monetary and credit conditions by their influence on capital flows and thus the money supply. By regulating the types of capital flow transactions permitted and the net foreign position of banks, the Bank of England did seek to make these consistent with its domestic credit policies. On the other hand, the way in which the Exchange Equalisation Account was operated prevented deficits in the balance of payments from reducing bank liquidity and the money supply. Sterling withdrawn from the banking system and paid to the Exchange Equalisation Account to acquire foreign exchange for remittances abroad was returned immediately to the banking system by using it to purchase Treasury bills to help finance the central government deficit. So far as the supply of Treasury bills to the banks was reduced by this procedure, their liquidity ratio was impaired. Subsequent efforts by the banks to restore their liquidity ratio tended to raise interest rates and depress prices of gilt-edged government stocks as banks contracted advances and sold gilt-edged

---

[19] See "Control of Bank Lending: The Cash Deposits Scheme," Bank of England, *Quarterly Bulletin,* June 1968, pp. 166–70.

securities. By purchasing gilt-edged securities to support their price, the Bank of England then restored liquidity to the banking system and neutralized the decline in domestic money supply that would otherwise have resulted from the balance-of-payments deficit. Thus, the balance-of-payments deficits did nothing to help check excessive expansion of the domestic money supply.

Other controls that influenced credit conditions in the period 1950–72 were regulation by the Board of Trade of down payments and maturities for consumer installment (hire purchase) credit and direct control by the government through the Treasury over the amount that local authorities, nationalized industries, and the central government could borrow.[20]

MONETARY AND CREDIT CONTROLS IN THE PREREFORM ERA (ca. 1951–1971)

The postwar history of British monetary policy until the credit reform of 1971 is the history of attempts to restrain aggregate demand without effective use of general monetary policy. Control of the money supply has not been a major concern of the Bank of England and the Treasury in postwar Britain. Evidence is manifold in the form of policy statements by officials; lack of interest in the collection and publication of official statistics on the money supply until 1966 and later; disregard for the money supply as an important variable in theoretical analyses; and the simple record of significant growth in the money supply, even during periods when the authorities believed they were vigorously restraining aggregate demand by monetary measures such as high levels of Bank rate, restraints on bank lending, Special Deposits, and hire purchase controls. Instead, the monetary authorities chose to rely on their set of conventional controls over short-term rates of interest, in combination with a gradually expanding supplementary set of direct credit controls that focused on lending by banks and other financial institutions.

At the root of official reluctance to rely on conventional monetary techniques such as Bank rate and open market policy to control the money supply was unwillingness to raise interest rates high enough to prevent monetization of government debt by the banking system, that is, to increase nonbank purchase of government securities. Behind this reluctance to raise interest rates were other concerns of the authorities: (1) a concern with maintaining government credit and public confidence in outstanding government securities; (2) a desire to keep down the interest burden (including the burden on the balance of payments) of financing the government debt at high interest rates; and (3) a set of policy objectives that stressed the need to meet urgent and long-deferred needs for schools, hospitals, and homes,

[20] Cf. National Board for Prices and Incomes, p. 37.

for the modernization of manufacturing industry, and for the encouragement of exports. The commitment of successive governments to social goals requiring government finance, together with the postwar nationalization of basic industries in Britain, has kept the volume of government and government-guaranteed debt high and has intensified concern with government credit, debt management, and the interest burden.

These inhibitions on general monetary policy as viewed by the authorities were supported and strengthened by the theoretical and conceptual views of the *Radcliffe Report* and other related writings. These theoretical views direct attention to the structure of interest rates, the maturity composition of the national debt, and credit flows as key variables in aggregate demand management. The money supply and the monetary and wealth effects of an overall government deficit are assigned almost incidental roles. In these circumstances, the authorities resorted increasingly to direct and selective controls in the two decades leading up to the credit reform of 1971. In effect, an entire system of such controls gradually developed to supplant the market-oriented and indirect techniques of intervention traditionally employed by the Bank of England. Paradoxically, it has been virtually impossible to find a comprehensive account of the new set of administrative controls viewed as an integrated system. Authoritative accounts of the techniques of British monetary policy have continued to stress the traditional policy instruments of Bank rate and open market operations as central, while treating new techniques as temporary anomalies adopted under the stress of emergency situations — all too frequent in recent years. Only in the discussions immediately preceding the credit reform of 1971 was the official line modified to acknowledge the inadequacy of the credit controls, their ill effects, and the need for greater reliance on control of the money supply coupled with the operation of financial markets less hampered by conventional and formal restraints on competition.

The key components of the system of credit controls as it operated prior to the reform were the Bank of England, the discount houses, the clearing banks, and the Treasury bill and gilt-edged markets for government securities. Other financial institutions and financial markets interacted with these components of the controlled system. Description and analysis of the way in which the system of credit controls actually functioned is complicated by the existence of informal understandings and agreements that effectively and systematically modified the business behavior of the clearing banks and discount houses away from the norms of short-run profit maximization. Thus one cannot understand the functioning of the system of credit controls by starting from the structure of institutions and markets and deducing behavior on the usual assumption of enlightened self-interest constrained only by formal regulations and prescriptions by the authorities. The formal and clearly defined rules of behavior are supplemented by informal agreements and conventions whose details and implications usually have not been made clear. Analysis of the functioning of the system reaches one set of conclusions when these informal aspects are ignored and a different set of conclusions when they are included. The metamorphosis of the market-oriented system into the credit-controlled system occurred gradually over the period from the mid-1930's on, with little outward change in institutions and markets and without public discussion and analysis on the part of the authorities of the significance of the changes taking place. The development was further masked by a theoretical doctrine, exemplified by the *Radcliffe Report,* that misinterpreted and obscured the workings of monetary policy in the institutional and regulatory environment of the United Kingdom.

Although the Bank of England is obviously the institution that operated the system of credit controls, the clearing bank cartel provides the key to understanding how the system functioned. The clearing bank cartel, with the sanction of the Bank of England, established the types and terms of clearing bank deposits, the pattern of lending rates on clearing bank loans, the form and degree of clearing bank participation in the market for Treasury bills and in other short-term credit markets, and the special relationship of the clearing banks to the London discount houses. By tying their deposit and lending rates to Bank rate by conventional differentials, the clearing banks provided the Bank of England with means for setting a network of short-term rates at desired levels. By withdrawing from competition with the discount houses for Treasury bills and honoring market prices on these bills that had been established by the discount houses, the clearing banks gave their support to the special role played by the discount houses in the Treasury bill and short-term money markets. Moreover, by continuing to lend call money to the discount houses at rates that permitted the latter to hold Treasury bills at a profit, the clearing banks in effect subsidized the discount houses on those occasions on which the Bank of England, by refusing to raise Bank rates, saw fit to keep controlled short-term rates, including the Treasury bill rate, below the levels that conditions would have established in free markets. In so doing, the clearing banks obviously departed from the goal of short-run profit maximization.

In this constrained behavior, the clearing banks were motivated partly by fear and partly by favor. By cooperating informally with the Bank of England, they made it unnecessary for the Bank to seek a more formalized and therefore more rigid set of rules and regulations to guide their behavior. Moreover, had they refused to cooperate, there was the possible threat of nationalization, a contingency not entirely remote under the Labor government. As to favor, one feature of the cartel arrangement sanctioned by the monetary authorities was the practice of paying no interest on sight deposits and of limiting interest rate competition for clearing bank notice or time deposits. Another was the absence of competition among clearing banks by means of interest rates for customer loans. Eventually other financial institutions and markets made competitive inroads on the clearing banks' cartel. But for a considerable period, there may have been a monopoly element in clearing bank profits as a result of their restrictive practices.[21] The authorities sought to shelter the clearing banks from some of the inroads made by other institutions at their expense when they extended quantitative loan ceilings to include other banks and finance houses and sent advisory copies of their requests for loan expansion limits to associations for insurance companies, pension funds, investment trusts, and the like. The latter capital market institutions were largely unreachable by the Bank of England in any more formal manner under existing legislation.

With this general orientation, we now turn to a more detailed account of the system of credit controls with particular attention to controls over short-term interest rates. Here the relationships among the Bank of England, the discount houses, and the clearing banks were of central importance. Deposit and lending rates of the clearing banks were tied to Bank rate by agreed differentials. The clearing banks paid (and pay) no interest on sight deposits. Until the credit reform, the only other deposit they accepted was a seven-day notice deposit on which interest was paid at 2 per cent below Bank rate. The official report on bank charges, cited above, summarizes the effect of the clearing banks' collective agreements on *lending* rates as follows:

... With the exception of personal loans extended on an installment basis, the variation in effective advances rates is largely contained within the range from Bank rate to Bank rate + 2 per cent. ...

It can be seen that the effect of these agreements is to lay down an agreed rate to be charged to certain specified borrowers — nationalised industries, local authorities, insurance companies, and building societies, to specify a minimum rate for hire purchase companies, and — because there appears to be no agreed definition of "first class" industrial and commercial borrowers—to specify a minimum rate, the so-called blue chip rate, for other borrowers. In addition there is a special agreement with respect to export loans; this falls into a different category from the others, having been obtained through the special mediation of the Bank of England.

Within the framework provided by these agreements the banks compete for advances business aggressively. That is, they seek out such business competitively and can bid down the rates to the minimum levels agreed for certain types of borrowers. Nevertheless, the framework of agreements inhibits rate competition by specifying the actual rates to be charged to

[21] See National Board for Prices and Incomes, *passim*, especially chap. 9, pp. 59–62; and Brian Griffiths, "The Welfare Cost of the U.K. Clearing Banks' Cartel," *Journal of Money, Credit, and Banking*, vol. 4, no. 2 (May 1972): 227–44.

certain classes of borrowers and by setting a floor to the rates to be charged for other classes of borrowers.[22]

All of the clearing bank lending rates mentioned above and their rate on notice deposits changed by stipulated amounts when Bank rate changed. This practice may appear to be merely a formalization of results that could be expected to occur as market forces reacted to a change in the cost of credit from the central bank. However, the matter is not that simple, since clearing bank deposit and lending rates of interest changed *only when Bank rate changed* regardless of market conditions. To understand the working of the system, it is necessary to incorporate the effects of the Bank of England's operations in the Treasury bill and gilt-edged markets, of the operation of other banks and credit institutions in parallel credit markets, and of demand for credit by various types of borrowers, including the central government and local authorities.

The *discount houses* are an important operational link in the monetary and credit system in the United Kingdom, but their independent influence on monetary and credit developments is virtually nil. They are closely circumscribed in their activities by their dependence on the clearing banks and on the Bank of England. The discount houses have traditionally been the central institutions in the short-term money market in the United Kingdom. In this role, their functions have included (1) purchase of new Treasury bills from the Bank of England at its weekly tender and subsequent resale of these Treasury bills to clearing banks and other purchasers; (2) redistribution of short-term liquid funds among the clearing banks and between these and other segments of the money market; (3) having the exclusive privilege (apart from three money brokers) of borrowing from the Bank of England; [23] (4) being the primary discounters of commercial and trade bills; and (5) dealing in and holding a portfolio of short-dated government stocks and commercial bills. The discount houses finance their portfolio of Treasury and commercial bills and short-dated government stocks by borrowing at call on a secured basis primarily from the clearing banks, to a lesser extent from other banks and firms, and marginally from the Bank of England. In recent years with the permission of the Bank of England they have also held a portfolio of sterling certificates of deposit financed by borrowing in the interbank market and of dollar and foreign currency bills financed by loans from the Eurodollar market.

Under this system, the link between the so-called "market rate" on Treasury bills and Bank rate was established via the rate charged by the clearing banks on call loans to the discount houses. The agreed minimum rate at which clearing banks lent money to the discount

[22] *Bank Charges*, pp. 36–37.
[23] Three new firms of stockholders were recognized as money brokers by the Bank of England in July 1972.

houses was Bank rate less 1⅝ per cent. The discount houses financed
their portfolio of Treasury bills and short-dated government stocks primarily by call loans from the clearing banks at this rate, known as "the
basic rate." In balancing their portfolios at the end of the day, the discount houses also could rely on the clearing banks for marginal sums
at a higher "privileged rate." Alternatively, if they found themselves
with excess cash, the discount houses could buy Treasury bills from
the Bank of England to hold overnight.

The discount houses obtained additional financing for their portfolio from the clearing banks and from other banks and firms at a
variable rate of interest determined in the interbank money market.
The proportions of the funds the discount houses obtained from the
clearing banks at the basic rate, the interbank market rate, and the
privileged rate varied for different houses and clearing banks, depending on personal relations, tradition, and market conditions. The
clearing banks informed the discount houses daily what they thought
the average cost of money to the latter would be. These practices
established the cost to the discount houses of carrying their portfolio
of Treasury bills. It should be clear that the average cost of funds to
the discount houses depended on decisions made by the clearing banks
and tied to Bank rate.

To see how this system determined the maximum yield on Treasury
bills both "at the tender" and "in the market," we must examine some
further practices. New Treasury bills are offered for bid by the Bank
of England at a weekly tender that takes place on Friday. The amount
to be offered is announced one week in advance. The Bank of England
accepts bids on these bills from four sources: the discount houses, the
clearing banks placing bids for their customers who wish to purchase
new bills, "other" banks, and foreign official monetary institutions
(for example, central banks and international monetary institutions).
The latter group's bid is placed by the Bank of England on their behalf. The clearing banks do not tender for bills for their own portfolios
but purchase bills from the discount houses after the latter have held
them for at least seven days. The discount houses had a commitment
to cover the tender (that is, serve as residual buyer for the entire
issue) at a syndicate price agreed on and submitted jointly by the
discount houses. Since bills are sold on a discount basis, the price paid
for them determines their yield. The Bank of England allotted bills to
highest bidders in descending order until the issue was exhausted.
Thus, the bid by the discount houses syndicate set the minimum price
and maximum yield at which bills were awarded at the tender unless
the issue should be exhausted by allotments to "outside tenderers"
before the price offered by the syndicate was reached. This has rarely
been the case. Accordingly, the "tender rate" on Treasury bills was
effectively the rate established by the bid of the discount house
syndicate.

The "market rate" on Treasury bills was the rate at which the discount houses sold bills to the clearing banks and such others as might wish to purchase them. The "market rate" on newly issued Treasury bills was set by the discount houses on Monday at ⅛ per cent below the "tender rate" of the previous Friday. Bills with less than three months to maturity had prices and yields adjusted to their maturity. The clearing banks would not buy bills at yields lower than Bank rate less 1⅝ per cent, that is, their minimum lending rate to the discount houses. The discount houses could not afford to tender at a price such that the effective yield on Treasury bills at the tender fell below Bank rate less 1⅝ per cent, or they would lose money on the carry. Thus the *minimum* tender and market rates on Treasury bills were firmly anchored to Bank rate.

It is important to recognize that the expression "market rate" in this context meant precisely the rate at which Treasury bills could be purchased from the discount houses. It was not a rate freely determined by supply and demand in a competitive market. Normally, any buyer or seller of outstanding Treasury bills had to deal with a discount house, since these provided the only organized market in Treasury bills. Clearing banks normally held Treasury bills that they had purchased from the discount houses until the bills matured. The clearing banks on occasion purchased or sold outstanding bills as an accommodation to a customer. In doing so, they did *not* depart from the prices and yields established by the discount houses.

What were the implications of these practices for the control exercised by the Bank of England over short-term rates of interest? We have seen that the level and structure of clearing bank deposit and lending rates were pegged to Bank rate, moved by predictable amounts when Bank rate changed, and *only* when Bank rate changed. The tender and market rates on Treasury bills were bracketed by Bank rate as a maximum and Bank rate less 1⅝ per cent as a minimum. Within that band they could move up and down slightly in response to the cost of borrowed money to the discount houses. This cost was directly determined by the amounts of call money lent to the discount houses at the basic and higher rates of interest by the clearing banks. It was indirectly influenced by operations of the Bank of England to increase or decrease liquidity in the banking system. Among these operations were varying the size of the weekly Treasury bill issue; the purchase and sale of outstanding Treasury bills by the Bank of England in transactions with the discount houses, bill brokers, and clearing banks; seven-day and shorter loans by the Bank of England to the discount houses and bill brokers; and purchase and sale of gilt-edged government debt by the Bank of England via its broker. By selling government debt, especially by setting the Treasury bill tender above the amount of finance needed, the Bank of England could decrease liquidity, cause interbank and other nonregulated interest rates to rise, and force the discount houses to resort to borrowing at Bank rate, a penalty rate above the Treasury bill rate, when the clearing banks reduced their call loans to the discount houses. This was the usual procedure followed by the Bank when it wished to give a signal to the discount houses to raise the tender and "market" rates at the next Treasury bill tender while remaining within the band established by an unchanged level of Bank rate. By reversing the procedure just described, the Bank could give an opposite signal to achieve a modest reduction in the Treasury bill tender and "market" rates.

More interesting is the situation that occurred when a strong demand for credit developed in the economy, accompanied by a tendency for interest rates to rise in markets outside or parallel to those in which interest rates were covered by the network of agreements and conventions tied to Bank rate. Among the interest rates outside the network rigidly tied to Bank rate were those on interbank funds and sterling certificates of deposit; on local authority deposits; on deposits and loans by merchant banks, overseas banks, and foreign banks; and on loans by finance houses; and the yield on gilt-edged government securities. The Eurodollar market also has exerted an important influence on domestic credit conditions in the United Kingdom.

An increase in demand for credit caused an increase in interest rates in these uncontrolled markets as well as an increase in loan demand at the clearing banks. In the competition for deposit-type funds to meet these increased demands for loans, the clearing banks were hampered by their agreement to pay no interest on sight deposits and to fix their interest rate on notice deposits at 2 per cent below Bank rate. They responded to competition for deposits partly by organizing banking subsidiaries to compete indirectly for time deposits at higher rates of interest than permitted by the cartel arrangements. In part, however, the clearing banks experienced a steady erosion in their share in total loans and deposits of credit institutions (see Table 7.2). In these circumstances, when faced by strong demand for loans by their customers, a sensible response of the clearing banks was to reduce their marketable government securities holdings and concentrate on an increase in customer loans.

The clearing banks' reduction of Treasury bill holdings faced two restraining influences in these circumstances. The first was their need to maintain their required minimum liquidity ratio of 28 per cent of their deposits. Treasury bills along with call loans to the discount houses, commercial bills, bankers' acceptances, and cash are the principal assets eligible to satisfy the liquidity ratio.

A second restraining influence came into play on those occasions when the Bank of England sought to hold down short-term interest rates by refusing to raise Bank rate as credit demands in the economy increased. With the peg of Bank rate unchanged, the tender and market rates on Treasury bills would have risen above Bank rate in response to market forces, but the clearing banks were committed to lend call money to the discount houses at 1⅝ per cent below Bank rate. Moreover, the discount houses were in turn pledged to cover the Treasury bill tender. Thus, a ceiling was established for the Treasury bill yield at the level of the rate implied by the syndicate bid of the discount houses. This bid level was in turn based on a differential above the cost of borrowed money to the discount houses.

By continuing to supply the discount houses with the bulk of their call money at Bank rate less 1⅝ per cent, the clearing banks kept the tender and market rates on Treasury bills at their customary level below Bank rate. Since these rates were below market-determined rates on competing short-term assets such as interbank deposits, sterling certificates of deposit, and local authority deposits, the demand for Treasury bills by outside tenderers tended to decline, so that few investors willing to hold Treasury bills could be found outside the clearing banks, discount houses, and foreign official monetary institutions. This was the situation during various periods in the 1960's when the Bank of England sought to hold down short-term interest rates to prevent upward pressure on yields (downward pressure on prices) in the gilt-edged market for government securities.

This system of conventions and informal agreements gave the Bank of England firm control over a network of short-term interest rates extending out to three months maturity. The system depended on extensive cooperation by the clearing banks. These made call loans to the discount houses at interest rates below competitive market levels and in amounts sufficient for the discount houses to continue to fulfill their pledge to cover the Treasury bill tender without incurring losses on the carry.[24] Moreover, the clearing banks — through their own purchases of Treasury bills, their call loans to the discount houses, and their observance in Treasury bill transactions with their customers of the market price on Treasury bills established by the discount houses — practiced a price support policy for Treasury bills to keep their yield tied to Bank rate.

The network of short-term rates controlled by the Bank of England via Bank rate and these conventional arrangements influenced other short-term interest rates via arbitrage. During periods of strong demand for credit, borrowers would first seek accommodation at the clearing banks, and would turn to other lenders (for example, other banks, finance houses, and capital market institutions) only after obtaining all the credit they could from the clearing banks. One source of funds to the clearing banks to help meet this loan demand from customers was liquidation of their holdings of gilt-edged government securities. The authorities responded to this leakage in the system of credit controls by establishing quantitative ceilings to regulate clearing bank loan expansion. The imposition of loan ceilings gave the

---

[24] For discussion and some quantitative evidence bearing on this practice, see G. O. Nwankwo, "The New Monetary Regulation and the London Discount Market," *The Bankers Magazine,* June 1972, pp. 279–83.

authorities control over both the maximum quantity for clearing bank loans and their interest rates. By exempting certain categories of loans from the ceilings, the authorities could then have an allocative effect on clearing bank credit while reducing the upward pressure on the interest charged to priority recipients of credit and on government debt. Exports, shipbuilding, nationalized industries, and local authorities all received favorable treatment under loan ceilings and directives concerning priority borrowers. When necessary, spending by nationalized industries and local authorities was controlled by administrative measures.

Under this system of credit controls, the clearing banks were prevented from maximizing their profits because they were unable to allocate credits to the highest potential bidders and because they were required to support the Treasury bill and gilt-edged markets in government securities. Witness this exchange between Mr. D. J. Robarts, then-president of the British Bankers Association and chairman of the Committee of London Clearing Bankers and the Select Committee on Nationalised Industries, during the latter's investigation of the Bank of England in 1969:

> Q. We now pass on to credit control. The ceilings on bank lending have no statutory force and the authorities, that is to say, the Bank of England, rely largely on — they use the word *suasion* instead of *persuasion*, which I am told is stronger, though I am not sure about that. Are the clearing banks satisfied with this method of controlling credit or would you sooner this was dealt with in a more precise manner?
>
> A. We think this is as good a machine as one can get because we try as hard as we can to carry out what the Bank of England asks us to do. We realize that we have a very big public responsibility in that we take all our money from the public and we must discharge our duty in that way. *Of course, sometimes there is no doubt that what we are asked to do is not in the interests of our shareholders in the short term,* but I think we can always say that in the long term the interests of the banks and the shareholders and the general public more or less coincide. Therefore, it is right for us to do these things. [Italics added.] [25]

This statement is quoted here to support our assertion that the clearing banks have had to forgo profit-maximizing behavior to support the credit (and interest rate) control schemes of the monetary authorities. Mr. Robart's acceptance of the coincidence of bank and public interests in the long term does not face the issue of how the burden of nurturing these common interests should be shared among the beneficiaries.

To assess the effects and effectiveness of the Bank of England's policy to restrict and allocate credit while keeping the network of regulated short-term interest rates below their market equilibria, we must consider the behavior of lenders and borrowers in credit markets

[25] *Select Committee on Nationalised Industries,* p. 81, para. 623.

other than those in the network directly tied to Bank rate. The more important of these markets are the interbank market and that for sterling certificates of deposit, the customer loan market for merchant banks, overseas banks, and foreign banks, the markets for deposits and loans of finance houses, the local authorities deposits market, and the market for gilt-edged government securities.

All of these markets are linked by substitution effects and arbitrage to the more strictly controlled markets. The general effect of controls over the clearing banks, the discount houses, and the Treasury bill market throughout the decade of the 1960's has been to expand the absolute and relative share of total credit flowing through these other markets. The diversion of credit flows to these other channels has produced a variety of effects. The interbank and sterling certificate of deposit markets are the primary domestic source of loanable funds for the non–clearing banks. These banks also have obtained loanable funds in the Eurodollar market for conversion into sterling within limits established by exchange controls. Until the credit reform of September 1971, the clearing banks did not participate in these markets. However, excess liquidity of the clearing banks lent to the discount houses on call sometimes was placed in the interbank or sterling CD markets by the discount houses. The other banks could pay higher rates on deposits than the controlled rates paid by clearing banks and suit deposit maturities to customer preference, and so could attract deposits from the clearing banks and expand loans at clearing bank expense. Local authorities and finance houses likewise attracted deposits from the clearing banks. The local authorities borrowed (in anticipation of later revenue) primarily to invest in housing, schools, hospitals, and similar projects. The finance houses borrowed to make consumer installment (hire purchase) and commercial loans with maturities some of which exceeded the conventional short maturities on clearing bank commercial loans.

The growth in importance of these other credit channels threatened both the competitive position of the clearing banks and the effectiveness of the authorities' system of credit allocation and interest rate controls. The clearing banks responded by organizing or acquiring banking and finance house subsidiaries to compete more freely for large, interest-sensitive deposits and to make longer-term installment and commercial loans. The authorities responded by extending the credit ceilings to include other banks and then finance houses, by developing the Cash Deposits required-reserve scheme for non–clearing banks, and finally by the credit reform of 1971. The familiar phenomenon of escalation of controls in response to evasion of existing controls is clearly evident in this pattern. So likewise are the familiar disadvantages of controls in the form of stifling of competition, protection for inefficient firms, and development of practices and organizations whose chief raison d'être is to escape controls so that organizational inefficiency results in waste of resources.

There was one other major defect in the system of controls used by the Bank of England. This was the authorities' policy with respect to prices and yields in the market for gilt-edged government securities. One purpose of the authorities' efforts to hold down short-term interest rates was to prevent a rise in short rates from being communicated to gilt-edged yields via market arbitrage and substitution effects. There were two considerations that the authorities felt dictated a policy to maintain low and stable interest yields on gilt-edged securities. One of these was to maintain investor confidence in the price stability and marketability of the large amounts of gilt-edged debt outstanding throughout the years from the end of the second world war in 1945. The second was to keep down the level of long-term interest rates generally so as to encourage productive capital investment in the economy and the low-cost financing of housing, schools, hospitals, and other forms of social overhead capital. In the end, the authorities' gilt-edged strategy was defeated by market forces but not before the emergence of several important undesirable consequences, including domestic inflation and devaluation of the foreign-exchange value of the pound sterling.

Throughout most of the years since the late 1940's, the authorities held with great conviction and tenacity the view that price stability was essential in maintaining investor confidence and willingness to hold the large amount of long-term government debt outstanding. They feared that a price decline accompanying a rise in yields on the gilt-edged debt would arouse investor expectations of a further decline and would precipitate a liquidation crisis by investors seeking to avoid capital losses. In these circumstances, they foresaw the Bank of England, as lender of last resort, having to purchase large amounts of debt for cash to prevent a general collapse of the financial system. Better, then, to hold gilt-edged prices fairly steady by the government broker's judicious intervention on the weak side of the market and thus avoid the risk of having either to flood the economy with liquidity or to experience financial chaos. On balance throughout the past two decades, this strategy has resulted in persistent support purchases of gilt-edged debt by the Bank of England accompanied by an expansion of the money supply that has worked against the evolving system of credit controls developed by the Bank of England to restrain credit, aggregate demand, and inflationary pressures.

Downward pressure on prices of gilt-edged securities (upward pressure on yields) arose in part from substitution effects consequent on short-term credit controls during periods of rising demand for credit, and in part from an increase in the quantity of government and government-guaranteed debt outstanding due to central government budget deficits and the borrowing needs of local authorities and nationalized industries. Thus, the system of short-term credit controls tended to shift the pressure of excess demand to the longer-term markets in the form of an increase in the supply of privately issued capital market securities accompanied by a reduced investor demand for gilt-edged government securities at fixed and less attractive yields. The growth in government debt by increasing the supply of gilt-edged securities outstanding added to the excess supply in the gilt-edged market. Purchases of gilt-edged securities by the Bank of England to support their prices added to the money supply and to inflationary pressures in the economy. Once investors began to anticipate further inflation, they began to require higher yields on long-term fixed-interest securities as compensation for the inflationary trend. In these circumstances the authorities' price support policy became clearly untenable because it was self-defeating. This is the background to abandonment of the credit control system and the positive steps of credit reform in 1971. (See the next section.)

Our emphasis thus far has been on the way the system of credit controls operated to keep interest rates below their market equilibrium levels in periods of economic expansion, with growing demands for credit. The strategy of the Bank of England for achieving this result was to refuse to raise Bank rate, so that the network of clearing bank and Treasury bill rates would not rise. On occasion, Bank rate was raised, sometimes drastically. The devaluation crisis of 1967 was preceded and followed by such increases in bank rate, accompanied by an immediate rise in the other short-term rates linked to it. When the system was operated in this alternate fashion, the response of managed short-term interest rates was immediate. Moreover, competitive substitution effects communicated the influence of these rate changes to the interbank, other bank, and local authority markets as well as to the gilt-edged market. This increase in clearing bank interest charges on loans (except for export and shipbuilding loans) reduced the reliance on nonprice rationing of credit but surely did not eliminate it, save for short recessionary intervals of slack loan demand. Moreover, from 1965 to 1971, loan ceilings were almost continuously in force for clearing banks, other banks, discount houses, and finance houses. Thus, these markets were not permitted to move to their equilibrium price-quantity relationships. Even at higher levels of Bank rate and related managed rates, the excess demand for credit was not removed, and it tended to spill over into the longer-term market. As longer-term investors such as insurance companies and pension funds responded to private sector demand in the longer-term market, they reduced purchases and sold gilt-edged government securities. In response to this weakness on the demand side of the gilt-edged market, the Bank of England usually bought gilt-edged securities, thus supplying cash to the market.

Here then was the Achilles heel of monetary policy in the United Kingdom prior to the credit reform of 1971. Having ceased to rely on price rationing of credit coupled with control of the money supply, the authorities were forced to use quantity rationing in an attempt to control credit flows and aggregate demand. But adaptive behavior by financial institutions and markets made existing controls less and less effective, provoking the authorities to a further extension of quantitative controls and direct regulation, and less reliance on market behavior. Basically, an expanding system of credit controls came to replace monetary policy as a check on the inflationary impact of deficit finance by the public sector in the form of heavy borrowing by the central government, local authorities, and nationalized industries.

The logic of such a system leads inevitably from partial to more comprehensive direct controls. No system of partial credit controls can prevent inflation so long as the authorities continue to permit the money supply to expand at a rate substantially in excess of that of the real gross national product. Yet this is what has happened in the United Kingdom as shown in Table 7.3.

TABLE 7.3 United Kingdom: Money Supply, Real GNP, and Price Indexes (annual percentage changes)

Year	Money supply [a] (% change)	Real GNP [b] (% change)	GNP deflator [c] (% change)	Retail prices [d] (% change)	Wholesale prices [e] (% change)
1960	....	....	....	....	....
1961	2.60	3.59	3.28	3.43	2.29
1962	2.66	1.29	3.34	2.62	1.98
1963	6.57	3.99	2.15	1.96	1.27
1964	5.15	5.22	2.62	3.28	2.70
1965	7.61	2.77	4.00	4.76	3.31
1966	4.13	1.76	3.44	3.92	3.20
1967	10.59	1.78	3.68	2.48	1.46
1968	7.24	2.84	2.83	4.69	5.04
1969	2.87	1.34	3.44	5.44	3.68
Compound Annual Rate of Growth					
	5.46	2.72	3.20	2.89	2.76

[a] Notes, coins, private sector deposits with banks and discount houses, public sector deposits with banks, minus transient items. 1961–63 figures calculated from Bank of England, *Statistical Abstract*, 1970, p. 78; and *Supplement to the Bank of England Quarterly Bulletin*, September 1968, p. 379. 1963–69 figures calculated from *Statistical Abstract*, p. 78.

[b] Calculated from Central Statistical Office, *Annual Abstract of Statistics*, 1970, p. 286.

[c] Calculated from real GNP and GNP at current prices series in *Annual Abstract of Statistics*, p. 279.

[d] Calculated from *Annual Abstract of Statistics*, p. 363.

[e] Figures calculated from *Annual Abstract of Statistics:* 1960–62 figures from 1967, p. 329; 1962–69 figures from 1970, p. 365.

THE CONCEPTUAL BASIS FOR
POSTWAR MONETARY POLICY

In their approach to monetary and credit policy in the years from 1945 to the late 1960's, the authorities were influenced and their actions endorsed by a set of views concerning the role of monetary policy in aggregate-demand management that found its most comprehensive expression in the famous *Report* made by the Treasury Committee on the Working of the Monetary System in 1959, known as the *Radcliffe Report*.[26] This document expressed the prevailing official view of how monetary policy works and what its limits are, and was endorsed by a substantial segment of the academic economics profession also. As recently as 1969, in an authoritative review of "The Operation of Monetary Policy since the Radcliffe Report," prepared by the Bank of England in consultation with the Treasury, there is mention of "considerable evolution in the methods and tactics of monetary policy," followed by this statement:

> Broadly, however, the approach to policy has been similar to that of the Radcliffe Committee in that the authorities have consistently believed that it was right to pay attention to and try to understand the general financial position of all sectors of the economy and insufficient to concentrate exclusively on a single variable such as the quantity of money, however that may be defined.[27]

This statement is quoted here for its explicit and recent acknowledgement that policy has been guided by views broadly similar to those of the Radcliffe Committee, which regarded the money supply as only of incidental importance. Official spokesmen are reticent in public regarding the theoretical rationale for monetary policy. Thus, the acknowledged similarity is useful, since it permits us to refer to the theoretical rationale for monetary policy contained in the *Radcliffe Report* and related writings as a basis for understanding official views on monetary and credit policy.

The *Radcliffe Report* was embroiled in controversy promptly following its publication, and much has been written both in criticism and in defense of it. For our purposes, it is sufficient to refer to a few of the key ideas and viewpoints contained within it or omitted from it. Its key conceptual deficiency is omission from its analysis of monetary policy of the monetary and wealth effects of a deficit in the budget of the government sector. Thus, its authors regard changes in the money supply as consequent on actions of the Bank of England to modify the composition of the outstanding and given quantity of public debt. The Bank is conceived as a "market operator" that may

[26] Committee on the Working of the Monetary System, *Report* (Her Majesty's Stationery Office, Cmnd 827: August 1959).
[27] Bank of England, *Quarterly Bulletin*, vol. 9, no. 4 (December 1969): 448.

redistribute the national debt among various maturity classes (including cash) by its transactions in the market. It is this view of the central bank as open market operator that becomes translated into the doctrine that the money supply as one component of a national debt of fixed size is relatively unimportant compared with the structure of interest rates. Omitted from analysis is the effect of an expansion in the national debt accompanied by central bank purchases to expand the money supply. From this omission comes the Radcliffe view that interest rates and money supply movements must always be inversely related when initiated by action of the authorities.

The *Radcliffe Report* also took the position that there are many highly liquid assets in a financially sophisticated economy that are close substitutes for money. This led to the declaration:

> Though we do not regard the supply of money as an unimportant quantity, we view it as only part of the wider structure of liquidity in the economy. It is the whole liquidity position that is relevant to spending decisions.[28]

And to the corollary view:

> The authorities thus have to regard the structure of interest rates rather than the supply of money as the centre-piece of the monetary mechanism. This does not mean that the supply of money is unimportant, but that its control is incidental to interest rate policy.[29]

By this line of reasoning, the stage was set for neglect of the money supply as a strategic variable in the implementation of monetary policy. Attention was focused on the level and structure of interest rates. Moreover, there was a substantial body of official and academic opinion that did not regard credit markets or spending on real goods and services as very sensitive to interest rate variations. Further, British monetary theory in these years largely neglected the commodity price level as a potentially significant variable in monetary analysis. This omission resulted in failure to distinguish between nominal and real (or price-level-deflated) money balances and interest rates. These distinctions are particularly important in analyzing the demand for money and for fixed-interest securities in a period characterized by inflationary expectations.

These theoretical views and deficiencies supported the inclination of British central bankers and Treasury officials about the need to control interest rates with little regard for the money supply.[30] They also provided theoretical support for the view that monetary policy

[28] *Radcliffe Report*, p. 132.
[29] Ibid., p. 135.
[30] For further discussion of the theoretical deficiencies, see D. R. Hodgman, "British Techniques of Monetary Policy: A Critical Review," *The Journal of Money, Credit, and Banking* (November 1971): vol. 3, no. 4 767–75, especially.

might well be a weak instrument for aggregate demand management, so that monetary policy might require assistance from various forms of direct control over credit and both consumer and investment spending. Thus, for the most part, British monetary theory as reflected in the *Radcliffe Report* and related writings tended to reassure the authorities in their approach to monetary policy. These writings encouraged the authorities to believe that they might simultaneously (1) manipulate short-term rates for balance of payments purposes; (2) keep long-term rates stable so as not to reduce investment or generate debt monetization from expectations of falling gilt-edged prices; (3) finance a budget deficit through the banking system without regard for the growth in money supply and wealth effects that it occasions; and (4) keep down the pressure of aggregate demand by fiscal policy supported by administrative controls over the volume of lending by banks and other financial institutions and through controls over the terms of hire purchase credit. This approach did not work, as evidenced by the British experience of continuing domestic inflation, continuing expansion of domestic credit controls of an administrative nature, persistent balance-of-payments deficits ending in devaluation, and the need for a stop-go monetary and fiscal policy that contributed to one of the lowest rates of growth in real gross national product of any large industrial nation in the world.

THE CREDIT REFORM OF 1971

Cracks began to appear in official confidence in the system of credit controls following the devaluation of the pound in 1967. That devaluation had been accompanied by draconian fiscal measures and a further tightening of credit controls but had not produced the expected improvement in the British balance of payments. During 1968, the money supply rose by 6.5 per cent despite the drain of an overall balance-of-payments deficit of nearly half that magnitude. As the Chancellor of the Exchequer remarked in his budget statement of April 1969, ". . . a balance-of-payments deficit is financed either by borrowing from overseas or by drawing down assets [and] is in this sense an extension of credit to the domestic economy. Such an increase in credit at a time when we are striving to switch real resources into the balance of payments was a great deal more than we could afford. We cannot allow credit to be supplied on anything like this scale in the coming year." [31]

Publicly announced restrictive measures continued to stress loan ceilings and priority uses of credit, but behind the scenes in the Bank of England and the Treasury the old methods of selective credit control were coming to be viewed with increasing skepticism. This process received a strong impetus from international financial circles.

---

[31] House of Commons, Official Report, *Parliamentary Debates* (Hansard), "Budget Statement," April 15, 1969, cols. 1007–8.

In May of 1969 as a condition for further financial aid from the International Monetary Fund backed by central banks in other countries, the Chancellor of the Exchequer was required to commit the monetary authorities of the United Kingdom not to exceed a specified rate of expansion in "domestic credit." Despite the use of the term *credit* in the concept of "Domestic Credit Expansion," this magnitude essentially "measures the change in the domestic money supply with account being taken of any reduction in the money supply resulting from an external deficit (or any increase resulting from a surplus) and is, therefore, an adjusted money supply indicator." [32] To put it bluntly, external advisors imposed on the Bank of England and the Treasury a discipline in terms of the money supply that these authorities had been unwilling to accept through their own initiative. At the same time, an intensive investigation and rethinking of monetary and credit policy techniques was begun in the Bank and the Treasury.[33]

By spring of 1971, this process of reexamination and discussion had reached a point within the Bank of England and the Treasury that made it appropriate to broaden participation in the discussion to include representatives of principal types of financial institutions. The new chancellor of the exchequer in his budget speech of that spring and in the context of his remarks on techniques of monetary control announced plans for such consultation:

The existing arrangements which we took over when we came into office are clearly defective on the score both of flexibility and of scope for competition. Despite the use of special deposits, these arrangements have continued to rely more than I believe most of us on both sides consider to be desirable, on quantitative guidelines and on ceilings applied to bank lending. The use of these techniques over a long period is bound to lead to rigidities, and it perpetuates a rationing approach which is inimical to innovation in banking and which tends to stultify competition. What I hope we can do is break away from this approach.

I believe it should be possible to achieve more flexible but still effective arrangements basically by operating on the banks' resources rather than by directly guiding their lending. As bank lending to the private sector is only one element, but an important one, for effective management, this means devising a scheme capable of influencing the monetary system as a whole and the interplay between the different sources of credit creation.

A great deal of preparatory work and study has been done during recent months towards a more flexible regime on these lines. These ideas will now be fully explored between the authorities and the banks and finance houses.[34]

[32] Bank of England, "Domestic Credit Expansion," *Quarterly Bulletin,* vol. 9, no. 3 (September 1969, supplement).

[33] Some aspects of this investigation are described in Samuel Brittan, *Steering the Economy: The Role of the Treasury* (Harmondsworth, England: Penguin Books (Pelican), 1971), pp. 156–67.

[34] House of Commons, Official Report, *Parliamentary Debates* (Hansard), vol. 814, no. 115, March 30, 1971, cols. 1371–2.

The authorities published their proposals and subsequent decisions in a discussion document and a series of articles and memoranda that appeared in the May, September, and December 1971 issues of the *Quarterly Bulletin* of the Bank of England.[35] The reforms became effective on September 16, 1971. The thrust of these reforms is to accord greater significance to control of the money supply as a policy objective, to increase reliance on price rationing of credit rather than quantitative rationing in communicating central bank policy to the economy, and to stimulate competition in banking and financial markets by removing certain official controls and requiring the clearing banks to suspend their cartel agreements on lending and deposit rates of interest.

The first public operational step in the reform had occurred on May 14, 1971, when the Bank announced the end of its policy of unqualified support for the long-term (gilt-edged) market in government obligations and simultaneously published a position paper setting forth its principal reform proposals to initiate discussion between the Bank's staff and the financial institutions affected. The Bank's and government's sources of dissatisfaction with the existing system are briefly described in the position paper and in an address by the governor of the Bank delivered at the International Banking Conference in Munich on May 28, 1971.[36] The shortcomings identified in these statements are these: (1) Restraints on bank lending may not result to the same extent in a restrictive credit policy because growth of credit through nonbank channels may be stimulated. (2) Distortions may be introduced into the financial system; competition and innovation in financial institutions may be impeded, with inefficient firms being protected and efficient ones prevented from growing. (3) Misallocation of real resources in the economy may accompany quantitative rationing of credit. (4) The big deposit banks have borne an inequitable burden relative to other banks and financial institutions by serving as the principal channels for credit restraint.

The reform removes all lending ceilings. It establishes a 12.5 per cent liquid asset reserve for *all* banks, to be held against deposit liabilities in sterling. Eligible reserve assets are specified and are those normally readily convertible into cash at the Bank of England. Within this 12.5 per cent reserve there is for clearing banks an understood minimum to the share held in the form of deposits at the Bank of England. The Bank may call Special Deposits at a uniform rate across the banking system as a variable supplement to this reserve requirement. It may require different rates of call for resident and nonresident deposits.

[35] These were subsequently republished in collected form by the Intelligence Department of the Bank of England under the title *Competition and Credit Control*.

[36] Both are contained in the publication *Competition and Credit Control*, cited in footnote 35.

Aided by this variable liquidity reserve requirement, the Bank will employ Bank rate and market operations to influence the general liquidity of the economy. It will rely on financial markets to determine interest rates and credit allocation. Interest rates, including those on government obligations, will be permitted to find their market levels. The policy of unqualified support for the gilt-edged market in government securities is ended. The big deposit banks "should abandon their long-standing cartel arrangements which have provided for uniform deposit rates linked to Bank rate, and also the convention which has governed the relationship of their lending rates to Bank rate." [37]

Discount houses are to be preserved under the reform. They will continue to cover the weekly Treasury bill issue but will no longer tender at an agreed price. They will have to maintain at least 50 per cent of their funds in agreed categories of government debt. Call money lent to the discount houses counts toward the banks' required reserve of liquid assets. Discount houses will continue to enjoy exclusive access to the Bank's last resort lending facilities (apart from certain limited direct dealings between the Bank of England and banks, discount houses, and money brokers undertaken at Bank initiative in day-to-day management of the money market). Installment credit finance houses, which take deposits, will be required to meet reserve and Special Deposit obligations similar, though not identical, to those of banks.

While acknowledging the influence on monetary and credit conditions of the budget position of the central government and of international, short-term capital flows, the Bank does not envisage these as limiting its ability to neutralize excess liquidity or to bring about sufficiently strong upward pressure on bank lending rates. The British system of exchange controls has been both comprehensive and flexible although it has not been able to insulate British financial markets from the effects of leads and lags and the ebb and flow of nonresident sterling. This exchange control system, operated by the Bank of England in cooperation with private financial institutions, accounts for the confidence expressed by the Bank of England in its ability to exert control in domestic money and credit markets despite international capital flows. There are those, even on the Bank's staff, who remain skeptical of the Bank's ability to enforce credit stringency in the face of large deficits in the central government's budget accompanied by downward pressure on the price of government securities. They foresee a return to the former policy of supporting the price of gilt-edged securities should the central government's budget be in substantial deficit position. As we have seen, this would result in loss of control over the money supply and might, therefore, bring with it

[37] "Key Issues in Monetary and Credit Policy," in *Competition and Credit Control*, p. 8.

a resurrection of other elements of the former system of credit controls.

Too little time has passed since the credit reform for experience with its effects to permit more than a very preliminary assessment of its implications. On theoretical grounds, it can certainly be applauded as a development that will strengthen monetary policy and the management of aggregate demand in the United Kingdom while contributing to the competitive vigor and efficiency of the financial system and the entire economy. Greater flexibility and competitiveness is already apparent in financial markets. The clearing banks have begun to enter actively and in their own names into the market for sterling certificates of deposit, the interbank market, and the Eurocurrency market — areas of business in which they had not previously competed in their own names. In effect, they have ceased to observe prior cartel restrictions on competition in these markets. Moreover, the clearing banks have altered their lending rates in response to market conditions without waiting for a signal from the Bank of England in the form of a change in Bank rate. The discount houses have modified their practice, as suggested by the authorities. While they still submit bids to cover fully the weekly tender of Treasury bills, their former syndicated bid has been repaced by individual bids.

In commenting on the reform measures, economists in the United Kingdom have noted some elements of ambiguity in their implications for the choice between administrative controls and market processes in credit markets.[38] There is a suspicion that the definition of assets eligible to meet the liquidity reserve requirement to include various short-term government or government-guaranteed securities has been designed to broaden the market for these securities and thus shelter the interest cost of public debt from competition from other borrowers. A similar charge has been leveled at the provision for Special Deposits.

In the reform documents, the Bank of England has reserved the right to regulate maximum interest rates payable by banks in competition with savings banks and building societies. This proviso has been interpreted as reflecting a willingness by the authorities to consider intervention in market processes to subsidize certain types of credit.

The 12.5 per cent liquid asset ratio to sterling deposits required of all banks is some 5 per cent below the ratio recently observed by clearing banks but above, sometimes substantially above, the same ratio recently maintained by other banks to which it now applies.[39]

---

[38] See "The Bank of England's Proposals" with comments by A. B. Cramp, Norman Gibson, and Jack Revell in *The Bankers' Magazine*, July 1971, pp. 1–13; "Competition and Credit Control: A Money Study Group View," with comments by M. J. Artis and J. M. Parkin, Harry Johnson, and G. T. Pepper, in *The Bankers' Magazine*, September 1971, pp. 109–26.

[39] See Gibson, pp. 7–10.

Thus the effect of the ratio may be to alter the competitive advantage among these groups somewhat, to favor the clearing banks, and may lead in time to the disappearance or absorption of some banks in these other categories. Economists in the United Kingdom also have expressed doubt concerning the effectiveness of Bank of England control over the money supply or comparable monetary aggregates through the required reserve ratio. The problem is whether or not the authorities can control the supply to the banks of such a heterogeneous group of assets as those eligible to fulfill the liquidity reserve requirement.

For these various reasons, the effectiveness in practice of the monetary control techniques introduced by the reform of September 1971 remains open to question. There is also the fundamental issue of the authorities' attitude toward government financing and debt management. To what extent will they be prepared in the future to finance the government debt, including new deficits, by noninflationary means, accepting in this process the interest rates on government debt determined by market forces? Since the reform, there has not been sufficient experience to put these matters to the test.

Recent policy measures by British authorities can be interpreted as reflecting a determination to rely more than formerly on market processes in domestic credit markets, to make vigorous use of monetary and fiscal policy in aggregate demand management to stimulate economic recovery, and to accord priority to domestic over balance-of-payments objectives. To reduce unemployment, unusually high in 1972 at 3.5 to 4 per cent of the labor force, both budgetary policy and monetary policy have been strongly expansionary since late 1971. During the first six months of 1972, the money supply expanded at an annual rate of over 20 per cent, far in excess of the 6 per cent rate of increase in gross national product. This rapid increase in money supply has resulted from an expansion in domestic credit and also from an inflow of short-term capital from abroad. Although a rationale for easy credit can be found in the high rate of unemployment, such a flood of liquidity into the economy can hardly be required and is likely to add to inflationary pressures in the future. From this perspective, postreform monetary policy does not appear to be less inflationary, at least potentially, than its predecessor.

Balance-of-payments policy has used both administrative and market-oriented techniques during late 1971 and the first half of 1972. Short-term capital inflows from abroad occasioned by flight from the United States dollar in the late summer and fall of 1971 contributed to domestic monetary expansion and resulted in tighter regulations on short-term capital inflows by the authorities. These prohibited the purchase by nonresidents of sterling-denominated securities issued or guaranteed by the British government, and their purchase of short-term money market securities such as commercial bills and acceptances. Regulation of the net foreign position of banks was tightened and payment of interest on nonresident sterling deposits was prohibited. These regulations were withdrawn following the re-alignment of exchange rates according to the Smithsonian agreement of December 20, 1971. A strong speculative run against sterling in June 1972 resulted in a government decision effective June 23, 1972, to abandon the fixed foreign-exchange parity of the British pound for a floating rate. This is a market-oriented solution, doubtless qualified in practice by intervention in the exchange market by the Bank of England. The decision to float the pound sterling also signals the determination of the Heath government not to permit balance-of-payments considerations to take precedence over domestic aggregate demand management to stimulate economic recovery in Britain.

The credit reform of 1971 has altered the approach of the United Kingdom authorities to monetary and credit policy in ways that are capable of making that policy more effective while simultaneously strengthening competitive market forces in the economy. Whether the authorities will remain steadfast in their new orientation under the pressure of difficult choices or will revert to the system of selective controls and administrative interventions that characterized their policy in the 1960's is far from clear at this time.

8 The Effectiveness of Monetary Policy: A Comparative Analysis

There are certain instruments, or techniques, of policy that constitute the domain of the monetary authorities in a narrow sense. In the countries studied, these fall into five categories: (1) discount policy; (2) reserve ratios; (3) open market operations; (4) loan ceilings; and (5) administrative control of interest rates paid and received by banks and other credit institutions. Each of these techniques, or instruments, admits of considerable variation in specific mode of application, as revealed in the country studies.

The main theme of this chapter is that the effectiveness of these instruments and of monetary policy in general depends on the goals selected for monetary policy and on a variety of other factors that constitute for each country the more general financial system within which monetary policy operates. These other factors may be grouped under four general headings: (1) the structure of financial institutions and markets as this affects the process of financial intermediation; (2) the scope of state administrative control over financial institutions and markets through regulation or direct state ownership and operation; (3) the role of the government budget and of government debt; and (4) exchange controls and other measures to influence international capital movements. These factors may remain fixed or change rather slowly in a specific national setting. In an international comparative study they can be seen to vary in ways significant for the effectiveness of monetary policy.

THE CHOICE OF OBJECTIVES

Since the effectiveness of monetary policy must be judged by relating techniques to policy objectives, it is necessary to specify these objectives to assess effectiveness. Four broad policy objectives have come to be accepted as the long-range goals of *economic* policy in most industrialized countries. These are the familiar goals of full employment, price level stability, economic growth, and equilibrium in the balance of payments. Quite clearly, these four primary goals constitute evaluative criteria for an entire national economy whose performance is strongly influenced by many domestic and international forces besides the actions of the domestic monetary authorities. Therefore, the monetary authorities must be judged by the *contribution* they make toward achieving these goals rather than by an economy's actual performance as measured by these criteria. Moreover, the linkage between these goals and the five categories of monetary policy instruments distinguished above is complex in reality and is the subject of vigorous theoretical discussion and debate. The battleground covers a substantial portion of monetary and macroeconomic theory for both closed and open economies.

A precise assessment of the effectiveness of monetary policy measures would be possible then only as judged within the context of a comprehensive and realistic model of the particular national economy in question. To construct and implement such a model sufficiently detailed to incorporate the variations in technique, objectives, and features of the more comprehensive financial systems identified in the country studies, let alone other differences in national economic structure, is too ambitious a task to be undertaken within the present study. Accordingly, we adopt a more modest alternative: to offer some insights and generalizations on the effects and effectiveness of monetary policy under various circumstances based on a comparative view of the national studies contained in this volume. Specific national episodes are used to illustrate these generalizations.

Monetary authorities in all countries find it necessary to select as policy targets objectives that are shorter-term and more immediate than the comprehensive goals of economic policy mentioned above. This is a consequence of the complexity of the linkage between the techniques of monetary policy and the comprehensive goals, and of time lags in the dynamic process that constitutes the linkage.[1] Three types of intermediate objectives as targets for monetary policy predominate in the countries studied. These are monetary aggregates, interest rates, and credit flows. In the category of monetary aggregates it is convenient to include not only the money supply in its various definitions but also the related quantities of monetary base (that is,

[1] There is substantial professional and technical literature that explores the interrelations of short- and long-term objectives, monetary targets and indicators, theories of the influence of monetary variables on major policy objectives, and the quality of information on relevant variables and economic processes available to the monetary authorities. For example, see Karl Brunner, ed., *Targets and Indicators of Monetary Policy* (San Francisco; Chandler Publishing Co. 1969).

claims or potential claims against the central bank) and of liquid assets held either by the banking system or by the economy at large. What these targets have in common, despite important differences in precise content, is an emphasis on control by the monetary authorities of the money supply or potential money supply. Uusually such emphasis is accompanied by a minimum of direct intervention in the processes of credit markets.

By contrast, concern by the authorities with the structure of interest rates and with credit flows always involves forms of administrative intervention into credit markets to modify the structure of interest rates and the allocation of credit that otherwise would result from market processes. Among the forms of intervention that may be mentioned for illustration are loan ceilings, administrative regulation of interest rates, earning asset reserve requirements for credit institutions, capital issue controls, and channeling of savings bank deposits through government-operated financial intermediaries.

Such differences in the choice of policy targets by national monetary authorities are clearly evident from a comparative perspective. In Germany and the Netherlands, the monetary authorities have been concerned primarily with monetary aggregates. In Belgium-Luxembourg, France, and the United Kingdom primary significance has been assigned to control of interest rates and credit allocation. Italian monetary authorites have chosen an intermediate position on the spectrum. These differences may be illustrated somewhat more explicitly.

In Germany, the central bank seeks to increase or decrease the liquidity of commercial banks and other credit institutions in its efforts to manage aggregate demand. It has not been deterred from these efforts by substantial movements in both short- and long-term interest rates. The authorities have not sought to regulate interest rates by administrative controls since the major but unsatisfactory attempts at such regulation in the period March 1965–March 1967. Apart from this one historical exception, administrative interventions by the German authorities into credit processes have been conspicuously absent in the postwar period.

Monetary authorities in the Netherlands pay particular attention to the stock of liquid assets in the economy defined as those assets that are, or at their holders' option could become, claims against the central bank (that is, monetary base). Administrative interventions by Dutch authorities into credit, capital, and foreign exchange markets have been undertaken primarily to aid in regulating the stock of liquid assets rather than to influence the domestic allocation of credit. Thus, in using credit ceilings, they have sought to curb aggregate spending without raising domestic interest rates, which would attract foreign capital or provide incentives to commercial banks to repatriate assets from abroad. Other regulations on commercial and savings banks have sought to preserve the authorities' distinction between noninflationary lending based on savings and inflationary lending that adds to the supply of liquidity in the economy. Restrictions on access by foreign borrowers to the Dutch capital market may involve an element of credit allocation between domestic and foreign borrowers. Within the domestic economy this allocative intent is absent.

In Belgium, the authorities have emphasized interest rate and credit allocation targets. A part of the purpose of the Securities Stabilization Fund has been to influence credit flows by stabilizing the prices and yields of preferred types of bonds. These include government and government-guaranteed bonds, local authority bonds and those of the Municipal Credit Institution, and bonds issued by the Telegraphs and Telephones Board and the Belgian National Railways company. Foreign trade acceptances enjoy a privileged rediscount rate. Bank deposit rates are set by the central bank in consultation with the Belgian Bankers' Association. Bank lending rates on shorter-maturity loans are tied by convention and official suggestion to the central bank's rediscount rate. Rates on longer-term bank loans take as a benchmark the lending rates of the National Industrial Credit Company. Lending rates for the public credit institutions that make longer-term investment loans are established by their respective administrations. New issues of fixed-interest securities on the capital market are subject to virtually complete control by the Ministry of Finance and the Banking Commission. Public sector issues take priority in the issue of publicly marketed securities.

In France, also, the goal of credit allocation and control of interest rates has taken precedence over control of any monetary aggregate, although the National Credit Council does pay some attention to the ratio of the money supply to gross national product valued at current prices. Privileged discounting at the minimum rediscount rate and in amounts "above ceiling" has been extended to banks offering paper representing export credit, grain storage bills, and medium-term loans to finance housing and industrial equipment. Rediscounting is the principal channel through which the central bank supplies credit to the French banking system. Thus, credit flowing through these privileged channels has been an important impediment at time to efforts by the Banque de France to contain inflationary pressures.

French national policy has emphasized low interest rates as a stimulus to investment and as a factor in keeping costs of French export industries competitive in world markets. The National Credit Council exercises pervasive administrative control over interest rates charged and paid by banks and other credit institutions. Ceilings have been imposed on the rate of expansion of bank credit with exceptions sometimes permitted for such priority categories as export loans and loans for construction and industrial equipment. Large loans to big borrowers have been subject to administrative review by the Banque de France to check purpose and terms. Savings deposited in savings banks are channeled through the government-operated Caisse des Dépôts et Consignations, which is the dominant financial intermediary.

The Ministry of Economics and Finance operates a "Treasury circuit" to collect and disburse funds to high priority uses at favorable interest rates. Priority access to the capital market has been controlled by the Ministry of Economics and Finance. These concerns with credit flows and interest rates have had priority over any central bank attempts to control bank liquidity or the money supply.

In the United Kingdom the monetary authorities, at least until smitten by doubts that culminated in the Credit Reform of 1971, also chose interest rates and credit flows as their principal intermediate objectives in seeking to contribute to the broader goals of full employment, economic growth, price stability, and balance-of-payments equilibrium. Through its understandings with the clearing bank cartel and the discount houses, the Bank of England exercised a form of administrative control over an array of short-term interest rates in the traditional money market and over clearing-bank lending and borrowing rates. By support of the gilt-edged market, it stabilized the price of longer-term government securities even when this action, by increasing the money supply, worked against credit restraint. By imposing loan ceilings on banks and finance houses, the Bank of England sought to reduce the flow of credit to the private sector while sometimes exempting loans for exports, and for shipbuilding, and to the nationalized industries and local authorities. The Bank also sent information copies of its requests for credit restraint by the banking system to such financial institutions as insurance companies, pension funds, and building societies. When it was deemed necessary, the government restricted borrowing by nationalized industries, local authorities, and the Treasury. The authorities exhibited no concern to control any monetary aggregate prior to the pressure from the international community that led to the adoption of an adjusted money supply target (that is, "Domestic Credit Expansion") in May 1969. In their commitment to interest rates and credit flows, the monetary authorities had the support of theoretical arguments advanced in the *Report* of the prestigious Radcliffe Committee.

In Italy, the monetary authorities stress a monetary aggregate as the principal target for central bank policy. Here emphasis is on the "monetary base." The Italian concept of the monetary base includes potential as well as actual claims against the central bank; the base is measured in a way intended to express this potential magnitude with due allowance for Italian financial structure and the Banca d'Italia's explicit or implied commitments to acquire assets or make loans to credit institutions and the central government. However, in Italy, the monetary authorities have exhibited also a great concern with the allocation of credit within the economy. This concern has expressed itself in various forms. Within prescribed limits, banks are permitted to substitute Treasury bills, and agricultural, mortgage, and other specified long-term bonds for cash deposits at the central bank in meeting minimum reserve requirements. The authorities set maximum interest rates and maturities for bank deposits. Comprehensive powers for the Interministerial Committee and the Banca d'Italia to regulate interest rates on bank loans and deposits and amounts and composition of bank balance sheets (for example, loan ceilings) are held in reserve. During the period 1966–69, the Banca d'Italia pegged the prices and yields on long-term government bonds in an effort to shift portfolio preferences of private sector investors from bank deposits to government bonds. New bond issues in the capital market are regulated as to timing, amount, terms, and purpose by the central bank. Priority is given to bonds issued on behalf of the Treasury and by special credit institutions that make loans for approved investment purposes.

IMPORTANCE OF THE GENERAL FINANCIAL SYSTEM: AN OVERVIEW

The degree of success achieved by monetary policy is significantly influenced by the characteristics of the general financial system within which it operates. This is true whether the monetary authorities approach their task by concentrating on control of a monetary aggregate or by seeking to control interest rates and credit flows. But there are important differences in the requirements for success that depend on the choice of policy objective.

Authorities may meet three principal sources of resistance when they pursue a strategy based on control of a monetary aggregate. First, deficit budgets by central and local governments may create strong pressures on the central bank to support prices in the markets for these securities. Such support results in increased claims against the central bank and attendant growth in the money supply. This problem may be accentuated if there is already a large volume of government debt outstanding. Second, efforts of the monetary authorities to control the domestic money supply may be partially or fully offset by capital flows through the balance of payments under a regime of fixed exchange rates. Third, the process of financial intermediation to redistribute the existing money supply from lenders to borrowers may raise the spending velocity of the existing money supply so as to offset the central bank's measures to restrain its growth. This process is facilitated by sophistication of financial structure in the form of variety, diversity, and flexibility of financial institutions and markets and also by the existence of large outstanding amounts of marketable, and hence tradeable debt, particularly government debt.

Central banks usually are not in a position to do more than deplore and protest inflationary deficits by central governments. With the aid of central governments they may exercise some restraint on deficit borrowing by local governments. In all seven countries studied in this volume, there are arrangements whereby administrative restraint may be imposed on local government borrowing. Balance or imbalance in the central government's budget remains, however, a potent influence on the effectiveness of monetary policy directed toward control of a monetary aggregate.

Both theory and experience bear ample testimony to the degree to which international capital flows, responding to interest rate differentials or to speculation on a change in exchange parities, can handicap or even frustrate control over monetary aggregates by domestic monetary authorities. The lower interest rates and easier credit terms that are produced by expansionary action of the authorities may induce an outflow of capital and attendant loss of foreign exchange that cannot be sustained. Should interest rate differentials be reinforced by speculative motives, vast flows of short-term capital may occur within a few days and may even force an exchange rate devaluation on the country experiencing the outflow.

In the opposite situation, that of a capital inflow, the monetary authorities may find the domestic money supply growing against their wishes as foreign exchange pours into domestic financial institutions and markets to profit from interest rate differentials or the prospects of an up-valuation of exchange parities. The technical ability of the monetary authorities to offset the increase in domestic monetary base and money supply occasioned by such inflows depends on their armory of techniques and instruments. These may prove inadequate to deal with the monetary effects of capital flows. When this happens in a country in which the monetary authorities rely primarily on control over monetary aggregates, ways must be found to reduce the capital inflow if some degree of independence in domestic monetary policy is to be preserved.

The degree to which a change in velocity of the money stock tends to offset the effect on aggregate demand of a decline in the money supply growth rate is determined partly by the deterrent effect that increases in interest rates have on borrowers. But it depends too on the variety and efficiency of the channels for credit intermediation so far as these determine the financial system's capacity to bring borrowers and lenders together promptly and at reasonable cost. Generally, also, the more varied the types of credit instruments, securities, or obligations of financial institutions that can be offered potential lenders, the more interest-elastic the supply of credit. Therefore, the rise in velocity that accompanies and tends to offset the effects of restriction on the growth in monetary aggregates will be less when channels of financial intermediation are fewer, more specialized, and more subject to measures by the authorities to block intermediation or to increase its cost.

From this perspective, the complexity of financial structure, the variety of credit institutions subject to central bank measures such as reserve requirements and loan ceilings, the size and breadth of distribution of government debt, and conditions of access to the organized money and capital markets for various types of lenders and borrowers have implications for the effectiveness of monetary policy even when the authorities focus on control of a monetary aggregate. Therefore, selection of a monetary aggregate as the chief target for monetary policy need not obviate all concern of the authorities for means to influence aggregate credit flows even when they have little concern for incidence effects.

Monetary policy that concerns itself with interest rates and credit flows as primary targets faces a much more complex task than that which selects a monetary aggregate as its principal objective. So far as the tasks of interest rate formation and credit allocation are not left to the play of market forces, the monetary authorities have undertaken to achieve multiple targets and will accordingly require multiple instruments. In this light, the commonly observed tendency for selective credit controls to proliferate is understandable as an increase in the number of instruments that the authorities find necessary to use in pursuing multiple objectives.

Various monetary authorities have adapted certain of the traditional instruments that constitute the narrow domain of monetary policy so as to influence interest rate structure and credit allocation. Examples include special discounting privileges for priority lending categories, special earning asset reserve requirements, permission to substitute certain securities for cash reserve requirements, exemption of some types of loans from ceilings on loan expansion, and direct administrative intervention to set lending and borrowing rates for credit institutions. This list could readily be extended. In general, however, the degree of success achieved in controlling interest rate structure and allocating credit is limited unless these techniques are strongly supported by other measures and by certain features of the general financial system.

Efforts by the authorities to control interest rates and to allocate credit are more successful the less the scope for evasion by private financial institutions and markets domestically and the less opportunity the system affords for nonapproved transactions with foreigners in the absence of flexible exchange rates. Among domestic factors that enhance efforts by the authorities to regulate interest rates and allocate credit are these: high degree of concentration in commercial banking; nationalized control of commercial banks; limited variety and high degree of specialization in credit institutions; breadth of coverage of types of private credit institutions by the authorities' regulations concerning discount rates, reserve ratios, interest rates on deposits and loans, credit ceilings, eligible investment assets and similar measures; and public operation of key financial intermediaries and investment funds. The capacity of the authorities to determine interest rates and allocate credit also is strengthened when participation in the money market is narrowly restricted to exclude individuals, business firms, and longer-term institutional investors, when there are no other short-term markets parallel to the central money market, and when there is official control over new issues in the capital market. These predominantly domestic factors can be given further support by exchange controls over financial transactions with foreigners to permit only those transactions that suit the objectives of the authorities. Finally, tax and subsidy measures by the central government can exert an important influence on effective interest rates, credit flows, and real resource allocation, but such budgetary measures take us out of the realm of monetary and credit policy.

Virtually all of the factors listed above, as well as those measures mentioned earlier as falling within the more restricted domain of the central bank, are features of national financial structure or practice that can be controlled, determined, or altered deliberately by a sovereign state. However, many of these elements are deeply imbedded in tradition and accepted practice and can be changed only slowly if at all so long as change depends on democratic political processes. Therefore, in the shorter run and from the perspective of the national monetary authorities, many of these factors must be regarded as given elements of the situation with which the monetary authorities must cope. Since these factors lie outside the traditional and more restricted domain of monetary techniques employed by central banks, and since they do tend to change only gradually in a national context, they are often neglected in systematic discussions of the methods and effectiveness of monetary policy. To clarify their importance, we shall examine these factors in somewhat greater detail. Subsequently, we consider their interaction with the objectives and techniques of monetary authorities as this has influenced the effectiveness of monetary policy in the individual countries we have studied.

THE STRUCTURE OF FINANCIAL INSTITUTIONS AND MARKETS

The phrase *financial structure* as we shall use it here is meant to cover three aspects of financial institutions and markets: (1) number and variety of channels for financial intermediation; (2) degree of specialization of financial institutions; and (3) availability of open market channels.

First, the importance of financial structure in determining the effectiveness of monetary policy may be expressed simply. The key question is *the number and variety of channels available* in the financial system to perform the service of financial intermediation that brings lenders and borrowers together. The closer the financial system approximates the extreme of a single channel for credit, the simpler the task for the central bank in controlling money supply, monetary velocity, and cost and availability of credit.

Perhaps the closest real-world approximation to the simplest system imaginable that performs the minimum essential monetary and financial functions is that of the state banking system in the Soviet Union.

Soviet commercial and savings bank functions are incorporated with central banking functions in a single nationwide branch banking system. There are no other credit-granting institutions except for the Investment Bank, which doles out construction credits according to plan. There is no money market, and no capital market, and the extension of credit by one enterprise to another through channels outside the banking system is illegal. There is a state monopoly of foreign trade coupled with comprehensive exchange controls. Thus, no leakages occur via transactions with foreign countries.

At the other extreme among the countries studied in this volume is the financial structure in the United Kingdom. A variety of financial institutions exist in that country that perform banking functions including both deposit and credit functions: clearing banks, merchant banks, foreign banks, overseas banks, and savings banks. Other institutions such as building societies and finance houses accept time and savings deposits. The money market is open to numerous and varied participants including nonbank businesses, individuals, nonresidents, and all sorts of financial institutions. Other short-term credit markets parallel the traditional money market, including the interbank, local authority, sterling certificate of deposit, and Eurocurrency markets. The capital market is large and not subject to administrative controls on the volume of new issues. Debt forms held as assets by investors are many and diverse and widely distributed. A variety of specialist institutions such as discount houses, brokers, and investment bankers provide financial services ancillary to these various financial markets. The complexity of this network of markets and institutions led the Radcliffe Committee to refer to the British financial system as sophisticated. Such a sophisticated system facilitates changes in the velocity of money and provides numerous paths of intermediation to frustrate the authorities' efforts to control interest rates and credit allocation.

A second aspect of financial structure is that of *the degree of specialization of financial institutions* as this influences the substitutability of one institutional channel for another in response to measures applied by the monetary authorities. Here it is useful to distinguish between customer-serving institutions on the one hand and open markets (see below) on the other. The more sharply differentiated the institutions are from each other in their activities, the less good substitutes they are for each other in meeting customer needs. For example, the more like commercial banks other banks and credit institutions become (that is, the more they provide checking accounts and make short-term loans), the more essential that the authorities should regulate these institutions like commercial banks. This is one consideration that led the British authorities to extend the application of reserve requirements and special deposits to cover all types of banks and not just clearing banks in the Credit Reform of 1971.

An alternative approach is for the authorities to apply regulatory, or statutory, controls to prevent institutions from duplicating each other's functions. In the past, this consideration led the French authorities to prescribe distinct functions for their deposit banks, business banks, and banks for medium- and long-term investments. The trend for other financial institutions, particularly savings banks, to evolve in the direction of commercial, or "full service," banks is evident in most of the countries studied in this volume. The Dutch authorities had to extend their voluntary short-term credit restraints to the Dutch savings banks when these, having attracted short-term deposits, began using the funds so obtained to make loans whose maturities put them just beyond the maturities to which short-term credit ceilings applied.

A related aspect of financial structure is *the degree of concentration in the commercial banking industry.* Typically, control by the monetary authorities over deposit and lending activities of commercial banks is more effective the more concentrated the commercial banking industry. Commercial banking is dominated in the Netherlands by two branch banking systems, in Belgium by three. In the United Kingdom, the clearing bank cartel has been an important instrument of central bank policy. There are now six English clearing banks, but only four are of primary importance. In Italy, banking is less concentrated, but even so there are only nine branch banking systems of national importance. Six are nationalized, and the state owns 80 per cent of the stock in the other three. Other Italian commercial banks are restricted by government regulation to local or regional geographic areas within which they may solicit deposits. Historically in Germany, three large branch banks have dominated commercial banking, but concentration is declining steadily with the diversification of savings banks into commercial banking activities. In France, three large nationalized branch banks dominate commercial banking.

When a highly concentrated commercial banking system occurs in conjunction with a small number of other types of financial institutions whose functions are relatively specialized and tend not to overlap those of the commercial banks, the effectiveness of policy measures that bear on the commercial banks is enhanced. This was the situation in the Netherlands in the late 1940's and 1950's, as it was to a lesser degree in other continental countries.

A point closely related to the structure of commercial banking and thus to the effectiveness of controls imposed on commercial banks is *treatment by the authorities of banking subsidiaries.* In the Netherlands, the balance sheets of commercial banking subsidiaries must be incorporated gross in those of their commercial banking parents. Thus, lending ceilings and interest rate ceilings applied to commercial banks cannot be evaded by the device of organizing subsidiaries. By contrast, in the United Kingdom, subsidiaries of the clearing banks were a principal means for the latter to evade ceiling interest rates on clearing bank notice deposits that were tied to Bank rate by an agreed formula of the banking cartel.

Third, *the extent to which open market channels can substitute for institutional channels* in the process of financial intermediation influences monetary policy effectiveness. The phenomenon of "disintermediation" is well known. It is the use of open markets by borrowers and lenders to replace institutional channels when the latter are squeezed by higher reserve requirements, credit ceilings, and other measures. The possibility for resort to open market channels depends on the availability of such channels and the extent to which they are regulated. The openness of the money market to various types of participants is an important consideration. If there is no section of the organized money market through which businesses may lend to and borrow from each other, as in the commercial paper market in the United States, controls on institutional short-term credit channels are more likely to be effective.

The option of going to the open market for credit by issuing bills and notes is available to businesses but not to individuals. However, financial institutions whose customers are individuals may borrow in the open market to relend to customers. For this reason, the types of institutions that have access to the open market and the terms of their access may influence credit terms to individuals as well as businesses.

Two other factors that contribute to the influence of financial structure on ease of financial intermediation are the size and distribution of government debt and the degree of openness of the market for long-term capital. The size of the government debt is taken up in connection with the role of the government budget. The degree of openness of the capital market is considered as it applies to state administrative control over financial institutions and markets.

SCOPE OF STATE ADMINISTRATIVE CONTROL OVER FINANCIAL INSTITUTIONS AND MARKETS

The scope of state administrative control over financial institutions and markets is important in assessing the capability of the state and its agencies to implement goals of monetary and financial policy. The relevant distinction is that between reliance on market processes, with attendant costs and benefits that official action must modify to influence the behavior of the private sector of the economy, and reliance on regulations and direct state participation to accomplish this end. All governments use some combination of these means. But the degree of reliance on administrative control versus market incentives differs substantially among different national systems. Administrative controls take diverse forms and may be strong in one dimension but weak in another within a particular country. For this reason it is not a simple matter to classify countries definitively along a scale denoting degree of administrative control available to the authorities. Nevertheless, France and Italy clearly are characterized by a substantial degree of administrative control in the hands of authorities; Belgium and the Netherlands, by somewhat less in that order; and the United Kingdom and Germany, less still.

Two principal forms of administrative control may be distinguished: (1) regulatory control, and (2) state ownership, possibly combined with state operation. By *regulatory control* is meant the capacity of the authorities to stipulate certain conditions or forms of behavior that must be observed by banks and other financial institutions and that can be varied for purposes of monetary or credit policy. The authorities in this context include not only the central bank but other appropriate government ministries and agencies such as the Ministry of Finance, the Banking Commission, other regulatory agencies, and the exchange control authority. Conditions that may be stipulated include the setting of minimum cash reserve ratios, and of reserves to be held in the form of earning assets, such as government securities and rediscountable commercial paper; establishment of ceilings on the level of loans of specific types or on their rates of increase; regulation of deposit and lending rates of interest; and proscriptions on types of financial services or of investments in types of earning assets.

The statutory provision of such regulatory powers to the monetary authorities or other agencies of the state varies widely among the countries studied. In the United Kingdom, the statutory provisions have been minimal, requiring the monetary authorities to rely heavily on voluntary agreements, tradition, and informal understandings. There is not even a clear statutory definition of what constitutes a "bank" as a financial institution to which the regulatory authority of the Bank of England applies. Until the Credit Reform of 1971, no effective reserve requirements were applied to the several varieties of banks other than clearing banks. Loan ceilings on the other hand were gradually extended during the decade of the 1960's to include non–clearing banks, discount houses, and finance houses. Yet until the Credit Reform of 1971, the Bank of England continued to depend on informal arrangements with the clearing bank cartel and the discount houses for key aspects of its influence in the shorter-term credit markets.

In Germany, by contrast, reserve requirements apply by statute to a wide variety of credit institutions defined as banks because they perform "banking functions" specified in the banking law. Covered are commercial banks, central giro institutions, savings banks, credit cooperatives and their central institutions, mortgage banks, installment sales financing institutions, and foreign banks. In Belgium and the Netherlands, banks and other credit institutions are clearly defined in law, and so is the scope of supervisory authority for each type of institution. However, in both countries the monetary authorities recently have proposed amendments to existing legislation to extend and clarify their statutory authority to apply certain measures such as credit ceilings without having to rely on periodic renegotiation of voluntary agreements with credit institutions.

In France and Italy, the principle of state control over money and credit in the service of national priorities is fully accepted and finds expression in statutory grant of comprehensive powers of regulation and control to designated state agencies as well as in nationalization or state majority stock ownership of the principal commercial banks. The primary difference in the organization of control powers in the two countries lies in the relative importance of the central bank and the Ministry of Finance. In the French system, the Ministry of Finance plays a dominant role in the allocation of longer-term investment funds and in supervision of the bond market. It also has an important voice in the formulation of monetary and shorter-term credit policy through its chairmanship of the National Credit Council, which sets policy lines for the Banque de France to implement. In the Italian system, the power of the state to regulate monetary and credit affairs is vested in the Interministerial Committee for Credit and Savings. The Minister of Finance is chairman of the Committee, but the Banca d'Italia is the executive agent for decisions of the committee and appears to exercise a dominant voice in the formulation of policy, owing perhaps to staff organization in the Banca d'Italia superior to that in the Ministry of Finance. In contrast to French arrangements, the central bank in Italy (rather than the Ministry of Finance) regulates issues on the capital market and thus has an important influence in the allocation of longer-term investment funds.

Administrative control by state authorities is most complete in the case of *nationalization, or state ownership.* Examples of this are nationalized commercial banks in Italy and France, state savings bank systems in Belgium, Luxembourg, and France, postal checking services in Belgium, France, Italy, and more recently the United Kingdom, and state-operated financial intermediaries such as the Caisse des Dépôts et Consignations and various investment funds in France, and special credit institutions in Italy, and the Rediscount and Guarantee Institute, the General Savings and Pension Fund, and various specialized investment funds in Belgium. Through its administrative control of such institutions the state can implement policies with respect to priority categories of loans and investments, set quantitative limits for the volume of loans, and establish interest rates on deposits and other obligations and on loans made by these institutions. Such power is not always fully exercised and is not infrequently subject to the Ministry of Finance or some credit council or other supervisory or regulatory body rather than the central bank.

Commercial banks that have been nationalized, or whose stock is largely owned by the state, are far more reliable executors of the authorities' policy decisions regarding interest rates on deposits and loans, preferred lending categories, and net lending or borrowing abroad than privately owned and operated commercial banks are. Officers who hold their positions at the pleasure of the state administration are likely to perceive their personal advantage defined in success as career officials. Private bankers are far more likely to seek imaginative and safe ways to defeat the regulations of the authorities when personal gain lies in doing so. The nationalized banks of France and Italy provide examples of financial institutions whose officer structure is firmly under state control.

In practice, the role of *state-owned financial intermediaries* is even more important than that of nationalized commercial banks in contributing to the effectiveness of monetary and credit policy. Such state-owned financial intermediaries play an important part in the financial machinery of Belgium, Luxembourg, France, and Italy. Particularly important in this regard is state control of the channel through which deposits made by private savers in savings banks and similar institutions are invested. A variety of methods for accomplishing this purpose exist. One is to confine savings banking to a state network of savings banks. This is the system in Luxembourg. A second approach is to operate a state savings bank network, with private or mutual savings banks permitted to function in parallel with the state system. The problem then becomes how to control the lending policy and to channel the investments of the private savings banks. In France, this is done by requiring these banks to redeposit their funds with the state financial intermediary known as the Caisse des Dépôts et Consignations. This organization also holds the liquid funds of the social security system and until 1967 held the liquid funds of insurance companies and pension funds. Loans and investments of the Caisse des Dépôts et Consignations are determined in accord with government policy.

In Belgium, the state-operated Rediscount and Guarantee Institute is the key intermediary in the bankers' acceptance portion of the money market. The privilege of borrowing net in the call money section of the money market is reserved to this institute and its companion state agency, the Securities Stabilization Fund. The institute discounts bankers' acceptances and commercial bills at favorable rates of interest to encourage the banks in this form of lending that is important for domestic and foreign trade.

State-operated financial intermediaries are important in making investment loans in a number of countries. Typically, they obtain loanable funds by issuing bonds on preferred terms in the capital market, and in some cases they also accept long-term deposits and receive grants from the state budget. Examples are the special credit institutions in Italy, a variety of specialized investment funds in France (for example, Crédit National and Crédit Foncier), and the National Industrial Credit Institution and the Municipal Credit Institution in Belgium. In the Netherlands, the Bank for Netherlands Municipalities, through which municipal borrowing in the capital market is centralized, falls into the category of state-operated financial intermediary. However, its purpose is more to regulate the volume of municipal borrowing in the capital market than to provide funds on a preferential basis to municipalities.

An aspect of state administrative control characterized by substantial differences in national practice is *control of access to the domestic capital market*. State regulation of access to the domestic capital market serves one or both of two principal motives. It may be undertaken as part of a program to allocate domestic credit flows or its purpose may be to help control international capital flows.

The purpose of altering the allocation of long-term investment funds within the domestic economy is most explicitly and vigorously pursued in Italy. In the Italian capital market, priority access is accorded to the issue of government bonds and bonds of various special credit institutions whose task is to finance approved investment projects at favorable terms to encourage economic development. The Banca d'Italia must give its approval for the issue of any stocks or bonds to the capital market through any of the banking or credit institutions subject to its control or intended for listing on any of the Italian stock exchanges. It uses this power to review purpose, terms, and timing of new issues. The issue of bonds by private firms is discouraged by a 38 per cent tax on bond interest payable by private issuers of corporate bonds. Finally, the market for government bonds and those of the special credit institutions is encouraged by making some of these eligible to satisfy reserve requirements stipulated for banks and other deposit-taking credit institutions.

In France, the Ministry of Finance maintains a calendar of new issues, to which a proposed issue of bonds must be admitted before it can be offered on the market. Here again terms and purpose are scrutinized before permission for the issue is granted. The degree of rationing by purpose and amount has varied over time. The official position as stated by officials in the ministry is that rationing has been minimal in the last year or two.

In Belgium, the Ministry of Finance controls public sector bond issues, and the Banking Commission must approve of bond issues by the private sector. Controls are rigorously employed to provide the central and municipal governments and various state-operated investment funds with priority access to the bond market.

In the Netherlands and the United Kingdom, the only restrictions on access to the domestic capital market are applied to nonresidents for reasons of balance-of-payments policy. Domestic borrowers and lenders in these two countries have virtually untrammeled access to their capital markets. The use of a calendar for new issues in the Netherlands appears to serve primarily to adjust timing rather than to deny potential borrowers access to the market. In the Netherlands, the bulk of new capital issues are private placements, on which the central bank's influence is limited to moral suasion. Nonresidents are not permitted to invest in private placements. The flow of domestic savings into the capital market tends to be directed into domestic uses. In neither country do capital market controls appear to be designed to influence domestic credit allocation.

In Germany, the domestic capital market is open to both resident and nonresident borrowers on an unrestricted basis. There is a Central Capital Market Committee composed of representatives of the major banks involved in the business of security flotation. This committee is supposed to regulate the flow of new issues so as to maintain orderly conditions in the bond market. At times it has been asked to restrict the volume of new foreign issues. The Ministry of Economics is empowered under certain circumstances to suspend new issues by public bodies at all levels of government, from central government to municipalities. Such suspension is intended to restrict government spending in an overheated domestic economy and to relieve downward pressure on security prices during episodes of especially tight central bank policy. Noteworthy is the subjection of the public sector rather than the private to administrative rationing in the German system as an aspect of domestic stabilization policy. The German capital market is free of controls for purposes of investment allocations.

THE ROLE OF GOVERNMENT BUDGET
AND GOVERNMENT DEBT

Substantial differences prevail among countries in the influence of budgetary policy and of government debt on the effectiveness of monetary policy conducted by the central bank. International comparisons of the modus operandi and effectiveness of monetary policy must allow for these differences.

Two aspects of budgetary policy are of primary importance for monetary policy. First, a central government budget that is chronically in deficit often puts irresistible pressure on the central bank to support the market prices of government securities by means that result in inflationary expansion of the money supply. The recent monetary experience of Belgium, France, Italy, and the United Kingdom all include significant episodes of this kind. Second, the degree of flexibility in budget taxes and expenditure programs helps to determine the burden assigned to monetary policy for domestic economic stabilization. Sufficient flexibility in taxes and expenditures lightens the task of the monetary authorities in managing aggregate demand and permits a more effective mix of monetary and budgetary policies for internal and external balance.

There is considerable diversity in capability for compensatory budgetary policy among the countries studied in this volume. In the United Kingdom, both theory and techniques of compensatory budget management are well developed. This is also true of Germany since the passage of the Law to Promote Economic Stability and Growth in 1967. Moreover, the German law permits the central government to alter expenditures by local and Lander governments as well as by the central government, and makes explicit provision for the deposit or

release of tax revenues in blocked accounts at the Bundesbank so as
to alter the liquidity of the banking system. In the Netherlands, the
theory of compensatory budget policy is well understood, and the
central bank has worked out empirical estimates of the amount of
borrowing that public authorities may undertake in the capital market
without dislocating that market or causing inflation. However, the
public authorities, especially the local authorities, frequently exceed
these limits, so that there is a gap between theory and practice.

In Italy, budgetary processes are so cumbersome that the capability
for compensatory adjustment in the budget of the central government,
not to mention the local governments, has been virtually nil. In Belgium, the budget has not in the past undertaken much of a compensatory role in aggregate demand management. Indeed, persistent
deficits in the capital budget of the central government have contributed to the difficulties faced by the monetary authorities in managing domestic monetary and credit conditions. In both Italy and
Belgium, some compensatory role for government finance has been developed in the practice of public authority borrowing abroad or repay-
ing foreign-held debt to exert a liquidity effect on the economy. This is
more nearly a measure of monetary policy or debt management than
of compensatory budgetary policy. Finally, in France, the role of a
balanced budget for the central government as an aspect of efforts to
contain inflation has come to be appreciated in recent years and has
been implemented with some success. Nevertheless, the central bank
continues to bear the primary responsibility for economic stabilization
policy. In summary, in the countries studied in this volume, with the
exception of the United Kingdom, monetary and credit policies rather
than budgetary policies have been used most actively for domestic
economic stabilization.

*The size of the government debt outstanding and the breadth of its
distribution* among types of investors are factors that influence the
effectiveness of monetary policy. In this context what counts is size in
relation to other significant economic magnitudes such as a country's
gross national product or the volume of other debts outstanding. The
larger the size of government debt in these relative terms, the more
likely are the authorities to be inhibited in applying restrictive measures.
They know that such measures would increase the interest cost of
refinancing the debt as it matures, depress the market value of outstanding debt with attendant effects on the liquidity and solvency of
institutions and individuals that hold the debt, and increase the burden
of interest payments to foreign holders of the debt. Attempts to stabilize the market price of long-term government debt hampered the
execution of monetary policy in the United Kingdom throughout much
of the past two decades and in Italy during the years 1966–69. By
contrast, repudiation of government debt inherited from the years of
World War II in Germany had as one result the removal of a comparable constraint on the vigor of monetary policy in that country.

When government debt is widely distributed, the market for government securities serves as an efficient channel of financial intermediation. By redistributing existing holdings of debt in exchange for money balances, transactions in outstanding government securities help to activate idle money balances and thus to raise the velocity of circulation of the money supply. This process is facilitated if the central bank stabilizes bond prices and thus prevents or minimizes capital losses that otherwise might accompany bond sales.

When strains between successful debt management and successful monetary and credit policies have become especially severe, authorities in various countries have occasionaly sought relief by measures to freeze certain holdings of government securities. Usually these measures have involved requiring banks and other credit institutions to hold government securities as a special liquid asset reserve. Both the Belgian and the French authorities have used such measures.

EXCHANGE CONTROLS AND OTHER MEASURES
TO INFLUENCE INTERNATIONAL CAPITAL MOVEMENTS

No account of the general financial framework within which a nation's monetary and credit policies are administered can be complete without some reference to balance-of-payments controls, and more specifically, to controls over capital movements. Since the establishment of the par value system of exchange rates under the Bretton Woods agreement at the end of World War II and the subsequent return by the late 1950's to convertibility of all principal currencies of the non-Communist world, the private institutional basis for international financial transactions has developed rapidly and comprehensively. Among the developments contributing to the efficiency of international financial mechanisms have been the growth of the multinational corporation, improved correspondent relationships and establishment of foreign branches by large commercial banks, and the growth of the Eurocurrency and Eurobond markets, more closely linking national money and capital markets.

One result of these improved financial mechanisms has been a substantial increase in the responsiveness of international capital flows to actual or anticipated profits to be gained by transferring funds from one national money or capital market to another. These profit opportunities may be in interest or equity yields or in anticipated gains from speculation on a change in exchange parities. This increasing sensitivity of capital flows to anticipated profit differentials tends to reduce the effectiveness of monetary policy in achieving purely domestic objectives. A restrictive domestic monetary policy by the raising of domestic interest rates attracts funds from abroad that offset the intended domestic restrictive effect. A relaxation of domestic credit conditions and lower interest rates than those in foreign money markets or the Eurodollar market may provoke an outflow of funds that neutralizes the intended easing of domestic credit conditions and threatens a country's foreign exchange reserves. Efforts of the authorities to allocate domestic credit to priority uses also may be weakened or thwarted by international capital flows. Investors may prefer foreign securities to domestic ones when domestic rates are kept low for policy reasons. Domestic borrowers may seek accommodation abroad when they are discriminated against by credit controls in domestic markets. Clearly, the effectiveness of national monetary and credit policies will depend partly on the way national authorities approach the problem of international capital flows.

Under the present international par value system, specific national measures to influence international capital flows may be classified in two broad categories: (1) exchange control measures that prohibit certain capital transactions or require a license for them; and (2) measures to alter the cost or rate of return on such transactions. The first category includes such measures as blocked convertibility of bank balances; prohibitions on banks from accepting nonresident deposits in foreign currencies for conversion to domestic currency; regulation of the net foreign position of commercial banks; setting of time limits for advance or delayed payments to and from foreigners so as to control swings in current account settlements (that is, "leads and lags"); limits to or prohibition of business borrowing abroad for conversion to domestic currency; restrictions on foreign investment by business firms unless financed by borrowing abroad; restricted access of foreign borrowers to the domestic money and capital markets; restrictions on the purchase of foreign-issued securities by resident individuals; and regulations, or more often prohibitions, concerning purchase of foreign money-market instruments and capital market securities by domestic financial institutions. This list could readily be extended.

The second category consists of measures to alter the cost or rate of return on international capital flows. These include the use of an interest equalization tax payable by foreign borrowers in domestic money and capital markets; special (non-interest-bearing) cash reserve requirements on foreign-owned bank deposits in domestic currency to increase the effective cost to the banks of these deposits as sources of funds for domestic bank loans; similar reserve requirements on loans received by domestic businesses from foreign lenders; prohibition of interest payments to nonresident holders of bank deposits, or even assessment of penalty interest charges on such deposits, payable to the government; and prohibition of the sale of money market assets to nonresidents on repurchase agreements and similar measures. Central bank "swaps" have been used to stimulate capital outflow. Such swaps involve the sale of foreign exchange in the spot exchange market for investment abroad coupled with a commitment by the central bank in the forward market to repurchase the foreign exchange at an attractive price to remove the risk and increase the profitability of the transaction for the domestic bank involved.

Flexible, or floating, exchange rates constitute another approach to the problem of destabilizing capital movements. A country may be said to have flexible, or floating, exchange rates when the pressure of supply and demand in the market for foreign exchange determines the value of its currency, with no official intervention. In recent years, such important countries as the United States, United Kingdom, Germany, Italy, Japan, Canada, and the Netherlands have resorted to floating rates for short or long periods of time. In addition, some countries such as France and Belgium–Luxembourg have employed a dual exchange rate system, or two-tier foreign exchange market, in which the authorities have intervened to maintain a fixed or very narrowly fluctuating rate for current account transactions while permitting the rate for capital account transactions to float in response to market pressures.

The advantage of flexible, or floating, exchange rates is that the price mechanism takes over from administrative controls the task of rationing the supply and demand for a currency in the foreign exchange markets. Indeed, under fully flexible exchange rates, capital account transactions cannot result in a *net* transfer of assets from one country to another unless they induce appropriate compensating changes in the current account through the effect of altered exchange rates on trade flows. Thus, under fully flexible, unitary exchange rates, a country's balance of payments will always be in equilibrium so that no net movement of official foreign exchange reserves can occur or is required to produce balance. By implication, international capital flows cease to interfere with the domestic monetary authorities' control over the money supply or other monetary aggregate. The two-tier exchange market with separate exchange rates for current and capital account transactions (the latter flexible) is a step in this direction. However, this system involves substantial exchange control administration to enforce regulatory distinctions between transactions designated for the current account and those for the capital account. For various reasons (to be explored more fully in Chapter 10), national authorities exhibit such a strong antipathy toward an *international system* based on fully flexible exchange rates that this solution appears to have little if any chance for adoption.

For the foreseeable future, then, national monetary authorities will continue to operate in an environment that includes fixed, or relatively fixed, exchange rates. Accordingly, the effectiveness of domestic monetary and credit policies will continue to be influenced by international capital flows and by methods the authorities use to cope with these flows.

DISADVANTAGES OF ADMINISTRATIVE CONTROLS

In this review of factors that influence the effectiveness of monetary and credit policy, consideration of various administrative controls has stressed the support they provide to the authorities' efforts to control monetary aggregates, interest rates, and credit flows. But there is also a negative aspect to such measures. Although credit controls become more effective as the scope of official regulation and intervention in financial processes becomes more comprehensive, such controls also involve certain disadvantages, which increase with the scope and rigor of official intervention into private economic behavior.[2] There is first the question of whether regulations and administrative interventions by the authorities can allocate credit to socially desirable purposes with results superior or even equal to those of free markets, which are subject only to minimum rules of behavior for participants. Next there is the effect of controls on the design and efficiency of the financial structure: inefficient firms preserved in the shelter of regulations that restrict competition, emergence of new financial practices and organizations whose only rationale is to evade existing controls, and stifling of innovation by means of restrictive practices. Undesirable effects on resource allocation may not be confined to the financial sector but may extend to other economic sectors both through the influence of credit flows on allocation of real resources and through the absorption of real resources into inefficient financial operations. Third, depending on the techniques used to control interest rates and alter credit allocation, there is the possibility that the monetary authorities will neglect or be thwarted in their attempts to halt an excessive expansion in the money supply, with the attendant consequences of domestic inflation, deterioration in the balance of payments, altered distribution of real income, labor unrest, and other undesirable manifestations of inflation. A low interest rate policy also may depress the level of domestic savings and encourage the outflow of capital by legal or illegal channels. Exchange controls pose their own problems in retaliation by other countries and general interference with international trade and capital movements. Thus, determination of the optimum degree of official administrative intervention into monetary and credit processes involves weighing complex considerations.

CONCLUDING OBSERVATIONS BY COUNTRIES

From our present perspective, we can offer some brief comparative and interpretive observations on the recent experience that the countries discussed have had with monetary and credit policy. In Germany, monetary policy has concentrated on control of the money supply, or more exactly, on the related monetary aggregate, bank liquidity. Credit flows and interest rates are market-determined. This choice of strategy is fully consistent with the absence of important state-op-

---

[2] For a more extensive discussion of these disadvantages, see D. R. Hodgman, "Selective Credit Controls," *Journal of Money, Credit, and Banking*, vol. 4, no. 2 (May 1972); 342–59.

erated financial intermediaries, the lack of controls on capital market issues, the limited size of the national debt, and the key role of banks in the money and capital markets. The principal difficulties faced by monetary policy in Germany in recent years have arisen from inappropriate budgetary policy and from international, short-term capital flows. Since passage of the Law to Promote Economic Stability and Growth in 1967, budgetary policy has been better coordinated with monetary policy. The principal remaining challenge to the effectiveness of monetary policy comes from international capital flows; these have been brought partially under control by recent measures to reduce their profitability.

In the Netherlands also, the monetary authorities focus their attention on a monetary aggregate: the liquidity of the economy. There is primary reliance on domestic financial markets to transmit the effects of monetary policy throughout the economy. However, the Netherlands economy is so open by virtue of its small size that the authorities have for some years had to adopt measures to insulate the domestic credit and capital markets to a degree from their international counterparts. Among such measures have been exchange controls of varying degrees of rigor over international capital flows, and use of ceilings on commercial bank loans. International capital flows involving nonresident deposits in Dutch banks and in commercial settlements have posed the greatest challenge to the authorities in their efforts to regulate domestic liquidity.

The Italian monetary authorities interpret the monetary base (defined to reflect Italian conditions) as their principal target variable, but in practice they also actively seek to influence interest rate structure and credit flows in the economy. In this latter endeavor, the central bank has available comprehensive stand-by authority for exchange controls, control over securities offered publicly in the capital market, a commercial banking system dominated by nationalized or publicly controlled banks, and the assistance of the specialized credit institutions for medium- and longer-term investment. The special credit institutions obtain the bulk of their funds from bond issues and are thus subject to policy control by the central bank at that point. The money market is heavily controlled, and various interest rates charged or paid by banks are regulated directly or via the banking cartel agreement. In short, the Banca d'Italia's authority for administrative intervention, together with other features of the comprehensive financial system, appears to constitute an adequate foundation for policy measures to influence interest rates and credit allocation.

The primary technical difficulties that the Italian monetary authorities face have arisen from lack of support from budgetary processes in compensatory stabilization policy and from inflationary deficits in the central government budget that had to be financed by the central bank. Pressures of central government finance have been responsible for prolonged episodes of central bank support for Treasury bill prices in the money market, and for a pegging policy on long-term government and government-guaranteed bonds in the period 1966–69 that had inflationary consequences.

In France, the organization of the financial system and the authority of the central bank, the National Credit Council, the Ministry of Finance, and other ministries to intervene administratively in credit and financial processes is realistically related to policy goals of credit allocation and control of interest rates. The most important commercial banks are nationalized. Private banks and other credit institutions are subject to administrative regulation as required. The Ministry of Economics and Finance has ample authority to regulate new issues in the capital market. A government "fund" is the dominant nonbank financial intermediary into which all savings deposits, whether in public or in mutual savings banks, must be redeposited for subsequent investment. Other state-operated investment funds help to channel capital market funds to priority uses. Throughout recent years, except for brief periods, exchange controls have regulated capital flows between French and foreign money and capital markets. In 1971, the French adopted a dual foreign exchange market with a flexible rate for all but a few current account transactions.

A defect in the French system has been the use of privileged discount facilities at the central bank to encourage the banking system to lend for certain priority purposes at low rates of interest. The availability of such discounting facilities at the minimum discount rate and "above ceiling" has in the past permitted inflationary expansion in the money supply that the central bank was powerless to stop. Inflationary financing of government budget deficits by the central bank has been another shortcoming of French monetary policy in certain periods. Again, the government rather than the central bank has been the agent responsible.

Monetary and credit policy in Belgium is strongly oriented toward control of credit flows and interest rates rather than any monetary aggregate. The Belgium system is noteworthy for the dominant role played by public institutions in the money and the capital markets. These include the Rediscount and Guarantee Institute, the Securities Stabilization Fund, and the public institutions specialized to various categories of loans for investment purposes. The investment of savings bank deposits is controlled for both the state and the private savings bank systems. Access of private and public borrowers to the capital market is closely regulated. Since 1955, Belgium has operated a dual market for foreign exchange in which the rate for capital account transactions has been permitted to adjust to market pressures, thus rationing capital transfers. Other administrative controls over international capital flows are being used or have been requested by the authorities. Thus, the goals of credit allocation and interest rate control are supported by a variety of techniques and conditions that supplement appropriately the more limited domain of traditional central bank policy instruments. Persistent deficits in the capital budget of the central government have at times posed an inflationary threat by requiring the Securities Stabilization Fund to borrow at the central bank so that government security prices could be supported. But these inflationary pressures have been moderated by the contribution of the capital investments to productive capacity in the Belgian economy.

According to the perspective we have developed, monetary experience in the United Kingdom during the past two decades provides a striking illustration of gross incompatibility of the intermediate policy objectives sought by the monetary authorities with the instruments at their disposal, given the characteristics of the comprehensive financial system within which monetary policy had to be implemented. The targets of monetary policy throughout this period were interest rates and credit flows. The instruments of monetary policy, inherited from an earlier epoch, were essentially those appropriate to control the money supply or related monetary aggregate. Initially these were rediscount policy and market operations in government debt. Only during the period were these supplemented by voluntary agreements under which the central bank could vary cash reserve requirements by calling Special Deposits or Cash Deposits from the banking system. The Bank of England's practice of setting limits to types of loans made by credit institutions also came to be accepted by voluntary agreement during the 1960's. These limits initially applied only to clearing banks but were gradually extended to include other banks, discount houses, and finance houses. The statutory basis for the Bank of England's authority over credit institutions was vague, applied only to "banks," and left that term ill defined.

Money and capital markets were well developed and open to all kinds of domestic participants in addition to banks, including business firms, individuals, local governments, insurance firms, pension funds, and other nonbank financial institutions. A wide variety of credit and financial institutions existed with functions that partially overlapped each other and also overlapped those of the commercial banks. Access by domestic borrowers to the capital market was not subject to government control, except for nationalized industries and local governments. There were no state-operated financial intermediaries functioning in the money and the capital markets to channel credit flows to priority uses. A very large amount of marketable government debt was outstanding to aid in redistribution of money balances via the government securities market and thus to facilitate credit flows through that market should other channels be restricted by the authorities. No variable asset reserve requirements were applied to credit institutions to influence the demand for government securities, although the minimum liquid asset position expected of clearing banks had some effect of this kind.

Taken together, these various elements constitute a description of a well-developed, diversified, and flexible financial system. Even with the "voluntary" cooperation of the clearing bank cartel and the discount houses, only a very restricted segment of this system was subject to central bank influence by means other than market processes. Yet although the authorities lacked the means to exert effective control over credit flows and interest rates, they deliberately ignored the alternative strategy of controlling the money supply and relying on market processes to spread the effects through the economy.

Lack of control over the money supply was accentuated by frequent and substantial deficits in the central government budget accompanied by a price support policy for government securities, which the Bank of England pursued. The resulting increase in the domestic money supply helped to frustrate the partial system of controls over credit flows, added to aggregate demand, and contributed to inflation and to persistently recurring deficits in the balance of payments. The international weakness of the pound also derived in part from the steadily declining role of London as a reserve center and of the pound as a reserve currency. Even an extensive and fairly rigorous system of exchange controls was inadequate to protect the monetary authorities on their international flank in these general circumstances.

Thus, with the benefit of hindsight, the failure of monetary policy in the United Kingdom in the two decades prior to the Credit Reform of 1971 can be attributed to lack of comprehension by theoretical economists and practical officials of the inconsistency between policy objectives and the means available for achieving these objectives. This inconsistency was far greater than that observable in any other country studied in this volume.

The study of national monetary policies is logically incomplete until extended to include arrangements for monetary cooperation among nations. Under a fixed-exchange rate system, forces operating through a nation's balance of payments constitute a significant challenge to the effectiveness of domestic monetary and credit policies even when means and ends of domestic policies are compatible in the sense that we have been considering. Increasing economic and monetary interdependence among nations has sharpened the issues in the choice of means available to national authorities to cope with this challenge.

The possible responses of national policy to problems of monetary and economic interdependence lie along a continuum reaching from autarkic isolation to full monetary and economic union. All seven of the countries studied are committed in principle to work toward monetary and economic union within the framework of the European Economic Community. All, also, are members of the International Monetary Fund and thus participants in the still more comprehensive system of international monetary cooperation to which the IMF is dedicated. Acting separately, the larger countries studied here can exert an influence on the outcome of the reform process for the international monetary system, a process launched at the annual meeting of the IMF in September 1971. Acting jointly within the framework of European monetary integration, they can influence international monetary reform even more strongly. Indeed, the simple fact that monetary union of Western Europe had occurred or was a realistic prospect might well alter the desirable characteristics of the broader international monetary system whose reform is now under study.

Chapter 9 evaluates the problems and prospects for monetary integration among the member nations of the European Economic Community. Chapter 10 discusses selected issues in the reform of the international monetary system.

9 European Monetary Integration

A crucial dilemma in the modern world is the organizational inconsistency between political nationalism and economic interdependence. The geography of national *political* organization does not coincide with that of efficient *economic* organization. Modern communications and transportation, together with the advantages of economic specialization and large-scale production, are steadily increasing the interdependence of national economies through the international movement of goods, services, money, financial assets, technology, entrepreneurial skills, and people.

National governments are held politically responsible for the economic welfare of their citizens but are finding it increasingly difficult to exercise effective economic management within the area of national political sovereignty. To turn back toward economic isolation would require too great an economic sacrifice. Unilateral efforts by national governments to manage national economies may be relatively ineffective, always influence the economies of trading partners, and may provoke offsetting, defensive measures by other governments, with a danger of international economic strife. These considerations provide the stimulus for various forms of international economic cooperation.

The seven European countries whose national monetary and credit techniques and policies have been studied in this volume are involved in two principal forms of international *monetary* cooperation. One is regional in scope, the other worldwide. The first is a plan for the regional monetary integration of Europe embracing those countries that are members of the European Economic Community or that become members. The second is the international monetary system established under the terms of an agreement adopted at the United Nations Monetary and Financial Conference at Bretton Woods, New Hampshire, in 1944. The International Monetary Fund, established under that agreement, provides the institutional framework for consultation and collaboration by its members in the cooperative management of the international monetary system.

Both systems of international monetary cooperation are now in the process of active evolution. Interactions among national, regional, and international monetary systems and policies are vitally important for the manner in which each functions. The shape of the evolving regional and international monetary systems will be mutually determined to an important degree and will influence and be influenced by the organization, techniques, and policy goals of the participating national systems.

THE EUROPEAN ECONOMIC COMMUNITY'S PLAN FOR ECONOMIC AND MONETARY UNION

On February 9, 1971, the Council of Ministers of the European Economic Community approved a plan to initiate a ten-year program leading to economic and monetary union of the six countries then participating in the Common Market: Belgium, France, Germany, Italy, Luxembourg, and the Netherlands.[1] On October 22, 1972, the general goal of economic and monetary union by 1980 was reendorsed at a summit conference of heads of state of these six nations and of the United Kingdom, Ireland, and Denmark, scheduled to join on January 1, 1973. Accordingly, the program leading to monetary and economic union remains a declared objective for the enlarged Community.

The blueprint for the program of monetary and economic unification approved by the Council of the EEC on February 9, 1971, emerged from study and consultation in which the Council, the Commission, and various specialized committees of the EEC participated together with ministers of finance and economics from the member states. The model proposed is that of a federal union characterized by a common currency, fully coordinated central bank and national budgetary policies, absence of internal barriers to the free flow of labor, capital,

---

[1] The European Economic Community, or Common Market, was set up under the Treaty of Rome in 1958. Its original membership included the six countries mentioned in the text. On January 1, 1973, Denmark, Ireland, and the United Kingdom joined. The Community's foremost achievements to date are a customs union and a common agricultural policy. The EEC's principal institutions include the Commission and its staff, the Council of Ministers, the European Parliament, and the Court of Justice. The Council of Ministers is the only Community institution whose members directly represent the member governments. Which ministers of the national governments sit in the Council normally depends on the subject under discussion. The Council normally decides by majority (weighted) vote. On certain fundamental questions, such as the plan for monetary and economic union, the approval of the Council is required.

goods, and services, a unified stance on monetary and economic issues under negotiation with countries not members of the union,
adequate centralized power of decision to determine and carry out
policies in the above areas, and establishment of political machinery
to guarantee democratic control over this centralized power of decision. The attractiveness of this model is that it provides *in principle*
a solution to a number of vexatious problems that trouble the member
states of the EEC while it simultaneously represents the logical ful-
fillment of the process of economic integration begun in 1958 with the
founding of the European Economic Community and currently expressed in a customs union and common agricultural policy.

In the discussions preceding the adoption of the program, the *logic*
of economic and monetary union was seen to arise from the desire to
create an economic market of sufficient size to accommodate economies of scale made possible by modern technology and to reduce
existing barriers to mobility of labor and capital in search of more
productive uses. The *necessity* for greater economic and monetary
integration was viewed as stemming from the decreasing ability of
national economic policy makers to cope with sources of economic
instability arising from international economic interdependence both
within and outside the Community.

The Council-approved plan for monetary and economic integration
within the EEC establishes certain agreed principles of procedure,
calls for a variety of specific measures to be undertaken, and des-
ignates other issues for further study and consultation.[2] Technically,
two different currencies are joined in a monetary union if they are
freely interconvertible for any purpose at a permanently fixed exchange rate. Full union requires costless conversion and absence of
discrimination by national origin of user regarding terms of use (for
example, no controls, direct or indirect, on capital market transactions). The Council resolution endorses the principle of fixed exchange rates both within the EEC and for the international monetary system, and calls on the central banks of the member states to
cooperate in reducing the margins within which the exchange values
of Community currencies fluctuate in relation to each other. This is
viewed as a step in the direction of irrevocable fixing of exchange
parities *within* the Community.

The ability of individual EEC countries to fulfill their commitments
to maintain fixed exchange parities and to keep fluctuations of market
rates within narrow bands around those parities depends on their
ability to avoid persistent deficits or surpluses in their individual

[2] "Resolution of the Council and the representatives of the Governments of the Member States on the achievement by stages of economic and
monetary union in the Community," reprinted in *Bulletin of the European
Communities*, vol. 4, no. 4 (1971): 19–26.

balance of payments and to finance temporary deficits by drawing on foreign-exchange reserves or international credits. Recognition of these relationships accounts for certain additional provisions included in the Council-approved plan. The likelihood of deficits and of their persistence depends partly on the degree of inflation a country experiences relative to major trading partners. This degree of inflation in turn depends strongly on aggregate demand-supply relationships, which are influenced by budgetary and monetary policies. Mutual commitments to maintain intracommunity exchange parities within narrower bands thus involve commitments to extend mutual aid in meeting balance-of-payments deficits. But the extent of the aid required will be related to domestic monetary and budgetary policies in the respective countries.

To meet the need for mutual aid, the Council, in a separate but related action, approved the establishment of a medium-term mutual aid fund with resources of two billion dollars to begin operation at a later date. This medium-term aid is to be available to supplement unconditional short-term monetary aid up to specified quotas that was put into operation among Community central banks in February 1970. Looking further into the future, the Council called upon the EEC Monetary Committee and its Committee of Governors of Central Banks to study and report on the organization of a European Monetary Cooperation Fund to serve as an agency for pooling foreign-exchange reserves and coordinating foreign-exchange intervention by the central banks of member countries. This fund is also viewed as a possible forerunner of a federated and highly coordinated central bank structure for the entire Community.

The degree of divergence in national economic trends in aggregate demand, price levels, and interest rates concerned the Council and the drafters of proposals submitted to the Council. Such divergence can have undesirable consequences, including the transmission of economic instability from one partner to the rest of the Community, the export of price inflation, and deficits in national balance of payments on trade and capital accounts requiring mutual aid in the form of foreign-exchange credits. In the process of consultation among member states leading to the Council resolution, the interdependence of these phenomena gave rise to a serious debate concerning the timing of steps toward monetary union relative to the timing of effective mutual consultation on aggregate demand management.

The compromise that permitted agreement to be reached on the issue of timing involved three elements: (1) acceptance of the principle that monetary steps and "harmonization" of economic policies in other areas should move forward in synchronized fashion; (2) commitment to the narrowing of exchange parity spreads on an "experimental" and hence reversible, rather than more permanent, basis; and (3) inclusion of a safeguard provision permitting the entire program of monetary measures (for example, narrower bands, and medium-term financial aid) to be suspended by January 1, 1976, should the Council, on the basis of a review by the Commission of both monetary and economic coordination measures (to be submitted before May 1, 1973), determine that the necessary degree of parallelism between the two types of measures had not been achieved.

To move toward the degree of economic coordination required, the Council endorsed the principle of Community-level consultation in the preparation of national budgets, particularly on "the margins within which the main items of all public budgets must be situated" and "variations in their sizes, the extent of the balances and the methods of financing and using the latter." [3] The Council also agreed to adopt "the broad outlines of economic policy at the Community level and quantitative guidelines for the essential items of the public budgets." Thus, in principle, the Council has undertaken to make quantitative recommendations to the member states regarding major budgetary magnitudes. To extend coordination to domestic monetary policy, the Council invited the central banks to work cooperatively within their authority so as to achieve better coordination of policies concerning interest rates, credit allocation terms, and bank liquidity trends.

Among the principal issues noted for future study and action in the Council-approved plan are the following: (1) harmonization of the instruments of monetary policy; (2) harmonization of the structure, and to some extent the level, of taxes, particularly the value-added tax, excise duties, tax treatment of interest on fixed-interest securities and dividends, company taxes, and the extension of tax exemptions granted to private persons crossing intracommunity frontiers: (3) integration of financial markets and the progressive coordination of the policies of member states on financial markets, such as policies concerning bond and stock issues by nonresidents in domestic capital markets; (4) policy toward the movement of capital to and from third countries outside the Community; (5) Community-level policy on structural and regional measures and the provision to the Community of appropriate means to administer such policy. Broadly speaking, these are areas of policy for which the general logic of monetary and economic union indicates the need for adjustments in diverse practices among member states, either to remove barriers to mobility of labor, capital, and entrepreneurship within the Community or to facilitate the coordination or implementation of economic policy in response to recommendations or decisions taken at Community level. Two other unresolved issues are the role and degree of independence of the central banking function at the Community level, and the transfer of power of decision in economic matters to a Community organization together with provision for democratic control over such economic decisions.

[3] Council "Resolution," p. 22.

DEVELOPMENTS SINCE THE EEC COUNCIL'S ADOPTION OF THE PLAN FOR MONETARY AND ECONOMIC INTEGRATION

Since February 1971, when the EEC Council formally launched the program of monetary and economic integration for the Community, two sets of events have significantly influenced the program. The first of these is the general turbulence in international monetary relations that characterized the period beginning with the floating of the German mark and the Dutch guilder in May 1971 and ending with the international realignment of major currencies in the Smithsonian agreement of December 18, 1971. Other important currencies also were floated for portions of this period, including the United States dollar, the Belgium-Luxembourg franc, and the Italian lira. These critical developments in existing international monetary arrangements subjected European currencies to speculative pressures that disrupted the timetable for measures by the Community's central banks to narrow exchange margins within the Community, initially set for June 15, 1971. On the other hand, the very turbulence in international monetary relations added to the incentive of EEC member countries to find a cooperative solution in coping with external pressures while maintaining internal stability of exchange rates.

The second set of factors that influenced the proposed program of monetary and economic integration was the successful conclusion of negotiations to admit the United Kingdom, Ireland, and Denmark to membership in the EEC to become effective on January 1, 1973. The admission of new members with new problems and new points of view might reasonably be expected to delay steps toward integration until the new and original members could exchange views and evaluate possible new issues associated with such membership.

Taken together, these developments are sufficient to explain why only very modest progress has been made in implementing the program for monetary and economic integration since the Council adopted it in February 1971. This explanation does not rule out the possibility that intrinsic difficulties in the plan combined with forces of resistance within the Community also may have contributed to the delay.

Following a pause of about one year, three positive steps towards monetary integration have now been taken. One was the initiation on April 24, 1972, of cooperation by the central banks of the six original EEC member countries and the candidate members to keep fluctuations of the exchange rates among Community currencies within a band whose width should not exceed 2.25 per cent. Successful implementation of this commitment has the effect of holding maximum fluctuations of exchange values between any two Community currencies to 4.5 per cent (if currencies at the top and bottom of the band change places), which is identical to the maximum possible

fluctuation of the exchange rate between any Community currency
and the U.S. dollar under the terms of the Smithsonian agreement.
When the British pound came under heavy speculative pressure in
late June 1972 and was set free to float, the pound moved outside the
stipulated band.

The second and third positive steps occurred during the October
1972 summit meeting of the original six and the three new members
scheduled for admission on January 1, 1973 (Norway's voters having
rejected membership in a national referendum during September
1972). The summit meeting reendorsed the goal of monetary and
economic union by 1980 and set various critical dates for additional
steps towards the union. It also announced agreement to establish a
European Monetary Cooperation Fund to begin operation by April 1,
1973. The Fund's stated purposes are to coordinate intervention in
the exchange markets by central banks of member countries undertaken to keep exchange rates for Community currencies within the
narrower band, to facilitate mutual clearing and credit arrangements, and to serve as the forerunner for an eventual Community-
level central banking organization. Most of the operational details of
this Fund were left unresolved at the summit conference.

Other aspects of intra-Community cooperation and coordination
called for in the Council-approved plan continue to languish. No visible progress has been made in the harmonization of domestic monetary policies among the EEC member states. Techniques and criteria
for coordination of budgetary policy remain ill defined and command
no general support within the Community. There has been as yet no
agreement within the EEC on *cooperative* methods for regulating international capital movements, although individual countries have
strengthened their measures to regulate capital movements over their
own borders. These measures have increased the barriers to free flow
of capital *within* the Community as well as *between* the Community
and the rest of the world. Longer-term projects such as reform of
financial markets and institutions, development of an integrated
European capital market to replace the Eurocurrency and Eurobond
markets, and tax reform to remove barriers to the intra-Community
mobility of labor, capital, and entrepreneurship have not advanced
since adoption of the plan.

EVALUATION OF ASPECTS OF THE PLAN FOR
EUROPEAN MONETARY INTEGRATION

To evaluate the prospects for further progress in European monetary
integration, it is helpful to look at certain key issues that arise when
the steps proposed in the plan are related to the existing national
monetary and financial systems studies in this volume. We shall also
explore more deeply the analytical rationale for certain of the monetary objectives and measures set forth in the plan and assess their

relevance and validity for the basic purposes the plan seeks to serve. The aspects of the plan selected for primary emphasis are these: (1) exchange rate policy; (2) the European Monetary Cooperation Fund; (3) regulation of international capital movements; (4) capital market policy; (5) coordination of budgetary policies; and (6) harmonization of domestic monetary measures.

Exchange Rate Policy

A main goal stated in the plan for monetary union is the progressive narrowing of exchange rate fluctuations and eventual fixity of exchange rates among members of the EEC. Fixed exchange rates within the Community would greatly facilitate the arrangements involved in the Community policy of common agricultural prices and price supports for farm income maintenance. Changes in intra-Community exchange rates alter price relationships in national currencies and disturb intra-Community trade in farm products. They also alter price relationships between Community markets and world markets. Thus, a change in exchange rates within the Community will disrupt the Community's common agricultural market unless complex adjustments are made at national borders in the form of taxes and subsidies.[4]

If fixed exchange rates can be maintained for lengthy periods, they will encourage mobility of capital and entrepreneurial talent and may even make a modest contribution to the mobility of labor within the Community. The ultimate goal of full economic integration with a Community-wide market for productive factors as well as goods and services will require fixity of exchange rates or a common currency.

There are also more immediate aims to be served by fixity of exchange rates. By keeping exchange rate fluctuations among Community currencies within a narrow band, the Community gives itself a monetary identity in the international monetary system. The band can be kept narrow enough so that maximum variations of effective spot rates for transactions between any pair of Community currencies do not exceed the potential variation in the exchange rate between any Community currency and the U.S. dollar under the Smithsonian agreement. By this means the Community seeks to provide an alternative to the U.S. dollar as a stable asset form for private and public exchange reserves. Moreover, if internal fixed rates can be combined with greater flexibility between the Community level of rates and external currencies, this flexibility can help to buffer Community capital markets from external influences and thus reduce the degree of interference by such flows with measures to regulate aggregate demand within the Community. Flexible external rates can also help to adjust

[4] For a detailed technical analysis, see H. Vittas, "Effects of Changes in EEC Currency Exchange Rates on Prices, Production, and Trade of Agricultural Commodities in the Community," *International Monetary Fund Staff Papers,* July 1972, pp. 447–67.

excessive deficits or surpluses in the Community's combined balance of payments with the rest of the world. Such cohesion within the Community would strengthen its voice in negotiations leading to reform of the international monetary system.

Beginning on April 24, 1972, the central banks of members of the Community have been intervening in exchange markets to keep intra-Community exchange rate fluctuations within a 2.25 per cent band. An agreement provides for mutual credit whose amount is subject to no set limit but whose term may not exceed 59 days. Repayment is to be made in reserve assets (that is, dollars, other currencies, gold, and special drawing rights) in proportions that match the relative importance of these assets in the debtor country's reserves. This latter provision is intended to produce a gradual harmonization of the composition of reserve assets among Community central banks. Subsequent to the agreement, the United Kingdom had to withdraw when it floated the pound in late June 1972. When the lira came under speculative attack at the same time, Italy agreed to continue its participation in the narrower band only if permitted to repay short-term credits in dollars rather than partly in other reserve assets. Thus, difficulties have already arisen in maintaining the narrower bands.

There are other problems. One immediate implication of narrowing exchange margins within the Community is restriction also of the potential margin of variation for individual national rates of exchange relative to the dollar unless the value of individual EEC national currencies should rise and fall in concert relative to the dollar. Diverse conditions affecting the balance of payments of individual EEC countries make this a most unlikely result if the adjustment of individual exchange rates is left to the influence of market forces. When bands are narrowed without adjustment in the Community level of the dollar, certain results are inevitable. A surplus country may find that the narrower intra-Community margin requires it to intervene to purchase foreign exchange at a lower market rate of exchange relative to the dollar and a deficit country at a higher rate relative to the dollar than is required by the terms of the Smithsonian agreement. This implies inflows or outflows of foreign exchange reserves in excess of those that need occur under the Smithsonian agreement.

The level of the entire Community band can be raised or lowered relative to the dollar by general revaluation or devaluation of Community currencies by a stipulated percentage. This will not make the problem of divergent trends in balances of payments of member states any easier to deal with, since any correction of an excessive surplus for one country is likely to be offset by accentuation of the deficit being experienced by its partner, whose currency is at the floor of the Community band. Instead of entering the exchange market to keep its own currency from rising, the surplus country will need to acquire its partner's currency to keep its exchange value from falling. The agreement to narrow bands makes no provision for adjustment of the Community level of the dollar outside the limits implicit in the parities for individual currencies established by the Smithsonian agreement. Within these limits, the band itself may be adjusted only by a coopera- tive decision of the central banks.

If a deficit country has an adequate stock of owned reserves, it may be able to support its own exchange rate for some period of time without help from its EEC partners. However, such independent self-support is not expected to suffice, as is evidenced by various credit arrangements that are or will become available. It is convenient to consider these together with the proposed European Monetary Cooperation Fund into which they may eventually be incorporated.

The European Monetary Cooperation Fund

Establishment of such a fund has long been an objective within Community circles. At the Summit Conference in October 1972, it was agreed to bring the Fund into operation by April 1, 1973, at latest but many of the details of the Fund's organization and operation remain unsettled. The Fund is to have its own unit of account defined in terms of gold content, to which member currencies will be related according to stipulated parities. The Fund will serve as an organization to coordinate the foreign exchange activities of its members, to facilitate multilateral clearing, and to extend mutual credit on a multilateral basis. The amount, basis, and duration of credit to be available through the Fund has not been fully determined and may undergo a progressive evolution toward a pooling of reserves under joint management, if the views of more ambitious proponents prevail.

Initially the Fund will incorporate the very short-term arrangements for mutual credit that apply under the agreement for cooperative narrowing of the band within which intra-Community rates of exchange may fluctuate. It will also utilize existing arrangements for short-term monetary aid among the central banks of member countries.

This latter agreement dates from a decision of central bank governors of the six on February 9, 1970, and appears to have been amended to include the central banks of new members of the EEC. Central banks contribute to the Fund by quotas ranging downwards from $300 million for the larger countries to $100 million for the smaller countries. These quotas also determine the limits of aid to be received, save in circumstances in which the governors permit an exception. Total resources unconditionally available for short-term monetary aid are $1.4 billion. On a conditional basis an additional like amount could be extended.

Credit to meet an unexpected balance-of-payments deficit is available for three months. Extensions for another three months are possible at the discretion of the governors and under agreed conditions. After using funds, the borrower must enter into economic consultations with the other member countries. Exchange risk on loans outstanding appears to be borne by the borrower, since loans are to be repaid in the means of payment in which delivered. The decision of the Summit Conference left these conditions governing short-term monetary aid intact in the approving of the Fund's establishment but called for reports by the appropriate Community bodies concerning possible adjustment in short-term monetary aid (report due by September 30, 1973) and conditions for the progressive pooling of reserves (report due by December 31, 1973).

An agreement also exists providing for mutual medium-term financial aid. This was approved by the EEC Council on February 9, 1971, at the time the Council endorsed the ten-year program to achieve monetary and economic integration within the Community. This aid is intended to supplement the short-term monetary aid. The maximum quotas are identical under the two systems. Credit is for two to five years and is decided upon by a majority (weighted) vote of the EEC Council. Credit is conditional on economic policy consultations and constraints on the borrower. The initial agreement to provide such aid is valid for the period January 1, 1972 to January 1, 1976. For the present this arrangement is not specifically related to the European Monetary Cooperation Fund.

The key issue in the establishment of the Fund is the basis on which a surplus country will provide reserves to a deficit country through the Fund. Much is being made currently of the advantage the Fund offers as an organization to multilateralize credit. But the ability of the Fund to extend credit on a fully multilateral basis depends on the absence of persistent balance-of-payments deficits and surpluses specific to individual countries. Under fixed exchange rates, economic forces are likely to produce persistent deficits for some countries while others experience persistent surpluses. Thus, the acid test for the Fund, and ultimately for the seriousness of the commitment by member states to internally fixed exchange rates, is whether or not the Fund becomes a channel for merging the reserve holdings of national central banks on the basis of some form of pooling or outright grants. Short of this, a country experiencing a persistent overall payments deficit through adherence to the Community level and structure of exchange parities faces growing foreign indebtedness on credit terms as the price of allegiance. Viewed from the perspective of a surplus country, the price is continued surpluses and continued credit extension. It is problematic whether EEC surplus and deficit countries will regard their economic welfare as sufficiently interdependent to support such a system. In current negotiations and forthcoming announcements about the European Monetary Cooperation Fund, this issue may be ignored or postponed. But ultimately it will be critical.

Regulation of International Capital Movements

The long-range goal of the EEC regarding international capital flows has aspects both internal and external to the Community. Reduction of barriers to capital mobility within the Community is a stated aim of the Council-approved plan for monetary and economic integration. So too is the development of a consistent Community-wide approach to capital flows between members of the Community and third countries. By implication, the Community's approach to capital flows involving third countries should be to regulate flows that do not serve the interests of the Community. In principle, such regulation might take place by a common flexibility in Community exchange rates, by exchange controls uniformly applied throughout the Community, or by other less comprehensive regulations applied to financial institutions and business firms engaged in capital transactions with third countries.

These long-range goals of the EEC countries regarding capital flows are supplemented by the more immediate objective of gaining control over short-term capital movements when these threaten the ability of domestic authorities to regulate exchange reserves and domestic monetary aggregates, to maintain fixed exchange rates, and to achieve domestic goals concerning interest rates and credit allocation. Clearly some complex problems must be resolved before the goal of greater capital mobility within the Community can be reconciled with control over capital flows that are "destabilizing" in terms of these other objectives.

In practice, at the present time each country studied in this volume intervenes in some way to regulate international capital movements, and the trend toward increased intervention is evident. Approaches to the problem extend from virtually comprehensive administrative controls over capital movements within the framework of foreign exchange controls as in Italy, the Netherlands, and the United Kingdom, to the use of a two-tier foreign exchange market with a floating rate for capital transactions in Belgium–Luxembourg and France, and to the German system of market-oriented controls such as special reserve requirements on nonresident deposits, special cash deposits that apply to corporate borrowing abroad, and regulations governing interest payable to nonresidents on deposits.

In principle, exchange controls do not represent a satisfactory solution to the problem of regulating international capital flows because of their discriminatory and arbitrary effects, which limit competitive market processes and reduce economic welfare. Moreover, application of exchange controls on an individual-country basis within the EEC is inconsistent with the avowed aim to integrate Community capital markets and with the process of monetary and economic integration generally. To apply a uniform set of exchange controls at the borders of the EEC with no controls on internal movements of capital would be administratively complex and would pose serious problems of policy regarding the character of the controls, priorities to be observed, and the like.

These considerations have motivated two alternative approaches to regulation of capital movements by Community countries: (1) the two-tier exchange market employed by Belgium since 1955, adopted by France in 1971, and urged by the French as a general solution for the Community; and (2) a set of measures to control inflows of short-term capital recommended by the EEC Commission for adoption by each member country. These recommended measures include the fixing of regulations for investments on the money market and the remuneration of the deposits of nonresidents, the regulation of the net external position of credit institutions, and special obligatory reserve requirements for nonresident deposits. Neither of these approaches to the regulation of capital movements is without shortcomings as a permanent solution for the Community.

A recent analysis of the two-tier foreign exchange market reaches conclusions favorable to the two-tier system as compared with widening bands or selective controls to reduce destabilizing capital movements.[5] The analysis concludes that variation in the exchange rate for capital account transactions is more effective than these alternative measures and less arbitrary. But adoption of this approach involving separately varying exchange rates for capital account transactions for individual countries would frustrate the declared EEC objective to create an integrated, Community-wide capital market so as to increase capital mobility inside the Community.

In principle, it is possible to combine freedom of capital movements at fixed parities within a group of countries with operation vis-à-vis the rest of the world of dual rate systems designed to keep each country in overall payments balance. Such a "discriminating regional system" also has been analyzed.[6] In this system each in-group country requires foreign exchange transactions to be classified in one of three categories: current account transactions, in-group capital account transactions, and rest-of-the-world capital account transactions. The advantage of the system is to permit in-group capital transfers at or near the current account parity while allowing each country to manipulate its rate of exchange for nongroup capital account transactions in order to achieve overall payments balance.

In practice, such a system if adopted by the EEC would have some distinct disadvantages. Extensive administrative controls would be required to prevent "leakages" from occurring among the three categories of external balances. Moreover, there is no assurance that the response of net flows of nongroup capital transactions to exchange rate variation in that market would prove adequate to redress imbalances in the other two accounts. This difficulty might well increase

[5] Vittorio Barattieri and Giorgio Ragazzi, "An Analysis of the Two-Tier Foreign Exchange Market," Banca Nazionale del Lavoro, *Quarterly Review,* no. 99 (December 1971), pp. 354–72.

[6] See J. Marcus Fleming, *Essays in International Economics,* chap. 12, "Dual Exchange Rates for Current and Capital Transactions: A Theoretical Examination," esp. pp. 314–17 (Cambridge, Mass.: Harvard University Press, 1971).

with the passage of time as current account net flows altered in response to differential domestic price trends and other factors. Further, should current account imbalances become large enough to arouse speculation on changes in current account parities, the authorities might find it very difficult to offset speculative capital flows from within the group as well as from outside simply by varying the rate of exchange in the nongroup capital account market. These problems, plus that of possible reprisals in the form of capital controls by nonmembers of the group, raise the distinct possibility that such a system would tend to degenerate into one of generalized exchange controls.

A partial alternative to general exchange controls or the two-tier market approach is provided by the set of selective measures recommended by the EEC Commission for adoption by individual members of the Community to regulate unwanted capital *inflows*. These measures are of two basic types. One involves direct prohibition, as in the case of regulations on the net foreign positions of financial institutions, of interest payable on the bank deposits of nonresidents, and of loans contracted abroad by residents. The other type of measure seeks to alter the effective terms of choice in private financial markets by imposing reserve requirements against funds obtained from abroad. A system of this kind can be made reasonably effective against undesired short-term capital inflows for short periods of time. It is subject to the usual attrition in effectiveness through increasing evasion in the longer run and may require escalation of controls towards full exchange controls should the perceived need for control persist.

These selective measures must be viewed as an ad hoc response to the special problem of recent massive inflows of dollars rather than as more basic tools geared to long-run solution of balance-of-payments problems for Community members. The market-oriented measures, like special reserve or cash deposit requirements, would be of limited effectiveness in controlling *outflows* of short-term capital as contrasted to inflows. Moreover, as applied by individual countries, these measures tend to decrease rather than increase the degree of integration of the Community-wide capital market, which is antithetical to the longer-run objective of the Community.

One fairly obvious point remains to be made about *any* system of Community-wide controls over international capital movements that seeks to combine the external controls with freedom of capital movement internally. For the external controls to be effective, they must be applied and enforced uniformly by *every* member state. Any breach in the dike anywhere will defeat the system and cause a reversion to the individual country controls that will in turn segment nationally the internal capital market.

No system of regulation that applies uniformly to the entire Community can remove the problem of reconciling diverse interests among individual members. Systems applied by individual countries are inconsistent with the goal of a unified, Community-wide capital market as a main feature of monetary and economic integration.

Capital Market Policies

The creation of a unified Community-wide capital market within which capital funds will move freely and without distortion of economic competition has been an objective of the EEC Commission for many years. Despite numerous Commission initiatives, there has been no progress in this direction for about a decade. A principal source of resistance to the creation of a Community-wide capital market has been the desire of national governments to influence the allocation of real resources to priority uses by domestic capital market policies. Protection of foreign exchange reserves by controlling the access of foreign borrowers to domestic capital markets and moderation or control of short-term capital movements to aid domestic stabilization policy are additional objectives served by national controls over international capital movements. These, too, may serve as obstacles to a unified, Community-wide capital market.

The country studies in this volume have described a wide variety of measures that national governments use to keep domestic savings at home and to allocate them to approved uses. Foreign borrowers are denied access to domestic capital markets save by explicit license, rarely given. Institutional investors are prohibited from purchasing foreign securities. Individual investors are discouraged from purchasing foreign securities by restricting information, limiting solicitation, prohibiting purchase of foreign-government obligations, or requiring that only foreign securities publicly issued on domestic exchanges be eligible for purchase. Access to the domestic market for fixed-interest securities may be subject to a calendar of issues in which timing, amount, and terms are governed by government policy. Credit and financial institutions are regulated in the types and terms of their obligations (for example, deposits and bonds) and in the earning assets they may purchase. Government-controlled financial intermediaries guide the investment of savings funds placed with them on an obligatory basis by the network of private and public savings banks. Tax measures are used to disadvantage private firms in the capital market or to encourage individuals to place savings with banks or other financial institutions rather than invest in corporate securities. The investment policy of these institutions is then regulated to guide credit and longer-term investments into approved uses.

To establish a unified and competitive capital market, all of these institutional, legal, tax, and regulatory measures will have to be reviewed and modified to remove discriminatory features. Not only is this a monumental task but it is profoundly important for the viability of particular financial institutions and for the complex of arrangements developed within certain individual countries to allocate capital by national priorities. In principle, a system of budget taxes and subsidies might be designed to take over the role of capital allocation from the existing complex of measures in different countries. Alternatively allocation might simply be left to market forces. In the latter case, the resulting allocation of investment funds would certainly be different from its present allocation in some of the EEC countries, notably Italy, France, Belgium, and Luxembourg. The intra-Community distribution of investment would probably also be altered. For budgetary processes to increase their role in capital allocation, taxes would have to rise and administrative burdens borne by central and local budget organizations would increase. This raises the question of how the absorption of new tasks by national and local budgets would be made consistent with the kinds of Community-level control over national budget proportions called for in the plan for monetary and economic union. Clearly, attempts to create a unified capital market for the entire Community face countless difficulties.

The Coordination of Budgetary Policies

A nation's budget is a principal expression and instrument of national policy in a great many areas of national life. It has pervasive effects on income distribution, aggregate demand management, and the allocation of real resources between consumption and investment and to specific geographic regions and forms of private and public investment. Combined with local authority budgets, it affects provision for social security and for socialized consumption in areas of public health, education, public buildings and roads, community services, and the like. Because of its central role in implementing national policy in these many areas, the national budget is a highly sensitive matter for which to advocate the principle of international cooperation. Nevertheless, the plan for monetary and economic integration regards coordination of national budgetary policies as a key area for cooperation. The Council *Resolution* of February 9, 1971, calls for aligning timetables of national budgetary procedures and states the following principle:

> ... As regards budgetary policy proper, the margins within which the main items of all the public budgets must be situated shall be determined at Community level with particular reference to the variation in their sizes, the extent of the balances and the methods of financing and using the latter.

The EEC Werner Report provides this amplification:

> To facilitate the harmonization of budget policies, searching comparisons will be made of the budgets of the Member States from both quantitative and qualitative points of view. From the quantitative point of view the comparison will embrace the total of the public budgets, including local au-

thorities and social security. It will be necessary to evaluate the whole of the fiscal pressure and the weight of public expenditure in the different countries of the Community and the effects that public receipts and expenditures have on the global internal demand and on monetary stability. It will also be necessary to devise a method of calculation enabling an assessment to be made of the impulses that the whole of the public budgets impart to the economy.[7]

The basic rationale for Community-level concern with the budgetary policies of member states appears to be the implication of such policy for aggregate demand management and for effects on domestic price levels. It is recognized that the size of the government budget and the balance between receipts and expenditures can affect the pressure of aggregate demand in an economy both directly in terms of income flows and indirectly via its influence on the growth rate of the domestic money supply. The Community seeks stable economic growth for its members, that is, economic growth with restrained amounts of price inflation. Inflationary national budgets in some member countries can disrupt stable growth throughout the Community. Moreover, coordinated anticyclical budgetary policy among the member states may be able to exert a more powerful influence in support of cyclical stabilization than uncoordinated efforts can. Also, under a system of fixed exchange rates with shared foreign exchange reserves, the distribution of real resources within the Community will be affected by differential rates of inflation and their influence on balance-of-payments deficits and surpluses for individual countries. The size of budget deficits or surpluses and their methods of financing or disposition will influence domestic money supplies, asset distribution, and inflation rates. Therefore, budgetary management has direct implications for the distribution of benefits under a reserve sharing plan. These are among the chief reasons for seeking coordination of budgetary processes among member states.

The difficulties that confront efforts to coordinate national budgets arc truly formidable. The diversity in present budget practices and responsibilities among member states is so great that it is difficult to make intelligent and meaningful comparisons let alone to establish conformity in budget procedures and categories. Budgets differ in size related to gross national product. The division of budgetary responsibility between central governments and regional and local subdivisions varies greatly. There are diverse trends in emphasis on centralization in contrast to decentralization. National budgets differ in distinctions recognized between current operating expenses and capital expenditures and in treatment of social security. Some countries prepare no cash budget distinct from an appropriations budget.

---

[7] *Report to the Council and the Commission on the Realization by Stages of Economic and Monetary Union in the Community,* October 8, 1970, S-11, 1970, p. 19.

The treatment of off-budget expenditures differs widely. The role of different types of taxes in budget receipts varies greatly. How this variation can be reconciled with proposed measures of fiscal har-- monization is completely unresolved.

Conditions related to deficit financing differ regarding size of the outstanding national debt, control over issue of local authority debt, direct purchase of government debt by government-controlled financial intermediaries, availability to the Treasury of a direct line of credit with the central bank, and freezing of a portion of outstanding debt in portfolios of credit and financial institutions. Practices concerning tax regulators and concepts of cyclical or structural budgeting to give the budget cyclical flexibility are far from uniform. In some member states they are well developed, in others totally lacking. Budget philosophies differ on the contribution the budget is expected to make to economic and monetary equilibrium and on the circumstances, if any, under which the central government or local authorities should borrow or repay debt abroad.

The staff of the EEC Commission has been engaged for some years in serious comparative studies of budgets of member states. In this effort they have been assisted by representatives of technical services from the member states. Their primary effort thus far has been to develop standard and useful classifications of receipts and expenditures and to fit into these classifications relevant data from the member states. In the course of these studies, they have grappled with many of the complications arising from diversity in practice that have been mentioned briefly above.[8] Among important problems the working group has encountered have been classifying budgetary activities of central governments and local authorities on a comparable basis for different member states that are substantially different in administrative structure and competence, and extending the budget accounts to include social security activities of the states with due allowance for large organizational differences relating to this sector.

These studies represent substantial progress in creating a statistical framework and factual foundation that will permit meaningful comparisons. Much work remains to be accomplished, however, in the areas of local authority and social security budgets and in obtaining data on a more current basis. Moreover, providing an adequate description of budgetary magnitudes is only the first step in the process of mutually agreed budgetary coordination. The authorities have emphasized that it is global magnitudes and not detailed allocations to which the guidelines of coordination must apply. But the size of the budget in relation to gross national product reflects the relative im-

[8] For a recent study published by the Commission's group for comparison of budgets, see Commission des Communautés Européennes, *L' Evolution des Finances Publiques dans les Etats Membres des Communautés Européennes de 1957 à 1966,* Collection Etudes, *Serie Economie et Finances No. 8, Bruxelles, 1970.*

portance of the state in resource allocation, both directly through taxes and expenditures and indirectly through income transfers. Therefore, budget size is related to such basic aspects of society as the degree of centralization of economic decision making and society's social welfare philosophy.

Constraints on global magnitudes imply constraints whose incidence must fall somewhere on categories within the global magnitudes. These restrictions may sharpen already difficult choices made by budget authorities. Further, the composition of a national budget as between consumption-related and investment-related expenditures can affect aggregate demand and price stability differently even for budgets of identical global size. Thus, guidelines confined to global aggregates may not accomplish their purpose. A budget deficit financed by borrowing abroad has different monetary effects from one financed by borrowing at home, but it also affects the balance of payments differently. Proposed fiscal harmonization requiring changes in the structure and level of taxes is certain to have important effects on budgetary receipts. The relation between budget size and tax structure will require systematic investigation.

Clearly there are many interrelated problems that will have to be considered and resolved in setting even global guidelines for budget coordination. These problems are extremely complex, lie close to the heart of the national political process, have not been studied in depth, and consequently can only have been evaluated superficially if at all by the Commission, tht Council, and the representatives of member states in adopting the plan for monetary and economic union.

Harmonization of Monetary Policies and Instruments

The basic questions in this area are, What is the meaning of *harmonization*? and, What is it that is to be harmonized? Close reading of the Commission memoranda, Werner Committee Report and Council-approved plan for monetary and economic union reveals an evolution from an early emphasis on harmonization, or coordination, of monetary and credit *policies* toward a later concern with harmonization of the *instruments* of monetary policy. Apparently, the more the various working committees sought to refine their ideas in this area, the more they were inclined to think about instruments rather than policies. This shift in emphasis is understandable. The concept of harmonizing instruments is much simpler to interpret than that of harmonizing policies, especially if the harmonization of instruments is understood to mean that the monetary authorities in each country should possess identical means of affecting monetary and credit phenomena. Moreover, from the perspective of ultimate monetary union, a convergence of national monetary and credit techniques towards a single, master set to apply uniformly in the accomplished union appears desirable and even necessary.

The difficulty with this approach is that it substitutes administra-

tive for economic reasoning and ignores both the crucial problems of
transition and that of stating the economic criteria by which use of
the instruments is to be guided. To illustrate the nature of the transition problems, imagine that all EEC members agree to provide their
monetary authorities with some established list of instruments. Likely
candidates for a minimum list are rediscount policy, required reserves in the form of deposits at the central bank, and open market
purchases and sales of securities to alter the liquidity of credit institutions. Under current circumstances, as we have seen in the
country studies, the degree of reliance on particular instruments from
this list in different countries varies greatly. These differences in
practice arise from differences in relative emphasis on national policy
objectives, differences in the availability and use of other policy instruments such as credit ceilings, interest rate controls, earning asset
reserves, differences in organization, and relative importance of financial institutions and of money and capital markets, and differences in
the extent of foreign exchange controls.

Individual countries cannot commit their monetary authorities to
substantial changes in techniques of monetary and credit policies
without profound implications for policies in these other areas and
quite possibly for their abilities to achieve important goals of national
economic policy. For example, in some of the EEC countries, confin-
ing the monetary authorities to use of these classical techniques of
monetary policy would imply giving up attempts to allocate credit
and capital flows to high-priority investment projects, or alternatively,
would imply the need to impose special new tasks on budgetary processes. Forgoing the use of credit ceilings and interest rate controls
might require extending exchange controls or regulations on the net
foreign positions of credit institutions. The transition from one system
of instruments to another poses many problems of this sort.

If, on the other hand, different countries combine the use of a
stipulated list of common monetary instruments with diverse assort-
ments of complementary instruments and controls, the meaning of
harmonization of instruments becomes even more ambiguous. A
change in the basic discount rate of a central bank has varying consequences, depending on such matters as the availability of other
channels for discount, the extent of customary indebtedness of credit
institutions at the central bank, the ability of banks to repatriate reserves held abroad in the form of liquid earning assets, whether the
government budget is in surplus or deficit, whether or not the authorities follow a price support policy for government securities, and so
on. Indeed, the problem is even more complex than this when viewed
from the perspective of economic analysis. Even for two economies
that were identical in all the policy and organizational respects just
listed as relevant, the significance of specific economic policy measures for economic performance could easily differ, depending on a
large list of economic factors such as quality and composition of the

labor force, characteristics of the existing capital stock, entrepreneurial skills, or savings habits.

These problems concerning the relevance of "harmonization" as
applied to the instruments of monetary policy suggest that it is the
effects rather than the techniques of policy that need to be harmonized. The Werner Committee Report recommends obligatory consultations within the Committee of Governors of the Central Banks
and the establishment for each country of guidelines ". . . principally
as regards the level of interest rates, the evolution of bank liquidity
and the granting of credit to the private and public sectors." [9] The
Commission memorandum prepared for the Council subsequent to the
Werner Report speaks of ". . . strengthening coordination of Member
States' monetary policies," and views the Monetary Committee of the
EEC and the Committee of Governors of the Central Banks as the appropriate forums for working out such guidelines. The Council-approved plan also asserts that "monetary and credit policies should be
closely coordinated."

None of these three official documents provides explicit criteria for
the coordination of monetary and credit policy among member states.
As noted, the Werner Report recommends establishing guidelines for
the level of interest rates, the evolution of bank liquidity, and the
granting of credit to the private and public sectors. But these phenomena are not ends in themselves, so the ultimate criteria must lie elsewhere. While these are never explicitly stated with reference to monetary and credit policy per se, it seems reasonable to seek them among
the basic purposes to be served by monetary and economic union.
Likely candidates are the coordination of price-level movements
among member states and minimization of destabilizing short-term
capital movements among member states for the contribution these
could make respectively to exchange-rate stability and domestic stabilization efforts. Here arises the familiar dilemma that these two
criteria may offer opposing counsels to a country's monetary authorities. The further complication exists that forces impinging on member states' balance of payments from outside the Community may
produce disparate effects in different member states, requiring the
choice of money and credit measures appropriate to cope with these
disturbances from outside but destabilizing within the Community.

This discussion suggests certain conclusions about the area of
harmonization of monetary and credit policy in the EEC plan for
monetary and economic union. First, harmonization of monetary and
credit *instruments* is of very little use of itself in accomplishing the
Community's basic economic objectives and may create far more
difficulties than it resolves. Second, the criteria for coordinating

[9] Council–Commission of the European Communities, *Report to the
Council and Commission on the Realization by Stages of Economic and
Monetary Union in the Community,* Luxembourg, October 8, 1970, p. 21.

monetary and credit *policies* to mutual advantage are complex, may involve familiar dilemmas of choice among conflicting aims, and differ from those facing national monetary authorities in nonmember states primarily by requiring more explicit evaluation of effects on other (partner) countries to the extent that this commitment is seriously undertaken. Significant progress in the area of monetary cooperation beyond that normally practiced by sovereign nations promises to be very difficult.

PROSPECTS FOR THE EEC PLAN FOR MONETARY AND ECONOMIC UNION

We have examined six interrelated aspects of the EEC plan to achieve monetary and economic union by 1980. These are (1) exchange rate policy; (2) the European Monetary Cooperation Fund; (3) regulation of international capital movements; (4) capital market policy; (5) coordination of budgetary measures; and (6) harmonization of domestic monetary measures. In each area, the difficulties to be overcome in achieving declared objectives of the union are substantial. Our attention has been confined deliberately to areas most directly related to *monetary* integration. Innumerable additional problems must be resolved by members of the Community in other areas essential to *economic* integration, such as national policies on taxation, social benefits, and regional development. Required adjustments in national policies in all these areas will affect many established practices, forms of economic organization, business and governmental procedures, and vested economic interests. Much resistance to the required changes appears inevitable.

Benefits foreseen from the union include greater economic efficiency, increased capability for stabilization policy within the union, less vulnerability to destabilizing economic forces emmanating from the rest of the world, and enhanced prestige and strength for the European Economic Community in international economic negotiations over such matters as trade and tariff policy and reform of the international monetary system. There are also those who view monetary and economic union as leading to the political union of Western Europe, which they regard as highly desirable.

In the formation of any coalition, there must be a balancing of prospective advantages and disadvantages by the participants. It is open to question whether the perceived mutual benefits of monetary and economic integration within the Community will be judged sufficient to outweigh the costs to participants in adjustments required of various economic interest groups and in loss of national economic sovereignty in various traditional areas of policy. Much may depend on the evolution of arrangements to distribute benefits and costs fairly within the Community. The sheer organizational complexity of the task must not be underestimated.

Steps taken to implement the plan for monetary and economic union up to and including the Summit Conference of October 1972 have involved limited commitments that are experimental and reversible and more symbolic than substantive. Despite the agreement in principle to synchronize initial steps toward monetary union with closer coordination of domestic monetary and budgetary policies, the operational decisions taken thus far are those to narrow exchange margins, to provide mutual short- and medium-term credit, and to establish the European Monetary Cooperation Fund. Coordination of domestic monetary and budgetary policies remains at the level of discussion and consultation without firm criteria or binding commitments to achieve results. National policies regarding international capital movements, domestic capital markets, regulation of financial institutions, taxation, and social welfare have undergone almost no modification in directions indicated by the plan since its adoption in February 1971.

One of the considerations capable of stimulating progress toward monetary and economic union within the EEC is the desire of member nations to strengthen their collective influence in international negotiations to reform the international monetary system. These negotiations were begun informally following the Smithsonian agreement in December 1971. They moved to a more formal phase at the annual meeting of the Board of Governors of the International Monetary Fund in September 1971. In chapter 10, we shall view prospects for reform of the international monetary system in the light of that system's relationship to plans for monetary and economic integration within the European Economic Community and to the national monetary systems and policies of the seven EEC member countries we have studied.

10 Perspectives on Reform of the International Monetary System

Reform of the international monetary system became an urgent issue in international relations in 1971 following suspension of gold convertibility of the United States dollar in August and the subsequent realignment in the Smithsonian agreement of December of parities among the principal currencies. During 1972, the process of international negotiation reached agreement on an acceptable forum for development of proposals for reform. This task was assigned to a newly created ad hoc "Committee of 20" of the Board of Governors of the International Monetary Fund. Among the committee's members, associates, and deputies are the finance ministers, central bank governors, and other high-ranking financial officials of the principal non-Communist industrial countries together with like officials representing groups of other countries that are members of the International Monetary Fund. The Committee of 20, relying especially on the work of its deputies, will seek to formulate generally acceptable proposals for reform of the international monetary system, to be submitted subsequently for adoption by the Board of Governors of the IMF.

The main purpose of this chapter is to contribute to understanding of why certain issues have become key issues in reforming the international monetary system and why national authorities differ in their preferred solutions to these issues. An effort is made to trace different preferences on key technical aspects of the international monetary system to differences in national situations that are based on the goals and techniques of monetary policy and economic policy generally and on other factors that appear to provide an analytical rationale for different preferences. Certain conclusions concerning these factors may be offered for orientation.

First, it is not possible to establish any close analytical correspondence between specific *instruments* of domestic monetary and credit policy used by particular countries and specific technical details of an international monetary system selected to be especially compatible with these instruments. This is somewhat surprising, since one can think of some obvious examples when one type of instrument is more effective than another in coping with problems raised by economic interdependence. For example, capability for substantial open market operations puts national monetary authorities in a stronger position to neutralize the effects of destabilizing international capital flows than primary reliance on discount channels for extending central bank credit to the economy does. However, differences in instruments do not establish per se an analytical rationale for preferring fixed to flexible exchange rates, for preferring gold or special drawing rights to dollars as the dominant reserve asset, or for other preferences on fundamental aspects of the international monetary system. This is partly because monetary authorities have displayed flexibility in adopting new and supplementary instruments and techniques to cope with problems for which their established techniques were inadequate. Most countries have developed over time a battery of instruments that are as effective as such instruments can be in dealing with problems posed by economic interdependence. Thus, differences in systems of monetary and credit instruments are not fundamental in accounting for differences in national approach to reform of the international monetary system.

Second, and by contrast to what has just been said, *systems* of instruments may be associated with attitudes on the issue of fixed parities with capital controls versus flexible exchange rates without capital controls. This association stems, however, from the *objectives* of domestic monetary and credit policy rather than its techniques. When national authorities pursue goals for domestic credit allocation and interest rate structure they must rely more heavily on techniques of administrative intervention in domestic credit and capital markets than when their objective is to control a monetary aggregate. Controls over international capital flows are a logical complement to a system that seeks to allocate domestic credit flows.

Other economic factors that appear to provide an analytical rationale for national preferences concerning specific features of the international monetary system are size and degree of openness of a nation's economy, and whether or not there are national goals concerning structure (for example, net capital export) as well as overall balance in a country's balance of payments. Finally, there is an indirect link between prospects for international monetary reform and national policy techniques and objectives via the relationship of each to the proposed monetary integration of Western Europe.

Possible variations on technical arrangements in an international monetary system are virtually endless. No attempt is made here either to describe and evaluate existing schemes or to add to their number. Rather we seek to clarify the nature of conflicting interests that must be resolved or compromised in any viable reform proposal. In doing so, we gain an appreciation for certain features that are likely to be present in any international monetary system on which agreement is ultimately reached.

FEATURES OF AN INTERNATIONAL MONETARY SYSTEM

The need for an international monetary system arises from the existence of separate national currency areas among which trade occurs in goods, services, and assets, giving rise to a need for international monetary payments. Unless barter is to be used, there must be some way of converting one currency into another and of determining the exchange value of one currency in terms of another. Foreign-exchange markets served by brokers, dealers, and commercial banks provide the exchange facilities.

The phrase *international monetary system* refers to the general set of procedures that are followed in determining the exchange parities of national currencies in terms of each other. One conceivable solution is to leave this determination entirely to the daily interaction of supply and demand in private exchange markets with no intervention by governments or central banks. This is the system of fully flexible exchange rates.

A second broad category of international monetary systems involves exchange parities that are officially declared by governments and supported in some fashion by government action. One conceptually simple system of this kind is the classic gold exchange standard, in which exchange values of national fiat currencies are established by declaring their official values relative to gold and are maintained by the price-specie-flow mechanism. Any system that involves officially fixed exchange rates requires a supply of reserve assets that can be used to settle international payments' imbalances when, as is usually the case, the value of receipts and payments from all other international transactions in goods, services, and assets in which a nation is engaged do not balance precisely within the settlement period prescribed by custom. Gold has been the traditional reserve asset, but other reserve assets have arisen to compete with gold either by usage, as in the case of the British pound and the U.S. dollar, or by the international agreement, as in the case of bookkeeping claims against the IMF (that is, drawing rights) or against the proposed European Monetary Cooperation Fund.

A basic problem for any fixed-rate system is how to handle persistent surpluses or deficits in the balance of payments of individual countries. The possible measures may be classified into five general categories: (1) alteration of exchange parities; (2) use of exchange controls to ration foreign exchange so as to redress the imbalance between payments and receipts; (3) changes in domestic aggregate demand and price levels to modify trade and capital flows until balance is achieved; (4) unilateral capital flows as grants from surplus to deficit countries; and (5) redistribution of population by migration.

Measures (4) and (5) on the list are of limited importance as international mechanisms of adjustment. They play a more important role as interregional adjustment mechanisms within individual countries. The adjustment problem is present when domestic regions trade and engage in capital transactions with each other. Since all domestic regions use the same national currency, this is equivalent to their being linked by unitary and permanently fixed exchange parities. A permanently deficit region may be aided by capital grants from other regions via the national budget or its population may gradually migrate to other regions where income prospects are more favorable.

Changes in domestic aggregate demand and price levels do serve as international mechanisms of adjustment. Limited downward flexibility of prices and attendant problems of unemployment when aggregate demand is depressed restrict the tolerance of national governments for these methods of restoring equilibrium in a nation's balance of payments. Thus, national governments have come to rely primarily on alterations in exchange rates and on various forms and degrees of exchange control or administrative intervention, which they use as adjustment mechanisms within the framework of an international monetary system, based on fixed but adjustable exchange rates.

The interdependence of national economies that cooperate in a world trade and payments system accounts for the sensitivity of governments concerning mechanisms of adjustment that partner countries use. National interests are affected by the form and intensity of use of alternative adjustment mechanisms and by the role assigned to various reserve assets and to international credit procedures. This interdependence provides the stimulus to cooperative international agreements on rules of good behavior for participants in an international monetary system. If it were not for the reciprocal aspects of interdependence, it would always be advantageous for an individual nation to preserve complete freedom for unilateral action in taking measures of adjustment.

KEY ISSUES IN REFORM OF THE INTERNATIONAL MONETARY SYSTEM

Certain key issues must be resolved in reaching international agreement on reform of the international monetary system. These are (1) the degree of flexibility in exchange parities and of market rates around these parities; (2) the extent of exchange controls and other regulations influencing capital flows; and (3) the form of reserve assets and their interconvertibility. Each of these issues concerns a fundamental aspect of international monetary arrangements and is the subject of divergent views among important nations.[1] In our discussion of each we shall indicate why it is important and why national governments differ from each other in their preferred solutions. Finally, we conjecture what the outcome of negotiations on these issues may be as the process of reform moves toward realization.

The Degree of Flexibility in Exchange Parities and in Market Rates

There is consensus that in practice excessive rigidity has characterized the par value system established under the Bretton Woods agreement. This inflexibility prevails despite the agreement's provision for moderate changes in parities at the initiative of individual governments and for large changes in parities with International Monetary Fund approval in circumstances of "fundamental disequilibrium." Under the par value system, changes in exchange parities have tended to be delayed until they could no longer be resisted and thus have usually occurred in conditions of crisis for national balance of payments and for the fabric of the international monetary system itself. When there are divergent national trends in national income, prices, and productivity accompanied by changing patterns of demand in international trade and in capital flows, more frequent and more orderly changes in exchange parities can ease the process of international adjustment. Moreover, permitting market rates of exchange to fluctuate in a somewhat wider band around official parities can increase the exchange risk involved in shifts of short-term capital from one country to another in search of profits from arbitrage and speculation. By thus deterring such capital flows, wider bands can provide domestic authorities with somewhat greater latitude within which to pursue independent national monetary and credit policies. The basic issue is how much flexibility of exchange parities is desirable and how automatic such flexibility should be.

An international monetary system based on fully flexible exchange rates determined in private exchange markets has broad support among professional economists as a system that would permit national economic authorities to regain autonomy in management of domestic aggregate demand while resolving automatically the problem of maintaining external balance. By permitting market-determined adjustment in exchange rates, such a system averts external imbalance

---

[1] These key issues are discussed in *Reform of the International Monetary System*, a Report by the Executive Directors to the Board of Governors, International Monetary Fund, Washington, D.C., August 1972. The divergence of national views represented among the executive directors caused the *Report* to describe a variety of alternative options without reaching firm recommendations.

and also insulates the domestic money supply completely from changes produced via the balance of payments by making net inflows or outflows of foreign exchange impossible.

Despite these apparent advantages, national governments and monetary authorities have consistently displayed great reluctance to adopt a system of fully flexible exchange rates in practice. Debate on the feasibility of a flexible rate system has tended to stress the system's possible vulnerability to destabilizing speculative activity and the potential depressing effect that increased uncertainty surrounding exchange transactions would have on the volume of international trade. These and other arguments have been thoroughly aired in the professional literature.[2]

Two other less discussed difficulties appear however to be the chief practical deterrents to adopting an international monetary system based on fully flexible exchange rates. The first difficulty is the vulnerability of such a system to breakdown through defection of members. The second is that the conditions required to achieve market determination of fully flexible exchange rates are incompatible with national credit policies to influence domestic allocation of economic resources.

Individual nations can always gain some advantage through covert official intervention in exchange markets to alter market-determined rates so as to achieve national policy objectives — domestic economic stabilization or encouragement of a current account surplus to support a capital export program. Any single important country can destroy a fully flexible exchange rate system by intervening to influence its own exchange rate. Thus, a system that relies on good behavior by participating nations is in constant danger of degenerating into competitive intervention by national authorities with results that may be inferior to those under a fixed-rate system with agreed adjustment procedures.

The ideal system based on fully flexible exchange rates is one in which private sector economic decisions determine the international trade and capital flows that in turn result in the pattern of exchange rates that emerges in exchange markets. It is well known that private sector decisions to import and export are influenced by tariffs and by a variety of nontariff restraints on trade.[3] Parallels to these influences

[2] For representative discussions, see (1) Richard E. Caves, "Flexible Exchange Rates," *American Economic Review*, May 1963, pp. 120–29; (2) M. Friedman, "The Case for Flexible Exchange Rates," *Essays in Positive Economics* (Chicago: University of Chicago Press, 1953), pp. 157–203; (3) Samuel I. Katz, "The Case for the Par-Value System, 1972," *Essays in International Finance*, no. 92 (Princeton: Princeton University Press, March 1972); and (4) Anthony Lanyi, "The Case for Floating Exchange Rates Reconsidered," *Essays in International Finance*, no. 72 (Princeton: Princeton University Press, 1969).

[3] For example, see Robert E. Baldwin, *Nontariff Distortions of International Trade* (Washington, D.C.: The Brookings Institution, 1970).

affect international capital flows. In addition to exchange controls over capital flows, there are a variety of domestically applied credit control measures and regulations on financial institutions and business corporations that influence inflows and outflows of capital. The ability of national governments to manipulate exchange rates by these means increases doubts concerning the workability of a system based on freely flexible exchange rates.

Thus, the reform of the international monetary system currently under discussion will probably involve endorsement of exchange parities that are fixed but adjustable. In this respect, the outcome of reform negotiations will not differ in principle from the system established by the Bretton Woods agreement. Practical differences in the functioning of the two systems will turn on how exchange adjustments occur. Under the Bretton Woods system, exchange rate adjustments tended to be undertaken reluctantly and after undue delay, to be accompanied by international monetary crises, and most often to involve devaluation by deficit countries.

Reform proposals put forward for discussion by United States officials have stressed the need for adjustments in exchange parities that are more prompt and more symmetrically shared by countries that are experiencing persistent surpluses as well as those subject to persistent deficits. To accomplish these purposes, United States spokesmen have proposed using an objective indicator such as excessive gains or losses of foreign exchange reserves to signal the need for a policy change by the country concerned. On such a signal from the indicator, the presumption would be that the government concerned would initiate policy measures to correct the persistent disequilibrium in its balance of payments, whether a deficit or a surplus was involved. The choice of measures would be left to the government and might involve monetary and fiscal policies to alter aggregate demand; tariff adjustments; altered controls on capital flows; or some combination of these measures as well as, or instead of, a change in exchange parity. An objective indicator might have the advantage of focusing world opinion on the need for adjustment by a particular country and also of strengthening the hand of that government to undertake a necessary but politically unpopular policy. The international community might apply economic sanctions of one sort or another if the responsible government failed to act when called to do so under these "rules of the game."

In the past, the measures referred to in this set of proposals other than changes in exchange parities have been available but have not prevented the emergence of persistent surpluses or deficits in the balance of payments of particular countries. The practical effect of the proposals if accepted by the international community would probably be an increase in the frequency and degree of automaticity in adjustment of exchange parities. Spokesmen for France, Japan, and Germany already have voiced reservations about the degree of enforced flexibility in exchange rates that they believe to be implied in the United States proposal. Difficult negotiations with an uncertain outcome appear to lie ahead in this area of international monetary reform.

Controls over Capital Movements

Controls over capital movements are thoroughly entrenched as policy instruments in some countries; other countries appear about to adopt such controls. Domestic credit and capital market controls are significant instruments of domestic economic policy in a number of countries we have studied. This is especially true of Belgium–Luxembourg, France, and Italy, and to a lesser extent of the United Kingdom. A system of exchange and regulatory controls over capital movements to and from foreign financial markets is a necessary complement to such a system of domestic controls. Without it, the interaction of domestic and foreign supply and demand pressures will modify the pattern of interest rates and credit flows in domestic markets even under a system of fully flexible exchange rates. But government intervention by exchange and regulatory controls on capital flows is incompatible with the laissez-faire requirements for a system of fully flexible exchange rates. Thus, domestic regulations and controls to allocate credit flows and determine interest rate structure are inconsistent with a system of fully flexible exchange rates.

In principle, domestic allocative objectives for credit and capital flows and for real resources can be implemented by budgetary tax and subsidy programs rather than by credit policy. These forms of government intervention are no less contrary to the laissez-faire rationale for freely fluctuating exchange rates than intervention by credit and capital market controls. Moreover, extensive reorganization of the operational aspects of budgetary policy would be required to achieve sufficient selectivity and enforcement of allocative decisions at the microeconomic level. National governments may not regard such reorganization as desirable or even feasible.

Thus, requirements for a system of fully flexible exchange rates are incompatible with forms of economic intervention that governments are unwilling to relinquish. This incompatibility guarantees that international negotiations will resolve the issue of fixed versus flexible exchange rates by favoring fixed but adjustable exchange parities. This outcome in turn will strengthen the case for exchange controls and other controls over capital flows. To the rationale for such controls to support the efforts of government policy to allocate domestic credit and determine domestic interest rates will be added the necessity for moderating short-term capital movements so as to support domestic policies to stabilize aggregate demand. The forthcoming reform of the international monetary system seems destined to confirm the recent strengthening of national controls over capital movements observable in all Western European countries we have examined.

One frequently discussed alternative to the straightforward choice between an international monetary system based on fixed exchange rates for individual countries and one based on flexible rates is a system in which countries may group into several separate monetary unions, each union having fixed exchange parities internally but being linked to other unions by flexible exchange rates. Criteria for the formation of "optimum currency areas" have been studied and are found to depend heavily on mobility of productive factors among participating economic regions.[4] If such mobility is absent, economic welfare of some participating regions or states is likely to be inferior within the union as compared with outside.

Practical obstacles to a successful monetary union from the voluntary association of independent nations are substantial, as we have seen in our discussion (in Chapter 9) of the proposed program for monetary integration within the European Economic Community. Indeed, the required infringement of national economic sovereignty is so great and the task of economic and political reorganization so profound that success in such an undertaking is doubtful. Similar doubts apply to formation of an international monetary system based on such currency blocs. Moreover, linkage of such currency blocs by flexible exchange rates free of the taint of manipulation by bloc authorities would require these authorities to abstain from allocative credit and budgetary measures. In view of these two sets of practical difficulties, it appears exceedingly unlikely that the reform of the international monetary system will lead to regional monetary unions linked by fully flexible exchange rates.

Reserve Assets and Their Interconvertibility

Another central issue in the reform of the international monetary system involves the forms of reserve assets and their interconvertibilit. If negotiations should reveal a serious and unbridgeable disagreement about the forms of reserve assets and their interconvertibility, such a disagreement could conceivably precipitate a breakdown in international monetary cooperation and formation of inward-looking currency blocs. Under these circumstances, formation of such blocs would almost certainly be accompanied by heightened protectionist barriers, or tariffs, and by exchange controls not only over capital movements but also over current account transactions in goods and services. Such developments would signal an end to the post–World

[4] See Robert A. Mundell, "A Theory of Optimum Currency Areas," *American Economic Review*, September 1961, pp. 657–65; Ronald I. McKinnon, "Optimum Currency Areas," *American Economic Review*, September 1963, pp. 717–25.

War II era of expanded world trade and increased international specialization.

Under the par value system as it functioned until the formal suspension of convertibility of the United States dollar on August 15, 1971, there were three principal forms of reserve assets: gold, drawing rights in the International Monetary Fund, and U.S. dollars. Gold and claims against the IMF served as reserve assets by formal international agreement. The U.S. dollar had evolved into its role as a reserve asset through usage resulting from such factors as the size and strength of the U.S. economy, the key currency role of the U.S. dollar as a standard for defining exchange parities under the Bretton Woods agreement, and the efficiency and convenience of having one principal vehicle currency for both private and official international payments.[5] Substantially less extensive reserve currency roles were performed by the British pound and the French franc within the sterling and franc currency zones. The widespread use of the dollar in private international transactions made it a convenient intervention currency for central banks to use in fulfilling their commitments to maintain market rates of foreign exchange within agreed narrow bands around formal parities. All these considerations combined to confer on the dollar its role as a reserve currency.

The dollar's role as a reserve currency had a unique consequence for the United States balance of payments. Overall deficits resulting from the combined effects of current and capital account transactions could be settled in a reserve asset of which the U.S. monetary authorities had an unlimited supply: U.S. dollars. So long as private and official holders in other countries were satisfied to accumulate dollar claims, the United States could continue to finance its balance-of-payments deficit simply by providing the rest of the world with additional dollar liabilities. Moreover, the counterpart to these dollar-financed deficits was the purchase by United States residents of goods, services, and financial and real assets in foreign countries. As long as the dollars so acquired abroad were held voluntarily by private holders, all parties to the transactions could be presumed to benefit. Moreover, central banks in other countries were for some years eager to accumulate additional dollar claims to serve as reserves with which to protect their currency parities in case of overall deficits in their own balance of payments. Eventually, however, as U.S. deficits continued, the foreign private demand for dollars was satisfied so that private holders began to convert dollars at an increasing rate into their own domestic currencies, thus adding to official holdings of dollars and increasing domestic money supplies in these countries.

---

[5] For an insightful essay on the key currency role of the U.S. dollar, see Alexander K. Swoboda, "The Euro-Dollar Market: An Interpretation," *Essays in International Finance*, no. 64 (Princeton: Princeton University Press, February 1968).

Under the par value system, dollars were convertible into gold at the fixed price of $35 per ounce. Consequently, when central banks in other countries, especially western continental Europe and Japan, began to experience what they regarded as an excessive accumulation of dollars in official holdings, they began to exchange dollars for gold, thus reducing the stock of monetary gold held by the United States Treasury. This stock, while large, was not unlimited. Persistent drains on the U.S. gold stock through conversion of official holdings of dollars to gold eventually reduced the stock to about ten billion dollars' worth of gold valued at its official dollar price. At this point, on August 15, 1971, President Nixon announced the suspension of dollar convertibility into gold or claims against the IMF. Since that date, the dollar has been officially inconvertible into other reserve assets.

So long as the dollar remained convertible into other reserve assets, monetary authorities in other countries possessed a procedure through which they could register their disagreement with the continued net flow of dollars abroad associated with continuous deficits in the United States balance of payments. By conversion of dollars to gold, they could deplete the U.S. gold stock in the hope of forcing U.S. authorities to undertake steps to end the balance-of-payments deficit.

Recent years have witnessed a lively debate among national monetary authorities and in other official and academic quarters concerning assignment of responsibility for correction of the U.S. deficit. United States spokesmen have favored the up-valuation of exchange parities for countries such as Germany and Japan that were experiencing persistent surpluses in their balance of payments; they have also favored lower tariffs and more domestic inflation in surplus countries to reduce their exports and increase their imports. Other countries have recommended to the United States such policies as higher interest rates and deflationary monetary and fiscal measures. Devaluation of the U.S. dollar relative to other currencies generally was not urged on the United States, possibly for fear that the competitive effects on other countries would be too strong and possibly out of concern for the uncertainties over the shock such a devaluation would impart to the entire international monetary system owing to the key currency role of the dollar in that system.

The situation created by the suspension of dollar convertibility into other reserve assets is unique. After an initial period of uncertainty and floating rates, central banks in other countries have continued to intervene in foreign exchange markets to maintain market exchange rates within agreed limits around official parities. By the Smithsonian agreement, these agreed parities were altered from their previous levels so as to produce an effective devaluation of the U.S. dollar in relation to other major currencies. The agreement also involved a 7.9 percent devaluation of the dollar in relation to gold from $35 to $38 per ounce. The revised parities are referred to as central rates rather than official parities, so as to reserve the right to further change or return to the former parities during subsequent negotiations.

The dollar remains convertible into other currencies at these new parities and hence into goods, services, and assets throughout the world. United States deficits have continued, at least for a time, and continue to be settled in inconvertible dollars. A net inflow of dollars into other countries continues to add to official stocks of dollars and to domestic money supplies in these countries. The world, or more precisely the 124 member countries of the International Monetary Fund that participate in the international monetary system, is effectively on an inconvertible dollar standard. Gold has ceased to be used actively in settling accounts among central banks because of uncertainty concerning its appropriate value in such settlements. This uncertainty stems in part from uncertainty over the shape of the international monetary system that will emerge from reform negotiations and in part from the substantial rise under speculative pressure of the free market price of gold.

Reform negotiations over the form and interconvertibility of reserve assets thus involve the fundamental issue of dollar convertibility and the present unique role of the dollar in the international monetary system. This role has emerged not by deliberate design but essentially through usage as an economically efficient arrangement in a world economy that is becoming increasingly integrated through private economic initiative. The size and strength of the U.S. economy have made the dollar the world's choice as the key vehicle, and intervention and reserve currency in international payments. Demands for restoration of dollar convertibility are motivated by a desire of governments in other countries to reduce the role of the dollar in the international monetary system to that of other national currencies and in doing so to replace the international dollar standard with another standard more subject to international control. Return to the gold exchange standard would permit individual surplus countries to exchange dollars for gold so as to exert pressure on United States economic authorities, whereas exclusive reliance on reserve assets in the form of drawing rights at the International Monetary Fund would transfer regulation of international reserves to political processes in an international organization.

The concern of other important industrial countries with this issue is reflected in three of the eight points put forward as a basis for international monetary reform by the nine countries that will constitute the European Economic Community as of January 1, 1973. In a joint statement these countries have agreed that the monetary reform should (1) reestablish general convertibility; (2) provide for international regulation of world liquidity; and (3) conform to the principle of equal rights and obligations for all countries.[6] For these

---

[6] "E.C. Group Outlines Money Reform Goals, Ignores U.S. Demand to Study Trade Link," *Wall Street Journal,* July 18, 1972.

objectives to be achieved, the dollar would have to become fully convertible into an internationally controlled reserve asset and cease to be itself used as a reserve asset. For United States authorities to assent to such arrangements would represent a substantial reduction both in advantages that accrue to the dollar as dominant reserve asset in the international monetary system and in the ability of U.S. economic authorities to pursue independent policies in the management of domestic aggregate demand.

The basic U.S. position on these issues was set forth in the speech of Secretary of the Treasury George P. Shultz at the annual meeting of the IMF in September 1972. In his speech, Secretary Shultz favored retention of a reserve asset role for the U.S. dollar together with an increasing reserve asset role for special drawing rights (SDR's) at the IMF and a gradually diminishing role for gold. On the closely related issues of exchange rate flexibility and capital and other balance-of-payments controls, Secretary Shultz called for a system of fixed but readily adjustable exchange rates, and he opposed in principle all balance-of-payments controls except as very temporary measures.[7]

PROSPECTS FOR INTERNATIONAL MONETARY REFORM

These divergent views on key issues in international monetary reform arise from the fundamentally different economic circumstances in which the United States and other important trading nations find themselves. All are relatively advanced industrial nations with high per capita living levels. But the sheer size of the continental United States economy guarantees that its international trade and capital transactions will be of far less domestic significance in comparison with its internal transactions and national product than those of smaller, and hence more open, trading economies. The size of the goods and capital markets in the U.S. economy compared with those of its trading partners also accounts for the unique role of the U.S. dollar in the international monetary system.

From the U.S. perspective, freer international trade and capital movements, free choice of the form in which countries hold their reserve assets, unitary and highly flexible exchange rates, and even inconvertibility of the U.S. dollar into other reserve assets are advantageous arrangements that confer benefits without significantly inhibiting the effectiveness of domestic economic policies. The situation is quite different for the other major industrial nations that engage extensively in international trade (that is, non-Communist industrial countries). These countries' economies are smaller, hence more open and more vulnerable to external influences, than the U.S. economy. Their currencies do not enjoy the international status of the U.S. dollar nor the benefits of that status. A number of these countries are

[7] Text of Secretary Shultz's talk, *The New York Times*, September 27, 1972.

accustomed to use techniques of government intervention in their domestic economies that are incompatible with a commitment to free international capital flows and thus to fully flexible, market-determined exchange rates. For such countries, neither an international monetary system based on fully flexible exchange rates nor one based on fixed but adjustable rates with the U.S. dollar inconvertible and continuing in its reserve asset role would represent a desirable conclusion to the reform negotiations. What they would prefer is a return to a modified par value system with fixed but adjustable (although not too adjustable) exchange rates, optional national controls over capital flows, and international control of reserve asset creation with the role of the U.S. dollar as a reserve asset sharply circumscribed, or even eliminated.

Reform negotiations must somehow reconcile these divergent views. The United States certainly will not restore convertibility of the dollar into other reserve assets at the sacrifice of autonomy in its domestic monetary and fiscal policies to manage aggregate demand. Minimum requirements for combining such autonomy with convertibility are (1) a substantial increase in flexibility of exchange parities including provision for unilateral alteration in the dollar's parity vis-à-vis currencies of major trading partners; and (2) some arrangement for funding a significant portion of dollar balances currently held abroad to prevent a run on U.S. nondollar reserve assets following restoration of convertibility. It is doubtful that the United States will agree to elimination of the dollar as a reserve currency since this would give up an advantage conferred automatically by international usage.

Other major trading nations such as EEC members and Japan will not accept fully flexible exchange rates and may even balk at the lower degree of "automaticity" in rate flexibility implied in the U.S. proposals. They will continue to regard a change in exchange parity as the prerogative of a sovereign government responsible for a nation's economic welfare. They will insist on the right to employ controls over capital flows as instruments of national policy. Indeed, the use of capital controls is likely to become more widespread and intense in the future than it was in the past. No technical reform of the international monetary system appears capable of reversing this tendency in the near future.

The role of gold as a reserve asset and its price are not key issues except in relation to international control of reserve asset creation and the role of the dollar as a reserve currency. So long as the dollar continues as a reserve currency whose supply is not subject to international control, gold will have its supporters as a rival reserve currency. An increase in the price of gold relative to the dollar and other currencies cannot alter by itself the fundamental characteristics of the par value system nor of the role of the dollar in that system. Thus, an increase in the price of gold would not get at the basic sources of dissatisfaction with that system that have led to efforts at international monetary reform. This situation appears to be appreciated now even by the French authorities, who until recently have been among the more ardent advocates of an increase in the price of gold as a solution to international monetary problems.[8] No doubt some serious rethinking of this position occurred in the light of events subsequent to the suspension of gold convertibility of the U.S. dollar in August 1971. At that time monetary authorities in other countries opted for an international dollar standard rather than a system of currency blocs or international monetary chaos.

The postreform international monetary system is likely, therefore, to look a lot like the prereform par value system with differences in degree predominating over differences in kind: exchange rates fixed by national governments but somewhat more adjustable; dollar convertibility restored with some provision for funding outstanding dollar balances; gold, the dollar, and claims against the IMF continuing to serve as reserve assets; and more extensive and intensive use of controls over capital flows.

An alternative outcome arising from failure of reform negotiations to reach a compromise of this character on the key issues of exchange rate flexibility, the form and interconvertibility of reserve assets, and controls on capital flows is a possibility that cannot be totally excluded. In this event, a likely successor to the par value system would be a world monetary scene consisting of a number of currency blocs formed around the dollar, some European unit of account, and the Japanese yen, with the Communist countries continuing to operate their individual state monopolies of foreign trade and payments. Links among the blocs might take the form of floating exchange parities, but there is also the dangerous possibility that competitive manipulation of exchange rates could occur, with a gradual deterioration of trade and payments relationships into systems of comprehensive exchange controls accompanied by high tariffs and other barriers to trade. Such a breakdown of world economic relations would certainly be injurious to all countries. Its very possibility should spur the efforts of all parties to the reform negotiations to reach a more satisfactory outcome by equitable compromise.

A final comment on the role of the enlarged European Economic Community in international monetary reform may be offered from the perspective of the studies that have occupied the bulk of this book. The EEC program for monetary and economic integration is motivated in part by the desire of European leaders to create a monetary and economic counterpoise to the influence of the United States in world economic affairs. This defensive motive supplements and recently may even have taken precedence over other projected benefits from eco-

[8] For evidence of altered French views on the gold-dollar question, see the series of four articles by Raymond Aron in *Le Figaro*, August 28–31, 1972.

nomic unification. Recent commitments to the principle of European economic union accompanied by tentative and largely symbolic steps towards European monetary union have been spurred by the desire to create the prospect of a viable European alternative to further dominance of the international monetary system by the U.S. dollar and thus to strengthen the bargaining position of EEC member states in negotiations over reform of the international monetary system.

Does this mean that the creation of an inward-looking European monetary bloc is imminent? Probably not, in view of the difficulties confronting European monetary union (see Chapter 9) including the ambivalent attitude of prospective participants. This conclusion carries the proviso that the United States not force the issue by taking an uncompromisingly hard line in the reform negotiations. But prudence on the part of EEC member nations suggests the desirability of their keeping alive the prospects for further meaningful progress towards monetary union in Europe to gain leverage in these negotiations.

There is, however, a more constructive, long-run aspect to the EEC's proposed program for monetary and economic integration. So long as the international monetary system remains the expression of an uneasy compromise among the conflicting interests of participating nations, just so long it will remain potentially unstable and subject to periodic crises that threaten to undo the progress that has been made in rational world economic organization. The challenge is to develop forms of political cooperation and governmental authority in economic policy matters that transcend purely national limits. The European Economic Community, as the most advanced of various potential regional economic unions, provides a laboratory for the development of such forms of supranational organization. In this innovative and forward-looking role, the efforts of the EEC to advance towards monetary and economic union hold a promise for the future and merit sympathetic attention.

Index

Radcliffe Report
  and British monetary policy,
    188–90
  theoretical views characterized,
    175
Rediscount and Guarantee Institute,
  influences interest rates, 17
Rediscounting
  by administrative rationing in
    Italy, 93
  channels for in Belgium, 11–13
Reform of international monetary
  system
  views of European Economic
    Community on, 258–60
  views of United States on, 259
Regulation of banks
  in France, 29–31, 32
  in Germany, 53–54
  in Italy, 87
  in the Netherlands, 128
  in the United Kingdom, 161
Repurchase agreement
  and effectiveness of German
    monetary policy, 80–81
  French central bank credit
    by means of, 37
Reserve assets, 256
Reserve ratios, in France, 38–40

Saving, and inflation in France,
  48–49
Securities Stabilization Fund, role in
  Belgium, 7, 13–14, 17, 20
Soviet financial system, character-
  ized, 205–6
Special credit institutions, role in
  Italy, 88–89
State budget
  importance for monetary policy,
    213–14

national differences in compensatory role of, 213–14
preparation in Belgium, 20–21
State budget's compensatory role
  in Belgium, 20–21
  in Germany, 73
State ownership of financial institutions. *See* Nationalization
Swap policy of central bank,
  in Germany, 66–68

Techniques of monetary and credit
  policy
  British reforms of 1971, 158–59
  market-oriented nature in
    Germany, 75
  recent reforms in France, 50–52
Traditional instruments of central
  bank policy, significance of in
  France, 44–45
Treasury circuit, role in France,
  34–35
Two-tier foreign exchange market
  Belgian, 19–20, 24
  French, 47
  implications for European Eco-
    nomic Community, 236–37

United States dollar
  convertibility suspended, 257
  implications of inconvertibility
    of, 258
  as reserve asset, 256
  role in international monetary
    system, 258

Werner Committee Report
  monetary "harmonization" recom-
    mended by, 244
  recommendation concerning bud-
    getary policies, 239–40